Barrymore • Busby Berkeley

yer • Frank Capra • Claudette

Cukor • Bette Davis • Olivia

Robert Irene Dunne •

Fitzgerald ming • Joan

Greta Garland •

Cary d Hawks

Ernst Lv d Niven •

Claude Reagan

urt Ro Norma

ne Billy William Wyler

HOLLYWOOD'S

GOLDEN YEAR

1939

Wuthering Heights. Laurence Olivier as Heathcliff.

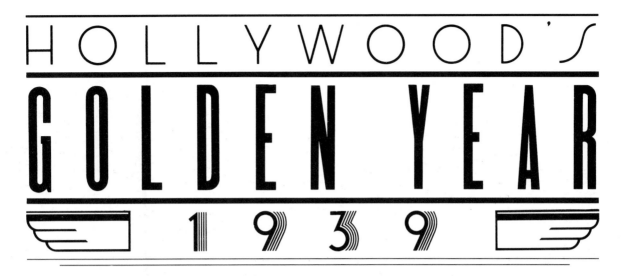

HOLLYWOOD'S GOLDEN YEAR 1939

A Fiftieth-Anniversary Celebration

TED SENNETT

ST. MARTIN'S PRESS ≡ NEW YORK

Also by Ted Sennett:

The Art of Hanna-Barbera: Fifty Years of Creativity
Great Movie Directors
Great Hollywood Movies
Hollywood Musicals
Masters of Menace: Greenstreet and Lorre
Your Show of Shows
Lunatics and Lovers
Warner Brothers Presents

Design by Glen Edelstein

Library of Congress Cataloging-in-Publication Data

Sennett, Ted.
    Hollywood's golden year, 1939 : a fiftieth-anniversary celebration
/ Ted Sennett.
      p.   cm.
    Bibliography; p. 263
    Includes index.
    ISBN 0-312-03361-3
    1. Motion pictures—California—Los Angeles—History.
    2. Hollywood (Calif.)—History. I. Title.
PN1993.5.U65S46 1989
791.43'75'0979494—dc20   89-32761
                                            CIP

First Edition
10 9 8 7 6 5 4 3 2 1

To all the talented people
—on both sides of the camera—
who made 1939 a golden movie year.

The Wizard of Oz. Dorothy in Munchkinland.

CONTENTS

Mr. Smith Goes to Washington. Senator Jeff Smith (James Stewart) at the point of collapse.

ACKNOWLEDGMENTS

I should like to thank all those who helped me with this book on the extraordinary movie year of 1939.

Once again, I am deeply grateful to Curtis F. Brown for his astute reading of my manuscript. I should also like to thank John Springer for providing me with prints of 1939 films, and for putting me in touch with that splendid actress, Geraldine Fitzgerald. My editor, Michael Sagalyn, has been helpful and supportive, and my agent, Peter Miller, has worked assiduously on my behalf. I also want to acknowledge the assistance of the staff at the Billy Rose Collection of the New York Public Library at Lincoln Center.

As many times before, I want to thank Jerry Vermilye for providing me with so many excellent photographs from his collection. I am also grateful to Michael King for his beautiful posters and to Robert M. Krauss and Ken Galente of The Silver Screen for their color material. Thanks are due, as well, to Jerry Ohlinger's Movie Material Store, the Billy Rose Collection at Lincoln Center, Mary Corliss and the Film Stills Archive at the Museum of Modern Art, Movie Star News, Photofest, Gene Andrewski, and Doug McClelland for their photographs. I should like to acknowledge Columbia Pictures, Universal Pictures, Twentieth Century-Fox, The Samuel Goldwyn Company, and Turner Entertainment for granting me permission to use photographs from their films.

I cannot imagine ever writing a book without expressing my deepest love and gratitude to my wife Roxane, and my children Bob, David, and Karen. Here's a toast raised in thanks from that man forever perched behind his typewriter.

The Women. Paulette Goddard, Mary Boland, and Norma Shearer on the train to Reno.

INTRODUCTION

1939: It was, by all accounts, an amazing year: a year of glaring and often ironic contrasts. Bright hopes for a golden future existed side by side with ominous threats of terror and violence. Dreams ˙and nightmares occupied the very same month. In late April of that year, the New York World's Fair opened on 1,216 acres in the borough of Queens in New York City, promising to make "The World of Tomorrow" a shining reality. As 600,000 listeners huddled in a chilly spring breeze, President Franklin D. Roosevelt formally opened the exposition, stressing the twin themes of progress and peace. Only a few weeks earlier, Adolf Hitler had ordered the conscription of all German youth. Only two days earlier, he had rejected President Roosevelt's proposal to meet at sea. And on the very day the fair opened, Russia had proposed a strong military alliance with France and England.

By the summer of 1939, as the clouds over Europe grew increasingly dark and sinister, the contrasts had deepened. On the one hand, *The Wizard of Oz*, reveling in a Technicolor domain where wicked witches melted, assured us that wherever we may wander, home and hearth are best. On the other hand, it was becoming evident that home and hearth were being threatened with extinction in a world about to burst into flames. In the month that *The Wizard of Oz* opened in New York City, Poland was rushing troops to its border; France and Holland were mobilizing their armies; and the Third Reich was sending U-boats to the North Atlantic. On the first day of September, while David O. Selznick was fretting about the length of *Gone With the Wind*, German troops stormed into Poland, and World War II began.

Despite the rumblings of war that echoed throughout Europe in the early months of 1939, America was not, at first, unduly alarmed. Americans are by nature optimistic and, after all, 1938 had been a hopeful year. The devastating impact of the Depression continued to linger, and many people still bore the scars of those bleak years when life had been cruel and hard. However, national unemployment had declined throughout the year, more money had been placed in circulation, and there had been no appreciable increase in prices. The banking interests that funded new ventures, including films, had become more lenient than they had been in many years.

It was not as if the American people were totally oblivious to what was happening across the ocean. Some foreboding news items may have been buried in back pages of the newspaper: In February, the German envoy to the Vatican asked the cardinals to elect a pope who favored fascism, and in Berlin, an order was issued requiring one hundred Jews to leave the Reich every day. Other news, however, could hardly have been avoided. In March, banner headlines screamed that Hitler's army had entered Czechoslovakia and raised the swastika in Prague. By May, Americans were reading about the "Pact of Steel" that Germany and Italy had signed, creating "an invincible bloc of 300 million people." At the signing, leading German and Italian officials, including Hitler, agreed that in time of war, Germany would rule on land and Italy on sea.

While these momentous events were taking place in Europe, life in America in that year of 1939 tended to be more comfortably concerned with the trivia of everyday living, or with the dreams and aspirations that involved one's own family and friends rather than power-mad dictators. People were being told about the miracles of cellophane and nylon. Everyone was admiring the quick knockouts by fighter Joe Louis, the "Brown Bomber." Families gathered around their radios to laugh at the stinginess of comedian Jack Benny, or to hear Kate Smith sing Irving Berlin's stirring anthem "God Bless America." A new car, a new refrigerator, or even a new house became the symbols of an improving economy for many Americans who had weathered bad times.

And then there were the movies. In the grimmest years of the thirties, movie palaces and neighborhood bijous had become darkened havens against the storm outside, a welcome escape into fantasy for a few coins. Performers who exuded glamour—Clark Gable, Greta Garbo, Jean Harlow, and many others—became the icons of their age, and an adorable, talented, curly-headed tot named Shirley Temple was proclaimed America's democratic princess. Photographed, interviewed, and gossiped about, they dominated the newspapers and magazines, often to the exclusion of political figures who were about to send the world reeling into war.

If the glittering stars lured audiences into the theaters, it was the films themselves that kept them there, enthralled in the darkness and ready to return again and again, often to the very same movie. By 1939, the film pioneers, who had forged empires out of fragments of dreams, had reached the peak of their powers. For over two decades, they had been creating an industry that, film by film, would offer an idealized vision of their adopted country. Coming with their families from oppressive countries, men such as Adolph Zukor, Carl Laemmle, Louis B. Mayer, and Samuel Goldwyn found an embracing freedom they wanted to celebrate in their movies. America had given them material success, and now they felt compelled to pay tribute to it with images of a beautiful, expansive land imbued with strong family values and unswerving patriotism, and inhabited by a proud, handsome, courageous people. Americans loved these flattering images, and they flocked into the theaters to see them.

There were, of course, other reasons besides gratitude for their creation of an idealized America in their films. Many of these pioneer figures had come from impoverished, bitterly struggling Jewish families in Eastern European countries, where their lives had often been dominated by harsh patriarchs with little affection or patience. They had arrived in a strange land, with scarcely any knowledge of its language, and they were odd-looking, "different." Now, in their new roles as rising movie moguls, they wanted to justify their existence, prove their worthiness to join the American mainstream. For some of them, this extended beyond filmmaking to their lifestyles in the burgeoning city of Hollywood. They relished becoming solid, affluent members of the community, giving lavish parties and contributing generously to respectable causes. Whether they clung to the strict religion of their fathers or assimilated into a nondenominational background, they had "made it" in the New World. Neal Gabler's book *An Empire of Their Own* (Crown, 1988) tells their story in absorbing fashion.

These men also had a fierce and abiding love for making movies. From the time they had started with nickelodeons and makeshift theaters, they had experienced a joy and a deep sense of satisfaction in placing those flickering images up on a screen. Coming from the masses, they knew what the masses wanted: at first the simple thrill of watching moving images and then a story that would make them laugh or cry. With little schooling, Zukor, Mayer, Goldwyn, and the others recognized and understood the visceral need of moviegoers to be taken out of themselves into a world of fantasy that might resemble a Western plain, a medieval castle, or a Park Avenue apartment. Some basic instinct told them the elements that went into the making of a good, and occasionally even great, movie. By 1939, they were often astonishingly on target.

These men clearly relished their work, but for some of those who would follow in their footsteps, making movies became a positive obsession. At MGM, Irving Thalberg, Louis B. Mayer's surrogate son and head of production in the twenties and early thirties, drove himself relentlessly, supervising every aspect of the studio's most polished and prestigious films. By 1936, his fragile health had deteriorated, and he died of pneumonia at thirty-seven. His legacy included such films as *The Merry Widow* (1934) and *Mutiny on the Bounty* (1935). Even more obsessive was Lewis Selznick's son David, who rose in the ranks from producer at RKO and MGM to his own production company. (As Louis B. Mayer's son-in-law, he was the rightful heir to the MGM throne after Thalberg's death, but he declined the role.) Continually working himself into a state of near collapse, Selznick made filmmaking the very heart of his existence. *Gone With the Wind* became his crowning achievement.

Of course, not all of the men who wielded studio power in 1939 were either founding fathers or their offspring. Some began to emerge in the early twenties, years after the pioneers had laid the groundwork, to establish their own place in the top echelon of the film industry. With his brothers, Jack Warner launched the sound era with his film of *The Jazz Singer* (1927), then went on to head Warner Brothers, a company that by 1939 was firmly established as a producer of gritty, fast-paced movies with such stars as James Cagney and Bette Davis. Darryl F. Zanuck, Warners' production head in the early thirties, left the studio to form his own company, eventually known as Twentieth Century-Fox. By 1939, that studio had achieved success with a series of lively comedies and musicals, and a brace of movies starring the nation's top movie attraction, Shirley Temple. At Columbia, Harry Cohn, perhaps the crudest and most ruthless of studio heads, had managed to turn his studio from a barely surviving resident of "Poverty Row" into a thriving company with a string of hit films.

What these men shared in common was a rough-hewn, blunderbuss style, a deep love for movies and moviemaking, and especially an uncanny instinct for weaving together the elements of a successful film. Much has been made of this ability (it is often used to excuse their personal excesses and vices), and it does, in part, account for the extraordinary number of durable films released under their aegis in 1939. But there is something more, something that may be far more important, and that is their ability to find and use the best people for actually creating their films: the directors, the writers, the cinematographers, and all the others who were, after all, responsible for what turned up on the screen. Goldwyn, Mayer, Zukor, and their colleagues had the undeniable gift for sensing what movie audiences wanted to see, but the people they hired had the talent and the skill. And these were the people who fashioned the lasting films that are celebrated in this book.

In 1939, many of the screen's finest directors were at the crest of their creative powers or were soon about to reach it. William Wyler capped a series of impressive films made under the banner of producer Sam Goldwyn (*These Three,* 1936; *Dodsworth,* 1936; *Dead End,* 1937) with a hauntingly beautiful adaptation of Emily Brontë's novel *Wuthering Heights.* Howard Hawks synthesized his abiding interest in men under stress with *Only Angels Have Wings,* concerning intrepid pilots who risk their lives to deliver the mail. George Cukor added another smoothly executed film to his string of credits with an entertaining version of Clare Luce's vitriolic play *The Women.* And Ernst Lubitsch's sophisticated, elegant touch helped to make *Ninotchka* a sparkling gem of a romantic comedy.

For John Ford, 1939 was an especially rewarding year. During the thirties, his films had ranged far afield, from a troubled Ireland (*The Informer,* 1935) to a tempest-tossed island (*The Hurricane,* 1937). However, his penchant for Americana had never really left him—he had directed two paeans to small-town life with Will Rogers—and during 1939 he was able to return triumphantly to American themes. In *Stagecoach,* his first Western since 1926, he brought a new vitality to the genre by giving full-bodied strength to the archetypal characters and situations, and by filming a few scenes in his beloved Monument Valley, on the Arizona-Utah border, with an open-air expansiveness. His *Young Mr. Lincoln* paid tribute not only to the Great Emancipator but also to the sturdy values he embodied. Only Frank Capra matched Ford in his admiration of the American experience; in *Mr. Smith Goes to Washington,* his patriotic fervor was blended deftly with warming humor.

Throughout 1939, directors with solidly professional credentials offered some of their best work. There were unmistakable echoes of Ernst Lubitsch's witty, tongue-in-cheek style in Mitchell Leisen's *Midnight.* George Stevens topped a decade of polished entertainments with the rousing adventure of *Gunga Din.* Leo McCarey's ability to veer from comedy (*Duck Soup,* 1933) to drama (*Make Way for Tomorrow,* 1937) found ideal expression in *Love Affair,* his charming mix of humor and sentiment. And English-born Edmund Goulding was able to guide Bette Davis through two of her finest performances in *Dark Victory* and *The Old Maid.* There were other directors as well (see the pages of this book), but the fact that all this first-rate moviemaking converged in a single year remains an astonishing fact of film history.

Director Victor Fleming deserves special mention, not only because he was the director of record on two major 1939 films but also because the two films happen to be among the most consistently popular, most revered of the past half-century. A blunt and burly man who had worked in films since 1910, Fleming inherited *Gone With the Wind* and *The Wizard of Oz* in that game of musical chairs frequently played by filmmakers. His work on these films was proficient, capable, and sometimes better than that, but so many other forces came to bear on both films, especially the unavoidable, overpowering force named David O. Selznick, who dominated *Gone With the Wind,* that neither film can honestly be called "a Victor Fleming movie." More likely, his own stamp can be found on some of his lesser films, such as *Treasure Island* (1934) and *Captains Courageous* (1937).

In addition to a gallery of outstanding directors, these top-ranking films of 1939 boasted an array of screenwriters who represented the pinnacle of this often overlooked art. As the colorful lives of the moguls are exposed, as directors are analyzed and revered, it is easy to pay scant attention to the men and women who created the lines for the actors to speak. In 1939, many of the best scenarists were hard at work at the studios, and if their words were sometimes mangled on their way to the screen, they still played a vital role in the movie year of 1939. Many of their names belong to movie lore: Dudley Nichols (*Stagecoach*); Ben Hecht and Charles MacArthur (*Wuthering Heights*); Sidney Buchman (*Mr. Smith Goes to Washington*); Charles Brackett and Billy Wilder (*Midnight*); Lamar Trotti (*Young Mr. Lincoln*), and Casey Robinson (*Dark Victory*, *The Old Maid*), to cite only a few among many.

Behind the cameras, men of exceptional skill gave these films their sharp or shimmering images. Many of the films boasted the finest cinematographers in the industry, whose work contributed immeasurably to the overall impact. At the Goldwyn studio, Gregg Toland's imaginative work with lighting brought an extraordinarily rich texture to *Wuthering Heights*. (Two years later, he photographed *Citizen Kane*.) At MGM, Hal (Harold) Rosson gave Oz its beautifully colored tones in *The Wizard of Oz*, while William Daniels, Greta Garbo's favorite cameraman, photographed her first comedy performance in *Ninotchka*. At Fox, John Ford saw *Young Mr. Lincoln* and the nineteenth-century American landscape through the eyes of cameraman Bert Glennon, who also photographed the awesome Western vistas of *Stagecoach*. For some cinematographers, a year's assignments could bring drastic contrasts: Ernest Haller was required to move from the black-and-white intimacy of *Dark Victory* to the Technicolor splendor of *Gone With the Wind* when he replaced Bert Glennon in March 1939. Other 1939 films gave work to such top cameramen as Hal Mohr, Joseph Walker, Tony Gaudio, and Joseph August.

Also behind the scenes were the art directors, who could conjure vanished worlds before our eyes, creating both lavish and intimate sets in amazing detail. Virtually every major MGM film of the period seems to have been designed by the indefatigable Cedric Gibbons; in this book alone he can be credited (or cocredited) with the art direction for *The Wizard of Oz*, *Ninotchka*, *The Women*, and *Babes in Arms*. Lyle Wheeler worked to numb exhaustion on the many sets for *Gone With the Wind* (in October 1939, in the last stages of filming, David Selznick apologized for "barking" at him so frequently), and Lionel Banks labored prodigiously to construct the elaborate Washington sets for *Mr. Smith Goes to Washington*. Other art directors who contributed enormously to the success of their films included Richard Day (*Young Mr. Lincoln*), Robert Haas (*Dark Victory*, *The Old Maid*), and Hans Dreier (*Midnight*).

And so it happened in Hollywood in the year 1939: Men and women of exceptional talent, skill, and imagination joined together to create an astonishing number of movies that have stood the severe test of time. Undoubtedly, the past and present visions of America and the world that they projected in their films had their origins in the minds of pioneers such as Zukor, Mayer, and Goldwyn, who wanted to show dreams and legends rather than truth. They insisted on giving the public a movie-eye view of reality in which scarecrows dance, love transcends death on the icy English moors, and the American South is a land of cavaliers and cotton fields. To carry out this view, they called on the most gifted men and women they could find and allowed them to lavish their gifts on every film.

They succeeded to an extent they could never have imagined. Audiences cherished their films, and a half-century later, they continue to treasure them. The best movies of 1939 have retained their hold on the imagination of movie fans, and this book is an attempt to account for that continuing fascination.

1939: Its movies marked one last gasp of sunlit innocence before the darkness of war descended. For at least the length of this book, we are happy to remember them, and to pay homage to their achievements.

Don Budge makes his professional tennis debut . . . The Golden Gate International Exposition opens in San Francisco . . . Singer Marian Anderson is denied permission to perform in Washington's Constitution Hall by the Daughters of the American Revolution . . . Pope Pius XI dies . . . 22,000 members of the German-American Bund rally in New York City . . . Louis Brandeis, America's first Jewish Supreme Court justice, retires from the Court . . . In Germany, Jews are forbidden to practice as dentists, veterinarians, or chemists . . . Wildly cheering throngs welcome General Franco's victorious troops into Barcelona . . . Neville Chamberlain meets Benito Mussolini in Rome . . .

. . . and the rousing adventure tale *Gunga Din* begins an auspicious movie year . . .

In the film's well-remembered climactic battle, the British regimental troops descend on the Thugs.

Men Will Be Boys:
Gunga Din

"Though I belted you and flayed you,
By the living Gawd that made you,
You're a better man than I am, Gunga Din!"
—Montagu Love, reciting Rudyard Kipling's poem in *Gunga Din*

ovie buffs enjoy many kinds of films. Yet whether they prefer lavish musicals or brooding, introspective dramas of alienation, most share a fondness for the adventure film in which characters, throwing caution to the winds, plunge headlong into danger. Often set in exotic or distant lands, the great adventure films satisfy one of our most visceral needs; they take us out of ourselves and allow us, at least vicariously, to shed the fears and inhibitions that keep us from experiencing "life" at its most perilous and exciting. At their exuberant best, these films have a tonic effect on our systems. Like an effective exercise machine, they keep our pulses racing and our hearts pounding. They give us a sense of well-being. Hopefully, we wait for films that make us think, that examine hidden corners of our lives or have something to say about the "human condition." But we often embrace adventure films for their compelling if artless narratives, their penchant for unabashed derring-do, and their colorful backgrounds, and when a truly outstanding one comes along, we continue to revel in it for many years after its first release.

George Stevens's *Gunga Din* is one of those films. By now, reams have been written about its blatantly imperialistic viewpoint and its condescending attitude toward the "natives." Years later, Stevens said that "the movie is so simplistic that if I'd experienced another year, I'd have been too smart to make it." Yet its shortcomings as a humanistic document fail to diminish its fifty-year status as a rousing tale of British warfare against a fanatical Indian cult in the late nineteenth century. We may wince slightly at the immature antics of the three heroes, but once they roar and bellow into action against the maniacal guru of the Thugs, we are caught up in their story, not once but many times. In the

Director George Stevens, behind the camera, assembles the troops on location near Lone Pine, California. The cast and crew suffered through intense heat and windstorms, but Stevens insisted on shooting in an area that resembled India.

early forties, *Gunga Din* became a fixture at neighborhood bijous, often turning up on a double bill with another evergreen perennial such as *The Bride of Frankenstein* or *A Night at the Opera.* There are those who can testify that *Gunga Din* remains a recurrent happy memory from their childhood. Along with Groucho, Chico, and Harpo, they recall Cutter, Ballantine, and MacChesney.

Rudyard Kipling's poem "Gunga Din" first appeared in 1892 as a tribute to a lowly but courageous water boy attached to a British regiment in India during the Victorian era. A fifteen-minute silent short dramatizing the poem had been made in 1911, but until the 1939 film, nobody had undertaken a feature-length production based on the story. In 1928, MGM had considered such a film and even developed a screenplay. There were several other attempts, all merely exploratory since the studio had made no deal with Kipling. Eventually, the project was dropped, and for a while independent producer Edward Small planned a movie derived from the poem. It was not until March 1936 that he finally bought the rights from Kipling's widow and assigned novelist William Faulkner to work on a screenplay. Faulkner's several versions had little resemblance to the film as we know it—in one, Gunga Din is characterized as a liar and a thief. Faulkner's work was never filmed and, later that year, RKO acquired the rights from Small, who joined the studio as a producer. Several new treatments were written, without success.

In the village of Tantrapur, Sgts. Ballantine (Douglas Fairbanks, Jr.), Cutter (Cary Grant), and MacChesney (Victor McLaglen) battle the marauding Thugs. An actual fanatical cult in India, the Thugs were robbers and murderers who offered human sacrifices to the goddess Kali.

In September 1936, director Howard Hawks signed a contract with RKO and soon became involved with the ongoing project of *Gunga Din.* A feisty, hard-bitten man who specialized in action movies, Hawks turned to his friends and collaborators Ben Hecht and Charles MacArthur for an entirely new approach. Hecht had written the screenplay for Hawks's *Scarface* (1932), and he and MacArthur had also worked with Hawks on *Twentieth Century* (1934) and *Barbary Coast* (1935). The studio executives had renewed their interest in *Gunga Din* after the recent success of such India-located adventure movies as *The Lives of a Bengal Lancer* (1935) and *Clive of India* (1935). Now they insisted that Hecht and MacArthur's script bear no resemblance to either of those films or to *The Charge of the Light Brigade,* which was about to be released. In October, the writers sent this wire to RKO's production head Sam Briskin:

HAVE FINALLY FIGURED OUT TALE INVOLVING TWO SACRIFICES, ONE FOR LOVE, THE OTHER FOR ENGLAND, WHICH NEITHER RESEMBLES "BENGAL LANCERS" NOR "CHARGE OF THE LIGHT BRIGADE." AND CONTAINS SOMETHING LIKE TWO THOUSAND DEATHS, THIRTY ELEPHANTS, AND A PECK OF MAHARAJAHS. WE HAVE THIS NOW IN A COCK-TAIL SHAKER AND HAVE POURED OUT SOME THIRTY-FIVE PAGES OF GLITTERING PROSE WHICH LOOK GOOD. BEST REGARDS.

Ultimately, the script they submitted contained many of the elements in the finished film. Basically, the story involved the boisterous and perilous adventures of three soldier friends and the water boy who longs to be a soldier. Their screenplay also contained hints of Kipling's *Soldiers Three*, his 1888 collection of stories about three British privates in India. The most direct influence, however, came from their own play *The Front Page*, the rowdy newspaper comedy that revolved, in part, about a newspaper editor's brazen attempts to keep his star reporter from marrying and leaving the paper. In Hecht and MacArthur's new script, Cutter and MacChesney try to thwart Ballantine's plans to resign from the service to wed his girl, Emmy, and go into the tea business. Their original version had Ballantine falsely arrested for desertion (similar to the device used in *The Front Page*), but in the completed film, Ballantine voluntarily renounces his fiancée for another hitch in the service.

As time passed, *Gunga Din* continued to resist production. By mid-1937, Hecht and MacArthur were no longer working on the screenplay; Edward Small had returned to independent production; and Howard Hawks, unhappy with the reception of his now-classic screwball comedy *Bringing Up Baby*, had also departed.* When Pandro Berman took over as RKO's new head of production, he had the Hecht-MacArthur script pruned by staff writer Anthony Veiller; then he made the most important decision: The movie would be directed by George Stevens, who had guided two of the studio's most successful films, *Alice Adams* (1935), with Katharine Hepburn, and the Fred Astaire–Ginger Rogers musical *Swing Time* (1936). His latest movie, *Vivacious Lady* (1938), had also been a critical and popular hit. Berman felt that Stevens could bring in the movie at a lower cost than Hawks, but he proved to be wrong. Stevens insisted that the film be shot on location near Lone Pine, California, in the middle of the High Sierras, where the rock formations resembled those in India. The studio agreed reluctantly, and with the project reactivated, writers Joel Sayre and Fred Guiol were assigned to rework the script with Stevens. (Guiol had worked with Stevens on the gags for the short Laurel and Hardy comedies in the director's early career.) Aside from some of the slapstick elements, their principal contribution was to introduce the Thuggee cult that existed in India. Assassins or "Thugs," dedicated to committing murder and mayhem in the name of the Hindu goddess Kali, had terrified the populace between the thirteenth and the nineteenth centuries.

Casting the film resulted in the usual number of false starts and changes. Early in the production, when Howard Hawks was still expected to direct, the

---

*RKO also ran into trouble when MGM asserted that the Hecht-MacArthur screenplay infringed on their rights to *Soldiers Three*, which they planned to film. The claim was discarded, but MGM offered to buy the rights and scripts of *Gunga Din* from RKO. The offer was rejected, and MGM didn't make *Soldiers Three* until 1951.

Surreptitiously, Cutter pours elephant medicine into the punch bowl at Ballantine's betrothal dance, while Sgt. MacChesney looks on warily. His intention: to make Ballantine's replacement ill so that their friend will be forced to join them on patrol.

superb British actor Roger Livesey was considered for one of the roles, and Hawks suggested that the studio try to borrow Robert Montgomery and Spencer Tracy from MGM for the roles of Ballantine and MacChesney. Production head Sam Briskin even tried to persuade Louis B. Mayer to lend him Tracy, Clark Gable, and Franchot Tone in exchange for the rights to the old musical *Rio Rita*. None of these transactions came to pass. When George Stevens took over as director, the casting procedure finally gained momentum. Cary Grant was suggested for the role of Ballantine and Jack Oakie, an RKO contractee, was considered for the cockney cutup named Cutter.

Grant, however, had a different notion. When Douglas Fairbanks, Jr., was asked to play the role of Cutter instead of Oakie, Grant went to producer Berman and suggested that he and Fairbanks exchange roles. He was convinced that he could bring a special quality of brash, energetic humor to the role, which would help the film more than if he were to play the conventional romantic lead of Ballantine. Berman finally agreed, and the roles were switched, giving Grant the chance to shine in one of his funniest, most unrestrained performances. Victor McLaglen, who had played many burly, rough-hewn military men (most

Ballantine bids farewell to his apprehensive fiancée, Emily Stebbins (Joan Fontaine). An RKO contract player since 1937, Fontaine made a rather pallid impression and was released by the studio. A year later, she became a star as the terrified wife in Alfred Hitchcock's *Rebecca,* and in 1941, she won an Oscar playing opposite Cary Grant in Hitchcock's *Suspicion.*

memorably opposite Shirley Temple in another Kipling-inspired story, *Wee Willie Winkie*), was signed to play MacChesney. Another RKO contractee, Joan Fontaine, was cast in the thankless role of Ballantine's fiancée, Emmy Stebbins.

For the supporting but extremely crucial role of Gunga Din, the clear first choice was the young Indian actor Sabu, who had appeared in *Elephant Boy* (1937) and *Drums* (1938). Producer Alexander Korda refused to lend him, however, claiming that *The Thief of Bagdad* was being prepared for him. For a while, tests were made of Indian actors, until Garson Kanin, then a writer-director at RKO, suggested that they test the seasoned Broadway actor Sam Jaffe for the role. Jaffe, who had made an impression as the ancient Lama in Frank Capra's *Lost Horizon,* was signed to play Gunga Din. More than three decades older than Sabu, Jaffe nevertheless patterned himself on the teenage actor.*

---

*Long after *Gunga Din,* Jaffe continued to give outstanding performances on stage and screen. His portrait of the mastermind thief in John Huston's *The Asphalt Jungle* (1950) was a memorable mixture of cunning and avarice, and he played the role of frizzy-haired Dr. Zorba in the long-running television series "Ben Casey" in the early sixties.

In the temple of the Thugs, a frightened Gunga Din (Sam Jaffe), the regimental *bhisti*, urges Cutter to make a hasty exit. Stage actor Jaffe was signed to play the role after the young Indian actor Sabu was unavailable. Previously, he had given a striking performance as the High Lama in *Lost Horizon* (1937).

Production began on location in the Sierras, several hundred miles northeast of Los Angeles. Imposing sets were erected, including the village of Tantrapur, a massive Thuggee temple, and military quarters and a parade ground for the British soldiers. The schedule called for six weeks of grueling location work, but the elaborate camera setups extended the time to eight weeks. While the screenplay was still being revised, the cast worked in blistering heat, with the temperature ranging from 105 to 115 degrees. There were other problems besides the heat: A windstorm damaged some of the sets, and three-day dust storms made everything but the closest objects difficult to see. Toward the end of the location shooting, dialogue and pieces of business were still being changed, and the schedule for each day's shooting was made up only the night before. Some of the cast members, especially Cary Grant, were permitted to improvise. Finally, before all the scenes could be completed, Pandro Berman, worried by the spiraling costs, ordered the company to return to Los Angeles, where much of the remaining material was shot. It was not possible, however, to stage the massive climactic battle on the RKO sound stage, and the company returned to the Sierras for two more weeks. This formidable scene required fifteen hundred actors, several hundred horses and mules, and four elephants, in addition to the principal players and the crew.

Other problems surfaced after the movie was finished. Composer Erich Wolfgang Korngold, whose stirring if bombastic scores for Warners films were widely admired, had been asked to write the score. Korngold turned down the assignment, presumably because the studio was unable to give him the time for which he had asked. He was replaced by Alfred Newman, who composed a score that mixed traditional and patriotic songs with original material, which included a memorable theme for Gunga Din. There were also difficulties with Rudyard Kipling's widow, who insisted that the scenes in which actor Reginald Sheffield impersonated her husband be eliminated from the movie. She claimed that he looked absurd in the context of an all-out adventure film. RKO obliged by removing Kipling from the release print, but the footage was later restored when it was uncovered by the American Film Institute. Even so, the references are oblique. Inexplicably riding with the troops, Kipling is addressed by the colonel as "Mr. Journalist," and his name is used only once, when the colonel expresses his admiration for the poem Kipling has written in honor of Gunga Din.

As might be expected, the completed film also ran into trouble with India and indeed was banned from being shown in that country. Its pervading attitude of white supremacy was not lost on Indian critics, and one, Khwaja Ahmad Abbas, writing in *Filmindia* magazine, condemned the movie as "imperialist propaganda of the crudest, the most vulgar sort," which depicted Indians as "nothing better than sadistic barbarians." The Bengal Film Board found the

At the left, Gunga Din and Cutter hide from the marching Thugs in their sacred temple. A few minutes later, as Gunga Din rushes away to summon help, Cutter descends on the Thugs, shouting brazenly, "You're all under arrest! . . . Her Majesty is very touchy about having her subjects strangled!"

looting of a temple by British soldiers thoroughly reprehensible, and it was also pointed out in a letter to RKO executives by the manager of the studio's office in Calcutta that although the cult of Thuggery attracted many Hindus, it was not confined to Hindus alone, nor was Kali a goddess exclusive to Thuggery; she was in fact a revered goddess worshiped by all devout Hindus. *Gunga Din* had deeply offended many orthodox Hindus.

If we can discount *Gunga Din*'s racist attitude and historical distortions, we can enjoy the film for its spectacular action, its boisterous if sometimes juvenile

Sgt. Ballantine is menaced by a Thug. Many years later, Fairbanks remembered that he and Cary Grant had tossed a coin to determine which roles they would play in the film. He also recalled George Stevens as "a very, very serious fellow" who would suddenly break into "great roaring laughter."

The diabolical leader of the Thugs (Eduardo Ciannelli) is about to teach his prisoner MacChesney "the error of false pride," while MacChesney's friends Ballantine and Cutter look on. With his baleful eyes and cries of "Kill for the love of killing!", Ciannelli frightened several generations of young moviegoers.

humor, and the broad strokes of the performances. It begins swiftly, with an attack by Thuggee cultists, disguised as humble pilgrims, on sleeping British troops, and then proceeds to the British station at Muri, where Colonel Weed (Montagu Love) worries about the ominous silence from the remote outpost of Tantrapur. He summons his three most reliable frontier veterans, sergeants Cutter (Grant), Ballantine (Fairbanks), and MacChesney (McLaglen). In the midst of a brawl with Scottish soldiers, the three men are introduced amusingly, with each one appearing at a window as his name is called. Cutter holds one Scotsman by the open window, and when ordered to let go of the man, he obliges, causing the man to plummet to earth. At the colonel's office, the three try to bluff their way through the inquiry, like small boys caught once too often at the jar of jelly.

In the movie's first large-scale action scene, the three lead a band of Indian soldiers and water-carriers (*bhistis*) to Tantrapur. The lowliest of the water-carriers is Gunga Din (Jaffe), who harbors the dream of one day becoming a true soldier. The men find the town strangely deserted, but come upon a small group of natives led by Chota (Abner Biberman). At first humble, Chota becomes defiant and suddenly wails to the goddess Kali. The cry brings forth a band of mounted Thugs, and a full-scale battle begins. With the aid of cameraman Joseph August, Stevens staged this sequence in fine bravura style, compensating for some lapses (unconvincing hand-to-hand fisticuffs, the too-perfect aim of the British soldiers) with vigorous, nonstop action. One startling moment has a Thug about to toss a lighted bomb, which blows up when a well-aimed bullet strikes the bomb. (Actually, the sequence's most memorable shot occurs just before the battle, when a bemused Cutter eyes the deserted post in the foreground, while an Indian soldier is strangled by a Thug in the distant background.)

The men fight the attacking Thugs fiercely and manage to escape by way of the river. They return to Muri, where the colonel worries about the reappearance of the murderous Thuggee cult, which at one time killed many thousands as part of their worship of the goddess Kali. At this point, the movie digresses from the action for some mildly amusing high jinks from sergeants Cutter and MacChesney. Dismayed by the fact that their pal Ballantine is leaving the service to marry Emmy Stebbins (Fontaine), they scheme to keep him with them. At the betrothal dance for Ballantine and Emmy, they spike the punch of Ballantine's replacement, Higgenbotham (Robert Coote), so that he is too drunk to leave with them on the mission to Tantrapur to rout the Thugs. Emmy pleads with Ballantine to stay behind, but he feels a loyalty to his friends, despite their maneuverings. They march off together, with little Gunga Din in tow. Earlier, in a crucial scene, Cutter had caught Din imitating a regimental drill with a rifle. Amused, Cutter instructs him in the proper drill and also allows him to keep his beloved bugle, for Din longs to be the regimental bugler.

The tables turned: MacChesney holds a knife at the throat of the guru, while his friends take a brief respite from the fray.

Gunga Din now moves into its longest and most exciting phase. At Tantra-pur, Cutter, who is forever looking to become instantly wealthy, is eager to search for the gold temple he has heard about from Gunga Din. When Mac-Chesney is forced to jail him to keep him from venturing out alone, Cutter breaks from his cell with the aid of Din and MacChesney's beloved elephant, Annie. Their flight leads them to the gold-domed temple, where Cutter whinnies with excitement at the discovery. (Cary Grant often used this sound to express a number of emotions.) His glee is short-lived, however. The temple turns out to belong to the Thugs, who assemble in a throng to hear the exhortations of their guru (Italian-born actor Eduardo Ciannelli in dark makeup). In a wild-eyed frenzy, the guru calls for his disciples to kill indiscriminately. ("Kill for the love of killing! Kill for the love of Kali! Kill! Kill! Kill!")* Sending Gunga Din off to find help, Cutter swaggers through the ranks of the surprised Thugs, shouting, "You're all under arrest!" He is taken prisoner, and the guru sneers, "Take him to the tower and teach him the error of false pride!"

After a long argument over whether the newly discharged Ballantine can accompany MacChesney on the mission to find Cutter—MacChesney tricks

*Ask any moviegoer of a certain age to recall this scene or the guru's speech, and he or she will oblige with a verbatim account. As usual, Hollywood of the day regarded any accent as all-purpose, and Ciannelli's Italianate line readings were never regarded as inappropriate for an Indian guru.

Ballantine into signing a re-enlistment paper—the two ride off together, with the camera tracking behind them for an exhilarating moment. Gunga Din leads the way to the temple, where they are all captured in a matter of minutes. They find Cutter, as flippant as ever despite the whip marks down his back. The guru threatens them with torture (including a nasty pit of snakes), but they manage to seize him as their prisoner in the torture tower. Here the stoic guru regales them with his plan to ambush the British troops that will surely come to rescue them, and how he will establish Thuggee cults throughout India and the world. "You're mad!" Cutter tells him. "Yes, and Caesar was mad," the guru cries, "Hannibal was mad, and Napoleon was surely the maddest of the lot!" (Many films of the period had the villain expressing a similar sentiment, suggesting that Hollywood was becoming aware of Adolf Hitler's threat of world domination.) To prevent the sergeants from using him as a shield, the guru hurls himself into the snake pit. The Thugs succeed in overpowering Ballantine and MacChesney, and they also bayonet Cutter and Gunga Din.

As the British troops approach, their music blaring proudly, Chota and the Thugs wait to ambush them. What follows is one of the most fondly remembered sequences in film history, even earning the distinction of being parodied in Blake Edwards's 1968 comedy *The Party*. Mortally wounded, Gunga Din staggers painfully to the top of the dome and, before he expires, uses his bugle to warn the soldiers of the impending ambush. A spectacular battle ensues in which the Thugs are routed. For Stevens, whose forte until this time was the lighthearted comedy or musical, this scene was an awesome challenge, and he acquitted himself admirably, giving a sense of scope to the sweeping action. Later, back at the fort, the colonel praises the heroism of the trio but reserves his greatest admiration for the heroic Din. "If ever a man deserved the name and rank of soldier, it was he," he says. "His name will be written on the rolls of our honored dead." As the men's eyes fill with tears, the colonel reads from the last stanza of Kipling's poem:

> . . . So I'll meet 'im later on
> At the place where 'e is gone—
> Where it's always double drill and no canteen;
> 'E'll be squattin' on the coals,
> Givin' drink to poor damned souls,
> An' I'll get a swig in hell from Gunga Din!
> Yes, Din! Din! Din!
> You Lazarushian-leather Gunga Din!
> Though I've belted you and flayed you,
> By the living Gawd that made you,
> You're a better man than I am, Gunga Din!

The film ends with the superimposed figure of Din, fully attired in his soldier's uniform and grinning proudly and happily as he salutes.

Gunga Din works so well as an ensemble film and stays so vividly in our minds as a rousing adventure tale that it is only after repeated viewings that one recognizes how much Cary Grant contributes to its rollicking, high-spirited tone. He had the right instinct in wanting to play Cutter (whose first name, Archibald, is the same as Grant's actual first name). Cutter is a fearless, childlike but eminently likable buffoon whose irrepressible ways cause most of the trouble for his best friends. He is the carefree cockney chap who Archibald Leach may well have been before he turned into Cary Grant. In his book *Romantic Comedy in Hollywood*, James Harvey aptly describes the character of Cutter: "He's the one with the greatest and zaniest energies . . . the most acrobatic and demented, with his cockney bravado and rolling sailor's walk, his straight-backed crouch and high whinny of excitement. It's an unrestrained comic performance and the closest he ever comes to playing an authentic crazy man, full of life and fun and a lunar isolation at the center of it all."*

Grant rides over the film's absurdities and distortions with glee. Joined amiably by Fairbanks and McLaglen, and hoisted by George Stevens's directorial skill, he helps to turn *Gunga Din* into a boy's dream of adventure that adults can savor and enjoy, even half a century after its release. Studios tried on occasion to remake *Gunga Din,* loosely in *Soldiers Three* (1951), with Stewart Granger and David Niven, and then abysmally in *Sergeants 3* (1962), with Frank Sinatra, Dean Martin, and Sammy Davis, Jr., which transferred the Indian setting of Tantrapur and Muri to the Wild West of Nevada. Neither version could approach the captivating fun of *Gunga Din,* or the cheeky bravado of Cutter, Ballantine, and MacChesney. Nor can we forget the wistful poignancy of the little *bhisti* who gave his life for the regiment.

Gunga Din. RKO. Produced by Pandro S. Berman. Directed by George Stevens. Screenplay by Joel Sayre and Fred Guiol; story by Ben Hecht and Charles MacArthur, from the poem by Rudyard Kipling. Photography by Joseph August. Art direction by Van Nest Polglase. Costumes by Edward Stevenson. Edited by Henry Berman and John Lockert. Cast: Cary Grant, Douglas Fairbanks, Jr., Victor McLaglen, Joan Fontaine, Sam Jaffe, Eduardo Ciannelli, Robert Coote, Montagu Love, Reginald Sheffield, and Abner Biberman. Loosely remade as *Soldiers Three* (1951) and as *Sergeants 3* (1962).

---

*James Harvey, *Romantic Comedy in Hollywood* (New York: Alfred A. Knopf, 1987), p. 305.

The New York World's Fair opens in New York City . . . The discovery of nylon promises to bring hosiery to the masses . . . The coronation of Pope Pius XII takes place in Rome . . . The Boston Bruins take hockey's Stanley Cup . . . Carole Lombard marries Clark Gable in Arizona . . . Mahatma Gandhi begins his fast to protest India's autocratic rule . . . Italy invades Albania without resistance . . . Adolf Hitler arrives triumphantly in Prague to claim Czechoslovakia for Germany . . . Nephew William Hitler calls his Uncle Adolf "a menace" . . . A half-million people stage a "Stop Hitler" rally in New York City . . .

. . . and memorable movies continue to arrive at an astonishing rate: *Stagecoach* and *Love Affair* in March; *Midnight, Wuthering Heights,* and *Dark Victory* in April . . .

Sheriff Curley Wilcox (George Bancroft) places the Ringo Kid (John Wayne) under arrest. In the driver's seat: Buck (Andy Devine). After years of appearing in many low-budget movies, including many Westerns, Wayne finally achieved stardom with *Stagecoach*.

Redemption on the Road to Lordsburg: Stagecoach

"There are some things a man can't run away from."
—John Wayne in *Stagecoach*

By the time John Ford's *Stagecoach* was released in the spring of 1939, few major Western films were being made. The genre that may well have been the screen's first—starting as early as 1903 with *The Great Train Robbery*—was no longer regarded as significant. Apart from an occasional large-scale Western such as *Cimarron* (1931) or *The Plainsman* (1936), most "sagebrush sagas" or "oaters," as they were called by the entertainment trade paper *Variety*, were confined to low-budget movies starring William ("Hopalong Cassidy") Boyd, Gene Autry, Hoot Gibson, Ken Maynard, and other popular, gun-totin' cowboys. A burly young football-player-turned-actor named John Wayne, a friend of John Ford's for several years, appeared in a batch of "quickie" Westerns that created no impression whatever. Western aficionados could only point to the silent glory of the best films starring William S. Hart, the dour, implacable hero of rugged pioneer tales.

Even John Ford, a director who deeply revered America's Western experience, had turned away from the genre. In the silent years, he had directed many Western films, including *The Iron Horse* (1924), a lavish account of the building of the first transcontinental railroad, but since *Three Bad Men* in 1926, he had moved on to other themes. Although his darkly brooding "black Irish" temperament led him to *The Informer* (1935), his first acknowledged masterwork, Ford was also drawn to the serenity and bedrock values of nineteenth-century American life in such films as *Judge Priest* (1934) and *Steamboat 'Round the Bend* (1935), both starring the "cowboy philosopher," Will Rogers. There were also routine studio assignments to fill, taking him from Shirley Temple in Rudyard Kipling's India (*Wee Willie Winkie*, 1937) to underwater action (*Submarine Patrol*, 1938).

At the start of the film, Dallas (Claire Trevor) is ushered out of town by the Ladies' Law and Order League. In films since 1933, Trevor specialized in women of dubious reputation, giving a brief but memorable performance as Humphrey Bogart's ex-sweetheart-turned-prostitute in *Dead End* (1937) and later winning an Oscar as an alcoholic gun moll in *Key Largo* (1948).

Ford's auspicious return to the Western after a thirteen-year absence began with "Stage to Lordsburg," a short story by prolific writer Ernest Haycox, which had appeared in an April 1937 issue of *Collier's* magazine. The story, which appeared to have been inspired by Guy de Maupassant's short story "Boule de suif," concerned a varied group of stagecoach passengers who make a treacherous journey through Indian country. Ford bought the story for $7,500 and, working with his longtime collaborator, screenwriter Dudley Nichols, he fashioned a screenplay that combined elements of Haycox's story with other influences, notably the stories of Bret Harte, whom both Ford and Nichols admired. No studio was interested in the script, until producer Merian C. Cooper, then vice-president of Selznick International, signed Ford with the company and decided to turn the property into his first personally supervised production, filming in the relatively new three-color Technicolor process. Ford and Cooper planned to star John Wayne and Claire Trevor—two actors who had been working steadily without achieving stardom—in the leading roles.

After consenting reluctantly to having the project move forward, company head David Selznick suddenly changed his mind, feeling that the movie needed two stars of the caliber of Gary Cooper and Marlene Dietrich. Since Ford and Merian Cooper had already made verbal agreements with Wayne and Trevor, they protested vigorously. Seldom willing to tolerate rebellion in the ranks,

Selznick wrote in a July 1937 memo: "He [Ford] is an excellent man, but there is no point in treating him as a god, and if he doesn't want to be here I'd just as soon have some other good director." Both Cooper and Ford left Selznick International, and Ford signed a nonexclusive contract with Fox and Goldwyn. Meanwhile, "Stage to Lordsburg" waited idly in the wings.

Finally, Ford and Cooper convinced independent producer Walter Wanger that they could make the film on a reasonably low budget, filming it in black-and-white rather than Technicolor, and using reliable second-string actors rather than stars in the leading roles. Ford would work out the details of the location and studio shooting. Wanger agreed to gamble on the project, and the movie, now called *Stagecoach*, went into production. Ford made revisions in the screenplay with Dudley Nichols,* and casting got under way. Major supporting roles were assigned to actors who had worked with Ford on other films. Thomas Mitchell ("Doc Boone") had been importantly cast in *The Hurricane* (1937), and George Bancroft ("Sheriff Wilcox"), a veteran of the silent years, had appeared recently in *Submarine Patrol*. Little Donald Meek ("Peacock"), reliably obsequious or cunning in scores of films, had been featured in *The Informer*, while gravel-voiced Andy Devine ("Buck") had worked for Ford as far back as 1919. John Carradine ("Hatfield") had appeared as a sadistic prison guard in Ford's *The Prisoner of Shark Island* (1936), and Berton Churchill ("Gatewood") had played blustering oldsters in Ford's tributes to small-town America, *Judge Priest* and *Steamboat 'Round the Bend*. Among the passengers aboard the stagecoach to Lordsburg, only Claire Trevor as Dallas and Louise Platt, as the pregnant army wife, Mrs. Mallory, had never been a member of the Ford acting company.

Although most of the film was made on the Goldwyn lot, using rear projection, Ford realized early on that, whatever the cost, some of the most important action scenes would have to be shot on location. In film lore, accounts vary as to how Monument Valley was chosen. Two thousand square miles of desert country astride the Utah-Arizona border, Monument Valley presented a vast and awesome vista of arid land punctuated by towering mountain peaks. The sense of isolation, of natural grandeur that was an integral part of the Western genre, was embodied forever in this Western tract. Many years after using it for the first time in *Stagecoach*, Ford commented casually, "I thought it would be a good place to shoot a Western."† John Wayne insisted that *he* told Ford about the valley. A man named Harry Goulding, who ran the Indian Trading Post at Monument Valley and was anxious to bring money to Indians,

---

*It has been said that Ben Hecht also worked on the script without credit.

†Apparently, Ford was modest about his part in restoring the economy of the poor Navaho Indians in the area. The money they received during the production was gratefully received, and Ford was named an honorary chief called Natani Nez, or Tall Soldier.

The cavalry escorts the stagecoach through Monument Valley. For many years, this majestic site was director John Ford's favorite location, representing everything he felt about the imperishable beauty and grandeur of the American West.

Three passengers on the road to Lordsburg: (left to right) Dallas, the crooked banker Gatewood (Berton Churchill), and the pregnant army wife Lucy Mallory (Louise Platt). The still suggests their disapproval of—and alienation from—each other.

claimed that *he* introduced Ford to the location. Whichever story is fact, there was one inescapable conclusion: Monument Valley became not only John Ford's favorite location for his Western films but also the very symbol and emblem of his deepest feelings about the indestructible majesty and power of America's Western frontier.*

Despite the importance it assumed in the Ford canon, Monument Valley was actually used for little of the footage in *Stagecoach*. The scenes inside the stagecoach were filmed on the lot, using the mock-up of a coach that was placed on rockers. The mock-up was then filmed in front of a screen showing background footage shot especially for the movie. The interiors were shot in dramatically lit sets that went against the common practice of the time by actually having low ceilings.† To represent the town of Tonto, as depicted at the start of the film, Ford used the Republic Pictures Western street for a few days, while the town of Lordsburg, where the climactic nighttime shootout occurs, was, in

---

*Several important sequences for *Stagecoach* were shot on California locations, away from Monument Valley. The river-crossing sequence was filmed at the Kern River near Kernville, and the climactic Indian attack was staged at Muroc Dry Lake near Victorville.

† A great admirer of Ford's, Orson Welles ran *Stagecoach* every night for a month soon after arriving in Hollywood. Two years later, he was praised for his effective use of ceilings in *Citizen Kane* (1941).

At the Dry Fork coach station, some of the passengers gather to eat. The disreputable gambler Hatfield (John Carradine, second from the right) waits on Mrs. Mallory, who, out of moral disapproval, refuses to sit with Dallas and Ringo. Except for Lucy Mallory, the stagecoach passengers exist apart from conventional, "respectable" society.

reality, a fragmentary exterior on the Goldwyn lot, for which lighting units were used from behind doors and windows to suggest a full setting.

As usual, Ford was the autocratic master on the set, insisting on controlling every aspect of the movie and loudly deriding the actors when they failed to give him what he wanted. For a relatively inexperienced actor such as John Wayne, it was both a difficult time and an invaluable learning experience. "Sure he got me angry," Wayne recalled many years later, "but he knew what he was doing. First of all—he was making me feel emotions. He knew he couldn't get a good job of work out of me unless he shook me up so damn hard I'd forget to worry about whether I was fit to be in the same picture with Thomas Mitchell. . . . By deliberately kickin' me around, he got the other actors on my side and hatin' him. . . . Mr. Ford only wanted to do one thing and that was to make good pictures, and to do this he would do anything, anything."* Claire Trevor affirms Ford's treatment of Wayne: "It was tough for Duke to take, but he took it. And he learned eight volumes about acting in the picture." When Wayne had difficulty in playing a love scene with Trevor, Ford told him to raise his eyebrows

*Quoted in Rudy Behlmer, *America's Favorite Movies* (New York: Frederick Ungar Publishing Co., 1982), pp. 109–110.

Sheriff Wilcox and Ringo pour hot coffee into Doc Boone (Thomas Mitchell) so that he can deliver Lucy Mallory's baby. A busy and capable character actor, Mitchell won an Oscar for his performance as the bibulous, philosophical doctor.

The thundering hoofbeats of the cavalry echo in the valley as the soldiers ride to the rescue of the stagecoach passengers. Ford's staging of the Indian attack and cavalry rescue had the pace, vigor, and excitement that always characterized the director's action sequences.

and wrinkle his forehead. Wayne used the same expression for four decades.

Apart from cameraman Bert Glennon and editor Dorothy Spencer, the most important member of Ford's behind-the-camera team was Yakima Canutt, a stuntman and double who had appeared in many earlier Ford Westerns. Canutt, who played a cavalry scout in the movie, performed two of his most spectacular stunts during the filming of the Indian attack sequence. In one, dressed as an Indian, he had to leap from his pony onto the lead horse of the stagecoach and try to seize the reins. The driver shoots him, and he falls between the lead horses; he is dragged a while, then lets go as the horses and coach pass over him. It was an extremely dangerous stunt that Canutt carried off with the help of Ford, who was able to get the shot in one take by placing the camera correctly. Canutt recalled: "It was kind of a tricky thing to do, because you only had two and a half to three feet between horses, and you had to be flat to get clearance under the stagecoach." In another stunt, doubling for John Wayne, he had to leap from one pair of horses to another, until he reached the lead horses and forced them to slow down. Much of the sequence was used as stock footage in later films.

The filming of *Stagecoach* was completed in late December 1938, only four days over schedule. Ford was able to hold to this tight schedule by cutting in the camera; that is, rather than shoot a scene from many angles so that the editor could enjoy flexibility in choosing the right frames, he shot and printed only what he knew in advance he wanted to use. In this way, there was simply no room for second thoughts. He used this technique in many other films, giving his sequences a crispness and clarity that few other directors were able to match. Also contributing to the effectiveness of *Stagecoach* was a musical score that included such favorite nineteenth-century songs as "Jeannie with the Light Brown Hair," "Shall We Gather at the River," and especially "Bury Me Not on the Lone Prairie," which was used whenever the stagecoach moved through the valley. (Frank Capra also played the latter song as a recurrent theme in *Mr. Smith Goes to Washington*, to suggest Jeff Smith's purely American roots.)

Stagecoach resuscitated the failing Western genre and brought new luster to Ford's reputation, presaging his even greater and more complex Westerns in the years to come. Yet its basic story is hardly fresh or original, and its characters could never claim to be newly minted. In a tradition that extended from *Grand Hotel* to *Ship of Fools*, Dudley Nichols's screenplay assembles a disparate group of people and sends them forth together on an experience that alters their lives. In this instance, the people are passengers on a stagecoach that moves through Apache territory in New Mexico of the 1880s. Not unexpectedly, they represent different strata of pioneer Western society: a seedy alcoholic doctor named Boone; Dallas, a prostitute forced to leave town by the community's high-minded ladies; a gambler named Hatfield, once the scion of a proud Southern family; banker

Gatewood, who is absconding with his bank's funds; a timid whiskey drummer named Peacock; and Mrs. Mallory, a genteel, rather lofty army wife who is expecting a baby. Also aboard are gravel-voiced Buck, the driver; and fair-minded Sheriff Wilcox (George Bancroft). Another passenger completes the contingent: When a wanted young outlaw called the Ringo Kid (John Wayne) turns up with a lame horse, Wilcox places him under arrest.

As the passengers interact, attitudes are exposed, secrets are revealed, and long-dormant feelings rise to the fore. It turns out that the Ringo Kid is bent on a mission of revenge, vowing at all costs to get to Lordsburg and kill the men who murdered his father and brothers. Scorned by the "respectable" passengers, the Kid and Dallas discover kindred souls in each other and fall in love. At the Dry Fork coach station, Mrs. Mallory gives birth to a baby delivered by a shaky but resolutely sober Doc Boone. Banker Gatewood tries desperately but futilely to conceal his crime, while Hatfield, summoning his last vestige of courtly behavior, offers his protection to Mrs. Mallory. In the inevitable Apache attack, Hatfield is killed and Peacock seriously wounded, and in the final confrontation in Lordsburg, Ringo exacts his revenge. With the complicity of Sheriff Wilcox, he and Dallas ride off together to begin a new life.

Dudley Nichols's lean dialogue moves the story ahead efficiently, and under Ford's reliable direction, the action scenes have an admirable pace and excitement. Yet if this were all, *Stagecoach* would qualify as a strong but conventional Western film, with little claim to classic status. What Ford was able to do, by way of his collaborators and his own belief in the material, was to give the characters and their predicament a surprising depth that made them fully rounded, fully credible figures. Within the framework of the standard Western saga, there are moments that make us care about the beleaguered stagecoach passengers: Doc Boone struggling to stay sober as he prepares to deliver his first baby in years; Ringo gazing at the Madonna-like view of Dallas holding the newborn child; Hatfield preparing to shoot Mrs. Mallory during the Apache attack, in order to spare her the horror of capture; Ringo confronting the Plummer boys in Lordsburg, his face tightly set in grim determination.

None of the major sequences in *Stagecoach* were new to the genre, yet Ford succeeded in crystallizing the conventions of the Western movie in a way that affected filmmakers in succeeding decades. The Apache attack on the stagecoach has been viewed as a model of its kind. As the camera tracks behind the coach roaring through the valley, we suddenly see the implacable faces of the Indians as they mass for the attack.* Just as Doc Boone raises a toast to the passengers,

---

*In *Stagecoach,* the Indians seem to be forces of nature rather than the painted, screaming savages in Ford's *Drums Along the Mohawk,* released the same year. Ford's Western films often betrayed an ambivalent attitude toward the Indians, which only resolved itself much later in the mournful, elegiac *Cheyenne Autumn* (1964).

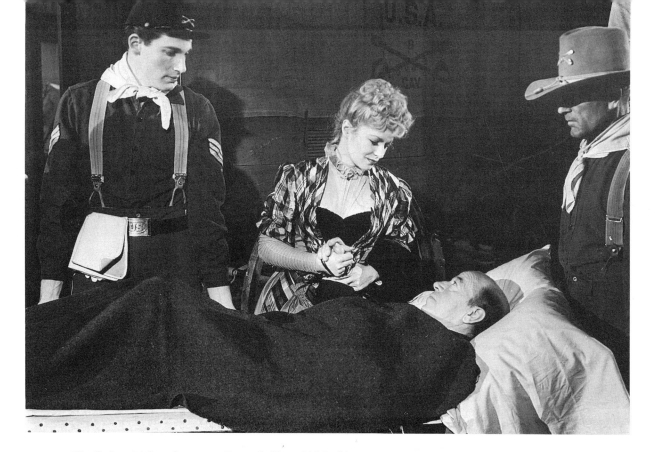

The little whiskey drummer Peacock (Donald Meek), wounded in the Indian attack on the stage-coach, is comforted by Dallas. During the film, Dallas displays the womanly, nurturing instincts that appeal to the Ringo Kid. Donald Meek appeared in scores of movies in the thirties and forties, usually in nasty or obsequious roles.

an arrow whizzes into Peacock, and the charge begins. The stagecoach hurtles toward the camera, with the Apaches in wild pursuit. During the ensuing melee, Yakima Canutt carried out the bold stunts that many viewers remember. At the point when ammunition is gone and the group faces inevitable slaughter, the stirring sound of the cavalry bugle tells them that help has arrived in the nick of time. Their flags flying, the cavalrymen rout the Apaches to the strains of "Battle Cry of Freedom."

The climactic shootout between Ringo and the Plummer brothers, filmed at night on the partial sets representing Lordsburg, has also taken on a mythic connotation with time. While the coach pulls safely into town, the Plummers learn that the revenge-minded Ringo Kid is on board. (An uneasy Luke Plummer is dealt "a dead man's hand.") Fearing for Ringo's life, Dallas tries to prevent the inevitable confrontation, but Ringo is not only determined to kill the Plummers but also convinced that he will survive to marry Dallas. Touched, Dallas tells him, "I'll never forget that you asked me, Kid." Soon, the wary Plummers gather in the darkened street, waiting for Ringo to appear. In the ensuing gunfire, the three Plummers are shot dead. Ringo expects to ride off with the sheriff to prison, but at the last moment, Wilcox allows him to leave for his farm with Dallas. Smiling at each other, pleased to share one small triumph over "the blessings of civilization," the sheriff and Doc go off together to have a drink. Throughout the scene, the images are spare and the dialogue minimal.

Over the years, *Stagecoach* has been regarded as a prototypical example of the genre. Yet without undue strain, the film can also be credited with a touch of profundity that raises it several notches above most other Westerns. One of John Ford's most persistent concerns over the years was with those who live outside the normal boundaries of society, the outcasts who ultimately achieve, often through pain and sorrow, their own redemption or salvation. We can recall, among others, Gypo Nolan in *The Informer*, finding forgiveness at the church's altar for betraying a friend; Dr. Samuel Mudd in *The Prisoner of Shark Island*, imprisoned, after public outrage, for setting the broken leg of Lincoln's assassin, then winning pardon by helping the victims of a yellow fever epidemic; and the renegade priest in *The Fugitive* (1947), who allows a hostage to be executed in his place, then forfeits his life by helping a fellow fugitive. In Ford's Catholic sensibility, no sins are so heinous that they cannot be absolved, no outcasts so lowly or humiliated that they are beyond God's mercy.

Although their sins do not include betrayal of their fellowmen, the principal characters in *Stagecoach* are also outcasts who are shunned and scorned by the world but who find a kind of redemption before their journey ends. Doc Boone may return to his liquor, but for one shining moment he is able to muster his skills as a physician and bring a new life into the world. Reviled by the townswomen (one of whom is married to the crooked Gatewood), Dallas reacts with gratitude when Ringo treats her like a lady, and she puts aside her bitterness to offer help to the woman who snubbed her. Later, her long-buried maternal instinct gives her a glow that makes Ringo love and appreciate her even more. The Ringo Kid himself, purged of his need for vengeance, discovers a hopeful future at the side of his transformed and redeemed Mary Magdalene. Even the gambler Hatfield has recovered some of his old gallantry before he dies. Clearly, Ford values these "sinful" outcasts much more than he does the "civilized" hypocrites who ride the stagecoach, especially Gatewood and the sanctimonious Mrs. Mallory.

So much has been written about the pivotal role of *Stagecoach* in revitalizing the Western genre that it has been easy to overlook the teamwork of Ford's cast. Many of the cast members (John Carradine, Berton Churchill, Donald Meek, Thomas Mitchell, Andy Devine), having worked at one time or another with Ford, were acquainted with his authoritarian directorial style. For others (Claire Trevor, Louise Platt), it was a new and sometimes difficult experience, but the result shows in the ease and skill of their performances. Wayne would later refine the laconic, determined Westerner, often under Ford's tutelage, so that he could eventually create a many-faceted role such as Ethan Brand in Ford's masterly *The Searchers* (1956). Here, in his first major role since *The Big Trail* (1930), he adds a becoming note of quiet gallantry to the standard character of the Ringo Kid. Trevor, who would finally find a part worthy of her talent in *Key Largo* (1948), at first overplays Dallas's desperation and rancor, but she finally turns her reformed prostitute into an affecting figure.

After *Stagecoach,* Ford would return often to the Western, deepening his themes and enriching the visual splendor of his canvas as he put his familiar stock company of players through its paces. Yet even in the best of his later Westerns, there are unmistakable echoes of *Stagecoach:* the same reverence and awe for the sprawling vistas of America's frontier, the same appreciation of pioneer courage and resilience, the same regard for the lost and unredeemed. Like the Ringo Kid, Henry Fonda's Wyatt Earp in *My Darling Clementine* (1946) learns that "there are some things a man can't run away from." Like the social pariahs in *Stagecoach,* Fonda's Colonel Owen Thursday in *Fort Apache* (1948) rides the hard road to redemption, ultimately sacrificing his life in payment for leading his men into an Indian ambush. Perhaps most important, in the few scenes set in Monument Valley, *Stagecoach* offers Ford's first use of the imposing stretch of land that would later become as essential as any character in such films as *She Wore a Yellow Ribbon* (1949).

In its day, *Stagecoach* won the approval of critics and the film industry. It was nominated in the categories of Best Picture, Best Director, and Best Cinematography, and it earned Oscars for Thomas Mitchell and its music score.* Over the years it has taken on a special cachet as a landmark Western. Filmmakers, including Ford himself, have borrowed liberally from its straightforward story, its unadorned characters, and its clean, direct, enormously effective visual style. Yet somehow moviegoers continue to remember best the stagecoach passengers who met their fate, or their future, in their perilous ride through the valley.

Stagecoach. United Artists. Produced by Walter Wanger. Directed by John Ford. Screenplay by Dudley Nichols, from the story "Stage to Lordsburg" by Ernest Haycox. Photography by Bert Glennon. Art direction by Alexander Toluboff. Edited by Dorothy Spencer and Walter Reynolds. Cast: Claire Trevor, John Wayne, Thomas Mitchell, George Bancroft, John Carradine, Donald Meek, Andy Devine, Berton Churchill, Louise Platt, and Tim Holt. Remade in 1966 and (as a television movie) in 1986.

---

*Honors were shared by Richard Hageman, Franke Harling, John Leipold, Louis Gruenberg, and Leo Shuken.

In the church on his grandmother's estate, Michel Marnet (Charles Boyer) and Terry McKay (Irene Dunne) undergo a near-mystical experience that deepens their love for each other.

Tender Emotions:
Love Affair

"I was looking up at the one hundred and second
floor. It was the nearest thing to heaven. You see,
you were there!"
—Irene Dunne to Charles Boyer in *Love Affair*

as romance vanished from the mov-
ies forever? There are those who claim that it has become obsolete, that ardent
embraces and kisses in the moonlight have been replaced by frantic, sweaty
couplings in the dark. Practical-minded filmmakers cite any number of "old-
fashioned" romantic stories that expired at the box office as surely as any heroine
stricken with the "movie disease." (Arthur Hiller's *Love Story*, a popular hit in
1970, probably succeeded because of massive publicity for the novel and film
rather than any emotional involvement with the dying Ali MacGraw.) If romance
hasn't disappeared entirely, then it has certainly taken a new form. Lovers can
still "meet cute," but now their mutual attraction evolves into more-or-less
explicit bedroom scenes, followed by lyrical ramblings through parks, meadows,
or city streets. Then come the bickering and the discussion of "relationships,"
ending with reconciliation or separation. Unlike movie lovers of past decades,
they do not suffer the condemnation of a "moral" society, and they are seldom
doomed by illness or imprisonment. Yet unlike past movie lovers, they can
never escape to their own back-street apartment, their secluded Garden of Allah,
their private Peniston Crag. The world is too much with them.

Once, in the days probably beyond recall, romance was a salable commodity
in films. Whether the movies involved lovers communing telepathically across
the miles—Chico calling to his beloved Diane in *Seventh Heaven*—or clinging to
each other after a single unseen night of passion—Christina embracing her
Antonio in *Queen Christina*—audiences surrendered willingly to their mood of
perfumed enchantment. If lyrical suffering was called for, who could move us
to tears more than Greta Garbo as Camille, coughing her last in the arms of

Terry, Grandmother (Maria Ouspenskaya), and Michel on Grandmother's estate in Madeira. In many films of the thirties and forties, tiny Russian actress Ouspenskaya exuded old-world charm and wisdom that sometimes contained more than a touch of steel.

Robert Taylor's Armand? Louis B. Mayer, overseer of Garbo's films, who understood the taste of American moviegoers of his day better than anyone in Hollywood, served up the romantic warblings of Jeanette MacDonald and Nelson Eddy and the romantic posturings of Leslie Howard and Norma Shearer as Romeo and Juliet. Love, ardent and passionate love, had a market on the screen; never mind that these popular performers were years too old for their roles.

Occasionally, a romantic film involved lovers who were not only past the first blush of youth but also beyond the early years of maturity. Fannie Hurst's novel *Back Street* became a 1932 film (remade twice) in which a nobly suffering Irene Dunne endures an over-the-years romance with married financier John Boles, earning her little more than the contempt of his children (which ultimately changes to admiration) and a perfectly marcelled gray coiffure. In *The Barretts of Wimpole Street* (1934), an ailing, tremulous Elizabeth Barrett (Norma Shearer), long dominated by her dangerously possessive father (Charles Laughton), finally escapes from his clutches and surrenders to the ardent attentions of poet Robert Browning (Fredric March). Many a sentimental romance of the thirties involved mystical ties between lovers that not only spanned centuries (*Berkeley Square*, 1933) but also the bridge between life and death (*Smilin' Through*, 1932; *Death Takes a Holiday*, 1934; *Peter Ibbetson*, 1935).

Terry McKay and Michel Marnet, the characters played by Irene Dunne and Charles Boyer in *Love Affair*, are hardly in their dotage but neither are they dewy-eyed innocents unaware of the consequences of their shipboard romance. In fact, when they meet, both are already involved with other people—she is engaged to be married, and he has an eager socialite waiting in New York. They exude confidence in their initial banter—she is a nightclub singer currently between engagements, and he is a debonair playboy with a long string of con-quests. With their eyes wide open, under the potent influence of moonlight and an unstated void in their lives, they drift into a love affair that surpasses any previous relationship. During the course of the film, in the Hollywood tradition, they share an idyllic romantic interlude, are cruelly separated by a tragic accident, and meet again for a happy ending.

When Dunne and Boyer were signed to play the leading roles in *Love Affair* under Leo McCarey's direction, both were established stars who had earned their popularity by the end of the decade. After a series of moist dramas, in which she played mostly high-minded, self-sacrificing women (how regally she endured scandal and abuse), and an occasional musical (notably *Show Boat*, 1936, in which she could use her trained singing voice), Dunne unveiled a talent for tongue-in-cheek romantic comedy with *Theodora Goes Wild* (1936) and *The Awful Truth* (1937), the latter film also under Leo McCarey's direction. If her tongue sometimes seemed planted too firmly in her cheek, her abundant charm and womanly appeal made (and kept) her an important star. After appearing in French films since the twenties, Boyer had settled in Hollywood in 1934, at-tracting more attention for his romantic good looks than for his acting ability, which was considerable. His role as a devious denizen of the Casbah in *Algiers* (1938) established his reputation as the Latin lover whose deep, accented voice and bedroom eyes could set women's hearts aflutter. Only in later years was he permitted to exercise his acting skill and versatility.

By 1939, director Leo McCarey's own versatility had already been proven. A master at blending comedy and sentiment (*Love Affair* is a first-rate example), McCarey had entered films in 1916, working as a gag writer and director of comedy shorts. By the early years of sound, he had directed many of the best comic entertainers of the period, including Eddie Cantor (*The Kid From Spain*,

Irene Dunne and Charles Boyer on the set of *Love Affair* with director Leo McCarey. McCarey had already proven his skill at directing comedy (*The Awful Truth*, 1937) and sentiment (*Make Way for Tomorrow*, 1937), and earlier he had survived the Marx Brothers with flying colors in the hilarious *Duck Soup* (1933).

1932), Mae West (*Belle of the Nineties,* 1934), and most gloriously, the Marx Brothers in their classic farce *Duck Soup* (1933). *Ruggles of Red Gap* (1935), his first important film, offered humor of a gentler kind in its story of a very proper British butler (Charles Laughton) who finds success and happiness in the wild American West. When the trend in film comedy shifted from raucous to romantic, McCarey directed Dunne and Cary Grant in the deft sophistication of *The Awful Truth.* Later, in the forties and fifties, McCarey's career turned erratic, shifting uneasily from genteel piety and sentiment (*Going My Way,* 1944, *The Bells of St. Mary's,* 1945) to political proselytizing (*My Son John,* 1952). Yet, as Richard Corliss has said, "Few other directors could skate so close to propaganda and bathos and end up with ankles straight and poise intact."*

Early in 1938, McCarey had conceived of *Love Affair* expressly as a vehicle for Dunne and Boyer, who admired each other but had never appeared together in a film. Boyer, in turn, admired McCarey, especially for his *Ruggles of Red Gap.* With Mildred Cram and Delmer Daves (uncredited), McCarey developed the original story, then had Daves write the screenplay. Donald Ogden Stewart,

*Quoted in *Film Comment,* Fall 1971, p. 59.

Back in New York after leaving the ship, Terry meets her fiancé Ken Bradley (Lee Bowman). Bowman made a career of being jilted by his leading ladies and was occasionally given a top role in a minor feature.

who received co-author credit, added some dialogue, especially for the early shipboard sequences. McCarey's style as a director was often improvisational, and, working with Daves, he made daily changes in the script, embellishing some parts and abandoning others. This approach created a problem for his stars, especially Boyer, who was used to memorizing his lines early on in the production, seldom having to veer from the printed text. Although the director's looser, freer style may have disconcerted Boyer, it also resulted in one of his best and most complex early performances, in which his "Great Lover" image is colored with a becoming grace and vulnerability. Dunne also moves with ease through the somewhat abrupt transition from comedy to drama.

Love Affair begins in the familiar vein of romantic comedy as Terry and Michel set sail for America, she to return to fiancé Ken Bradley (Lee Bowman in another of the thankless "other man" roles he played during those years), and he, according to rumor, to marry rich, frivolous Lois Clarke (Astrid Allwyn). When Terry and Michel meet, their exchanges, at first, are flippant and teasing. While they are clearly attracted to each other, they are too sophisticated to take the traditional banter of flirtation all that seriously. Terry, in particular, appears to back off nervously from revealing too much of herself, or giving the wrong impression. Finally, she cannot resist deflating his practiced charm by asking, "Have you been getting *results* with a line like that? Or would I be surprised?" Her remark leads to a flurry of disagreement, but only a flurry, since they evidently are strongly attracted to each other.

The effectiveness of these early sequences depends as much, if not more, on the acting of Dunne and Boyer as on the dialogue. Although Dunne claimed that she never enjoyed playing comedy as much as drama, she was one of the screen's most elegant comediennes, investing her lines with a light, tongue-in-cheek tartness that refused to accept pompous or foolish behavior from anyone. Like many of the best thirties actresses, Dunne combined beauty and intelligence in such a way that one complemented the other. When a role called for her special qualities, as did Terry McKay in *Love Affair*, she was peerless. Boyer, too, responding to McCarey's improvisational technique, gives his Michel Marnet a perfect blend of debonair charm and bemused self-awareness. Throughout this essentially comic first section, Terry's American breeziness plays well against Michel's European courtliness.

The film's first and most important transition from light to serious romance occurs when their boat trip is interrupted so that Michel can take Terry to his grandmother's home in Madeira. Grandmother, played by wizened Russian actress Maria Ouspenskaya with her familiar mixture of benignity and old-world wisdom, shows Terry another, deeper side of Michel, a talented artist who has been wasting his time in frivolity. Her serene, beautiful house—"a good place to sit and remember," according to Grandmother—casts a nearly mystical spell over Terry. At the same time, Terry's gentle way with the old woman enchants Michel. When she sings to his grandmother's piano accompaniment, his eyes reflect a growing love for her. Ostensibly to smooth the change from comedy to drama, McCarey built up this long, languid sequence with Ouspenskaya, photographing much of it in a misty glow. The sequence also contains a touch of the religiosity that would later permeate many of McCarey's films. Terry and Michel first sense their deep attachment to each other while praying in the church on Grandmother's estate.

This same wistful mood extends to Terry and Michel's first important love scene. Back on the ship, they finally talk about their deepening relationship. Standing at the ship's rail, as the camera moves in closely, he tells her that he needs six months to find out whether he's worthy to say what is in his heart. They agree to meet at the end of that time atop the Empire State Building—if they still feel the same way about each other. The stars' acting in this sequence is so skillful—they play against each other with such muted tenderness—that a viewer has barely enough time to question the illogic of their decision. Why,

Crippled by an accident while rushing to meet Michel, Terry sings "Wishing" with a group of visiting children. Although the film's sentiment comes perilously close to turning treacly, McCarey manages to keep it in reasonable control.

we may ask, must he prove his "worth," presumably as an artist, before he can claim her love, especially since it's readily apparent that he has already won her heart? The decision becomes more of a plot device than a logical extension of their relationship.

At this point, *Love Affair* leaves comedy behind and moves directly into romantic drama, heavily laced with sentimentality. As the months pass, Terry resumes her singing career, while Michel pursues his serious art and finally sells one of his paintings. On the day of their planned reunion in New York, an elated Terry rushes to meet Michel, but in her happily distracted state, she is hit by a car and critically injured. Disappointed and saddened, Michel waits for hours at their rendezvous, then decides that she must have married Ken after all. The motivation again becomes cloudy as Terry, now permanently crippled, refuses to contact Michel to tell him what has happened to her. With little apparent regard for the pain she must be causing him, without even entertaining the possibility that his love for her may be stronger than pity, she erases Michel from her life. Even later, when he sees her seated in a theater, she affords him nothing but a curt greeting. (She tells Ken, who is still her loyal fiancé, "Unless I can walk to him someday, he'll never know. And I mean *run!*")

While Michel's reputation as a painter increases, Terry works at an orphanage, where she leads the children (actually dubbed by the Robert Mitchell Boys Choir) in a rather treacly rendition of Buddy De Sylva's song "Wishing." Inevitably, however, love will find a way, and in the film's last scene, they are reunited. Michel goes to her apartment, where Terry tries desperately to keep him from learning that she is crippled. He gives her Grandmother's shawl, and Terry realizes that the old lady has died. On the wall of Terry's apartment, he sees the painting he had made of Grandmother and remembers that he had been told that the girl who bought it was wheelchair-bound. Suddenly, Michel understands her secrecy and her unwillingness to see him. They embrace ardently as she tells him, "I was looking up at the one hundred and second floor. It was the nearest thing to heaven. You see, *you* were there!" Terry's faith in the future, and their lives together, is now complete: "There doesn't have to be a miracle."

Once again, *Love Affair* demonstrates the efficacy, or even the impact, of star acting. The second half of the film, so solemn and sentimental in comparison with the first, asks the audience to make a rather abrupt change from laughing with two sophisticated people who find unexpected romance to commiserating with their plight, especially hers. In fact, Leo McCarey was acutely aware of the schism, and called in several writers to make a smoother transition. Yet it works surprisingly well, and the reason is largely due to the skill and conviction that Dunne and Boyer bring to their roles, especially in their climactic scene. Both actors respond with a rare intelligence and perceptiveness to the changing moods of the screenplay. Dunne's performance earned an Oscar nomination; and there were other nominations for Best Picture, Best Supporting Actress (Ouspenskya), Writing (Original Story), and Best Song.

The extent of the film's achievement becomes even more evident when one compares it with Fox's 1957 remake, *An Affair to Remember*. Directed again by Leo McCarey, the movie starred Cary Grant and Deborah Kerr, two equally attractive performers, as the lovers whose shipboard romance grows into something permanent. The screenplay remained the same; only the production values were expanded to meet the grandiose requirements of CinemaScope. Yet *An Affair to Remember* seemed lacquered and lifeless, and exposed to the light of an expensive new production, the story's lapses in logic and reason became all the more noticeable. Still, it was the acting that made the most crucial difference. Whereas Dunne and Boyer conveyed the sense of two mature people finding themselves giddily in love, Kerr and Grant glitter like stars rather than people, proving that star *presence* is not enough.

In the film's closing sequence, Terry tries to keep Michel from learning about her crippled condition, but he soon realizes the truth. The lovers are reunited for a happy ending.

It may be that more than eighteen years separates *Love Affair* and *An Affair to Remember*. Attitudes change, and perhaps we are no longer able to accept without question the dubious romantic assumptions of the original film. Perhaps romance, or a certain sort of romance, has vanished from the movies forever. In any case, *Love Affair* stands as a pleasing remembrance of things past.

Love Affair. RKO. Produced and directed by Leo McCarey. Screenplay by Delmer Daves and Donald Ogden Stewart, from a story by Mildred Cram and Leo McCarey. Photography by Rudolph Maté. Art direction by Van Nest Polglase. Edited by Edward Dmytryk and George Hively. Cast: Irene Dunne, Charles Boyer, Marie Ouspenskaya, Lee Bowman, Astrid Allwyn, and Maurice Moscovich. Remade in 1957 as *An Affair to Remember*.

Eve Peabody (Claudette Colbert), penniless in Paris, finds refuge from the rain at a musicale, where she hands in a pawn ticket to gain admittance. One of the best comediennes of the period, Colbert infused her performances with grace, wit, and a touch of irony.

Eve in Paris:
Midnight

"Every Cinderella has her midnight."
—Claudette Colbert in *Midnight*

On February 28, 1933, one day after Hitler's henchmen burned the Reichstag, Germany's parliament building, blaming the fire on the Communists, an Austrian-born Jewish journalist, film writer, and man about town named Billy Wilder fled Berlin to Paris.* One of the first to leave the German film industry in that troubled time—more than fifteen hundred movie personnel would flee in the following six years—Wilder had made his reputation with his screenplay for a talked-about film called *People on Sunday* (*Menschen am Sonntag*), codirected by Robert Siodmak and Edgar Ulmer. He soon began working in French films, coscripting and codirecting a movie called *Mauvaise Graine,* starring Danielle Darrieux. The following year, he entered the United States, his ultimate destination, on a tourist visa, working on a project for Columbia Pictures with another emigré director, Joe May. When the project fell through and his visa expired, Wilder went to Mexico before being readmitted to the States. For a while, he wrote original stories in German, until he perfected his English. Eventually, he acquired a writer's contract at Paramount, where he was responsible for several lightweight screenplays.

On one screenplay, *Bluebeard's Eighth Wife* (1938), Wilder collaborated for the first time with another Paramount staff writer named Charles Brackett, who had studied law at Harvard before turning to writing. From the start, they made an unlikely team: Wilder's caustic and cynical European style contrasted with Brackett's suave and courtly manner. They enjoyed working together, however,

---

*Many years later, Wilder remembered that he knew Hitler was not "an unpleasant joke" when he saw the elevator boy at UFA, the MGM of Berlin, in a storm trooper's uniform.

In her posh hotel room, Eve receives flowers from her new admirer, Jacques Picot, while Georges Flammarion (John Barrymore) reads the card. Eve has agreed to George's plan to distract the amorous Jacques away from his wife Helene. Barrymore was uncharacteristically reserved during the filming, having been weakened by illness and heavy drinking.

and *Bluebeard's Eighth Wife,* directed by Ernst Lubitsch, was a modest success. A lightly risqué, slightly acidulous romantic comedy, it revolved about an American millionaire (Gary Cooper) who marries the daughter (Claudette Colbert) of an impoverished French aristocrat. Blinded by love, he consents to a premarital agreement: If they are divorced (he has had seven previous wives), he will pay her $100,000 a year for the rest of her life. Much of the comedy involves her blatant and rather cruel attempts to frustrate him sexually and drive him to a divorce. He not only agrees to a divorce but also suffers a none-too-hilarious nervous breakdown. Ultimately, of course, they are reconciled, although one wonders why he would want her back after such nasty treatment.

Lubitsch's wry, worldly directorial style would seem to mesh ideally with Brackett and Wilder's sharp-edged, witty dialogue (and indeed they did mesh superbly only a year later in *Ninotchka*). In later years, in fact, Wilder acknowledged that he owed his greatest debt of gratitude to Lubitsch, whose unique, slyly insinuating "touch" on film reflected his mischievous personality. Yet in *Bluebeard's Eighth Wife,* the humor has the flat, stale taste of inferior champagne. Ironically, the very next Brackett-Wilder collaboration, under a much less skillful director than Lubitsch, proved to be one of the best and brightest romantic comedies of the decade. The film was *Midnight.*

The story of this movie's journey from script to screen contains more than

At the Flammarion chateau, Eve leads the guests in a conga line, as Georges looks on. The two actresses behind Mary Astor in the line are Elaine Barrie, then John Barrymore's wife, and Hedda Hopper, who, the year before, had started her long career as a gossip columnist.

the usual share of troubles and traumas, involving people both behind and in front of the camera. After Brackett and Wilder completed the script, drawing on a story written for the screen by Edwin Justus Mayer and Franz Schulz, they gave it to producer Arthur Hornblow, Jr., who, in the accepted way of the time, decided that another writer was needed to polish off the rough edges, a process called "writing behind the script." He gave the assignment to Paramount staff writer Ken Englund, and when he was disappointed with the result, he asked Englund, "Who do we have under contract who writes like Brackett and Wilder?" Englund replied, "Charles Brackett and Billy Wilder." The script was returned to them, at which point they blithely retyped the original manuscript and returned it to Hornblow, who had really loved it from the start.

There were some difficulties with the cast. Playing the leading role of Eve Peabody after Barbara Stanwyck was forced to withdraw, Claudette Colbert, as always, insisted that the difficult angles of her face required special attention from the cameraman—he was ordered to photograph only the left three-quarters angle of her face. The right side of her face was known as "the other side of the moon" because nobody ever saw it. A different sort of problem involved Mary Astor, who was playing straying wife Helene Flammarion. As her pregnancy was becoming more evident every week, she had to be swathed in furs, and she was photographed behind a bridge table or presiding at luncheon. When she was supposed to lead a conga line at a party, the script discreetly had her called to the telephone.

John Barrymore, playing Astor's husband Georges Flammarion, presented a more serious dilemma. Weakened by long bouts with alcohol and illness, he was uncharacteristically quiet and reserved on the set. Frequently, he was unable to remember his lines, and for many of his scenes he needed prompt cards, held off-camera by the prop man. He was helped by his wife Elaine Barrie, who had a featured role in the film. His professionalism, however, remained intact, and with prodigious effort, he succeeded in giving a flavorsome comedy performance, laced with wit and irony. He loved the script and later told Billy Wilder that it was the most fascinating screenplay he had ever read. He felt it was an authentic piece of literary comedy.

The most severe problem in making *Midnight* could not be alleviated by prompt cards or an artful cameraman. It was clear from the beginning that the film's director, Mitchell Leisen, and Billy Wilder simply despised each other. Leisen, who for years had been a prominent costume designer and art director, especially for Cecil B. De Mille, had been directing films for Paramount since the early thirties. Proudly and flamboyantly gay at a time when homosexuals tended to remain in the closet, Leisen often placed the décor of his films—their settings and costumes—above the films' story content. A highly competent although uninspired director, he apparently had an intense dislike for writers; as did many others in Hollywood at the time, he regarded them as a necessary evil. Writers were, indeed, low figures in the production pecking order. Wilder, however, was not one to surrender meekly to any director's whims and wishes.

And so Leisen and Wilder clashed over the screenplay for *Midnight*. Sequence by sequence, and even line by line, they argued bitterly. Many years later, Leisen accused Wilder of vulgarity and arrogance, a man who would scream if one line of his dialogue was altered. He claimed that he sat in the room with the writers, helping them construct the characters from his own knowledge of psychiatry. (He had been in analysis for eight years.) For his part, Wilder insists that Leisen "spent more time with Edith Head worrying about the pleats on a skirt than he did with us on the script."* Leisen, he maintains, was too ignorant of story construction to understand that a line or piece of action was being inserted for a reason and not merely as an idle whim. According to Leisen, it was Brackett who refereed their quarrels; Wilder claims it was Arthur Hornblow—"Charlie hated [Leisen] as much as I did. . . . There were these voids in most of his films where any screenwriter could see Leisen had been chopping. *Midnight* is perfect because I fought him every inch of the way."

---

*Quoted in *Billy Wilder in Hollywood* (New York: G.P. Putnam's Sons, 1977), p. 69.

Marcel (Rex O'Malley) and Helene examine Eve's luggage for some evidence of her true identity. Helene can hardly restrain her glee ("Oh, Marcel, this is heaven! Baroness Czerny indeed!"). Three years earlier, O'Malley had played a similar role with Greta Garbo in *Camille* (1936).

Midnight is, indeed, close to perfection in its cynical wit and stylish performances. If it is not necessarily vintage champagne, then it is certainly a bracing glass of superb wine, with a twist of lemon. (In later years, Wilder added another twist of Lemmon to his films, with outstanding results.) Whatever entanglements occurred on the set, the resulting movie sparkles in virtually every scene. It is only when a viewer has finished laughing that the sardonic tone of the screenplay becomes increasingly evident. Most of the characters in *Midnight*, for all their charm and playfulness, are a selfish and grasping lot. The humor of the situations in which they find themselves cannot obscure the fact that we are watching a gold-digging nightclub singer; a cheating, promiscuous wife; her fickle, light-headed playboy lover; her cuckolded husband—sad rather than comic because he *knows* he is being cuckolded—and a society leech who will attach himself to anyone who can relieve his boredom. Without the deft playing of the cast, the laughter would probably stick in our throats.

As it is, *Midnight* manages to bubble along merrily while keeping its cynicism fairly muted and under control. A reverse, also perverse, Cinderella tale, the movie has its not-so-guileless heroine given the chance to have her very own prince and castle, then turning them down for a man from the lower classes. It begins with Eve Peabody (Colbert) arriving in a rain-swept Paris from Monte

Eve introduces her "husband," "Baron" Tibor Czerny (Don Ameche) to Helene, while George registers amusement at Jacques's obvious annoyance with the intrusion. Charles Brackett and Billy Wilder's screenplay sparkled with a wit that made the essentially selfish characters palatable.

Carlo without any money or any possessions other than the evening gown she is wearing. She is spotted by taxi driver Tibor Czerny (Don Ameche), who agrees to drive her around the city as she searches for a job. Evidently, she is no wide-eyed innocent—"at this time of night," she confides to Tibor, "I'm not looking for needlepoint." He takes her for a meal at a local restaurant, where she openly admits her proclivity for gold-digging. She tells him that when the mother of an English lord she was about to marry offered her a bribe, she didn't throw her out. "How could I," she asks, "with my hands full of money?" Nevertheless, Tibor is attracted to her and offers her his room for the night. Jumping quickly to the wrong conclusion, Eve hurries away, leaving Tibor in consternation. In her flight through the rain, Eve is mistaken for a guest at a swank musicale and goes along with the ruse by handing in her pawn ticket.

Thus begins one of the film's brightest sequences, in which Wilder and Brackett not only poke fun at the absurd pretensions of such highbrow activities but also send the plot spinning into orbit. From the first, Eve is spotted as a phony by Georges Flammarion (Barrymore), who eyes her even as he half-dozes through the music. Just when Eve is certain she has been found out, she is swept into a bridge game with three bored guests: Georges's wife Helene (Astor), her current lover Jacques Picot (Francis Lederer), and Marcel (Rex O'Malley),

Eve's countermove: When Tibor turns up in his taxi driver's uniform, Eve explains that he is subject to sudden bursts of "eccentricity." It runs in the family, she explains: "Why else would his grandfather send us as an engagement present one roller skate covered with Thousand Island dressing?"

the eternal party guest, who is given some of the script's wittiest lines. Marcel considers himself a telephone worshiper: "Whenever a day comes without an invitation, I pray to my telephone as though it were a little black god. I beg of it to speak to me . . . to ask me out whenever there is champagne or caviar."

To her astonishment, Eve, who introduces herself as the Baroness Czerny, finds her pocketbook filled with money. Even more surprising, when she is taken to the Ritz Hotel by the infatuated Jacques, she discovers that she has a suite of rooms! The next morning, when she finds in her bedroom trunks containing an entire wardrobe in her size, and her "chauffeur" waits outside the hotel with her "car," Eve feels as if she has become Cinderella transported into a luxurious dreamworld. Then it all becomes clear: All this unexpected beneficence comes from Georges Flammarion, who offers her an irresistible deal—steal his wife's lover Jacques and Eve can have not only an unlimited bank account but also snare Paris's richest and most eligible playboy. At the same time that Eve agrees, she also receives flowers from Jacques, with a card reading "Hosannahs to the high gods for throwing us together." Georges notes, "I should resent that. To my wife he only wrote, 'So glad we met.' " Meanwhile, Tibor Czerny has organized his fellow taxi drivers to find Eve.

With Georges's collusion—he invites "Baroness Czerny" to a gala weekend

In *Midnight* and other comedies of the period, Claudette Colbert exuded a matchless charm and sophistication.

party at his château in Versailles—Eve begins her campaign to seduce Jacques away from Helene. Meeting them at a chic hat shop (the owner is played by Barrymore's then-wife, Elaine Barrie), she blithely "borrows" Jacques for the day, leaving Helene suspicious and angry. The stage is now set for the artfully contrived series of ploys, counterploys, and surprises that make up most of the film's diverting second half. Arriving at the château, Eve tells Georges privately about Jacques's dogged pursuit ("He ought to have his brakes relined"), while Helene frets about losing her lover. When Eve's suitcase arrives from Monte Carlo (Marcel has sent for it), Helene is determined to expose her as a fraud. Marcel joins her in looking through Eve's belongings, and for a while, things look bleak for Eve. "Every Cinderella has her midnight," she tells Georges.

By now, the cabdrivers have discovered Eve's whereabouts. The jig is apparently up when suddenly Tibor Czerny appears, dressed to the nines and posing as "Baron Czerny," newly arrived from Budapest to see his "wife." When they are alone, Tibor confesses that he loves her, but Eve, following the bent of many thirties heroines, is determined to marry Jacques for his money. She refuses to be poor like her parents, and Jacques is the man she's been waiting for all her life. Eager to upset her gold-lined apple cart, Tibor begins his maneuvers the next morning. He announces that their little daughter "Francie" has been taken seriously ill in Budapest and they must return home at once. As a countermove, Eve pretends to call Budapest, actually speaking to Georges, who plays both "Francie" and Eve's "mother-in-law." Here, Barrymore's gift for playing antic farce surfaces as he announces that "Francie" is only suffering from "alcohol poisoning," or imitates "Francie's" baby talk to hilarious effect.

When Eve's ruse is almost found out, she declares that her "husband" is sadly prone to sudden fits of insanity: They have no daughter, and Czerny, during these fits, can assume any disguise or occupation. (One of the less appealing tenets of thirties comedy was that wildly eccentric or even demented behavior could draw easy laughs.) When Tibor turns up dressed in his taxi driver's uniform, everyone assumes he is having a spell. Enraged, he must be knocked unconscious by Jacques. When he revives, Eve admits that she loves him, but they soon launch another quarrel. There remains only one recourse that will now free her to marry Jacques: With a remarkable lack of logic, they decide they must get a "divorce."

This leads to the final sequence in a favorite setting of thirties comedy— the courtroom. The "divorce" proceedings of Baron and Baroness Czerny are presided over by Monty Woolley, the Yale professor-turned-actor who would soon create the memorable character of Sheridan Whiteside in the original stage production of Kaufman and Hart's play *The Man Who Came to Dinner*. In his richly acidulous style, Woolley begins by ordering another couple to settle their petty differences, which, he asserts, amount to very little "in a time of vast world unrest." (This is the movie's only reference to the world beyond its proscribed limits.) He then turns to the Czernys' tangled "marriage." Told that Eve is claiming mental cruelty, he retorts, "Oh, *that* again!" and he offers his own rule of law: It's permissible for a wife to be beaten, as long as she's "struck not more than nine times with an instrument not larger than a broomstick." Tibor, at first, agrees not to contest the "divorce," but when he is alone with Eve in the "reconciliation" room, he obviously has one last ploy in mind. He pretends to become insane again, suddenly insisting on shaving. The furious judge refuses to grant a divorce—there can be no divorce as long as one party is deranged—and he urges Eve to go home with her "unfortunate husband." Now ready to settle down with a taxi driver instead of a playboy, Eve sets Jacques free ("You must never get married. It would disappoint so many women.") and leaves the courtroom with Tibor, fully reconciled.* But, of course, they cannot resist telling the flabbergasted judge that they are going off to get married!

In essence, *Midnight* follows the accepted pattern for romantic comedy in the thirties: A down-on-her-luck or working-class heroine suddenly finds herself projected into a world of luxury, where she gets the chance to live in plush forever. (In *Fifth Avenue Girl*, 1939, Ginger Rogers says, "I've got my claws in plush and I like the feel of it.") According to the pattern, however, love wears no dollar signs, and the heroine finally goes against her mercenary instincts by choosing the poor working stiff who has always adored her. The Hollywood concept that it's better to be poor and happy than rich and miserable permeated so many films in the thirties—and not only romantic comedies—that by 1939 it had taken on the power of a myth. Perhaps in no film is the concept advanced more blatantly than in Frank Capra's adaptation of the Kaufman and Hart play *You Can't Take It With You* (1938), in which the wealthy and snobbish Kirbys learn to shed their stuffiness and enjoy and appreciate the lovable eccentricities of the insolvent Sycamores.

If *Midnight* retains the familiar thesis, it does so with a sharp-edged wit that must be attributed largely to the Brackett and Wilder screenplay. The dialogue throughout has an exceptionally brittle style that occasionally becomes a bit heartless—learning that the "imaginary" child Francie supposedly has the measles, the foppish, ever-glib Marcel remarks, "Measles can give a child's skin a

---

*Throughout the decade, Colbert, like other leading ladies of the period, settled down with the lower- or middle-class hero instead of the idle playboy, thereby comforting all the marriageable Depression maidens who did the same. In *The Bride Comes Home* (1935), she gave up rich Robert Young for poor Fred MacMurray, and in *I Met Him in Paris* (1937), she again deserted playboy Robert Young, this time for playwright Melvyn Douglas. Occasionally, Cinderella won her prince—in *Easy Living* (1937), another Mitchell Leisen comedy that benefited from a bright screenplay (by Preston Sturges), Jean Arthur ends up with rich young Ray Milland—but only after she thinks he's poor.

Eve tends to Tibor after Jacques has knocked him down. Georges still feels that Eve would do best by marrying Jacques for his money: "Every time somebody orders champagne, Jacques's income bubbles."

nice polka dot effect." There is also an underlying hint of old-world melancholy in the screenplay that might be attributed to Wilder. Georges Flammarion genuinely loves his wife, despite her indiscretions, and his plan with Eve to bring Helene "back to her senses" smacks of desperation in spite of his arch high-comedy manner. There is, in fact, a touching moment at the end when Georges, who has succeeded in his goal, remarks to Helene, "This means the end of Jacques as an extra man. Do you mind very much?" With a smile, she replies, "Surprisingly little." *Midnight* mixes a touch of rue with its laughter.

Today, Cinderellas—even gold-digging Cinderellas such as Eve Peabody—may be in shorter supply than in other years, and many of them may own their own magic wands called credit cards. But *Midnight* serves as a happy reminder of a time when a pawn ticket could serve as a girl's introduction to affluence and romantic adventure.

Midnight. Paramount. Produced by Arthur Hornblow, Jr. Directed by Mitchell Leisen. Screenplay by Charles Brackett and Billy Wilder, from a story by Edwin Justus Mayer and Franz Schulz. Photography by Charles Lang, Jr. Art direction by Hans Dreier and Robert Usher. Costumes by Irene (with Edith Head). Edited by Doane Harrison. Cast: Claudette Colbert, Don Ameche, John Barrymore, Mary Astor, Francis Lederer, Rex O'Malley, Hedda Hopper, Elaine Barrie. Remade in 1945 as *Masquerade in Mexico*.

Ecstatic in their love, Cathy (Merle Oberon) and Heathcliff (Laurence Olivier) race across the British moors.

Passion on the Moors: Wuthering Heights

"I killed you! Haunt me then! Haunt your
murderer! I cannot live without my life! I cannot die
without my soul!"
—Laurence Olivier as Heathcliff in *Wuthering Heights*

n old Hollywood, a place that once existed halfway between a dream and an hallucination, "legends" could sometimes seem as numerous as seeds from a Burpee catalog. Many of the people who were considered legends sprang full-blown from the fevered imagination of a hardworking press agent: a brassy blonde turned into a sparkling luminary by way of *Modern Screen;* a megalomaniac with a megaphone transformed into a creative genius through the size of his ego and his budget. Others developed into legends through a combination of self-promotion, chutzpah, and either a bona fide talent or a genuine instinct for making the sort of movies audiences wanted to see.

By 1939, Samuel Goldwyn was one of the more durable of those legends. A true pioneer of the film industry, he had succeeded in weathering the storms and upheavals surrounding its birth. Goldwyn had been an independent producer since 1923, when he formed his own company after years of bitter wrangling with other pioneers such as Adolph Zukor and Jesse Lasky. A self-taught man, Goldwyn may have been unschooled and unlettered, but it was not long before it became amply evident that he had intuitive ability to assemble the right creative team to produce films of quality and prestige.

Most of Goldwyn's best films lay ahead when he finally turned, reluctantly, to *Wuthering Heights*. Yet despite such costly mistakes as *Nana* (1934), he had already produced a number of worthy films by 1939. They included *These Three* (1936), a scrubbed but reasonable adaptation of Lillian Hellman's "shocking" play *The Children's Hour;* an admirable, visually striking version of Sinclair Lewis's *Dodsworth* (1936); and a vivid screen transcription of Sidney Kingsley's play *Dead*

End (1937). It should be noted that all three of these estimable films had the benefit of director William Wyler's increasingly well-honed craftsmanship. If Sam Goldwyn's well-publicized "touch" was evident in these films, Wyler's clear fingerprints could hardly be ignored.

At first, when it was time to consider Emily Brontë's *Wuthering Heights* for possible filming, Goldwyn could well have uttered his most famous line, "Include me out." Like many Hollywood stories, the tale of how Brontë's passionate Gothic romance came under Goldwyn's aegis lies hidden under a cloud of conjecture. Apparently, the novel, which in its day was considered "too abominably pagan even for the most vitiated of English readers," had come to the attention of producer Walter Wanger, who thought of making a film version as a vehicle for Sylvia Sidney and Charles Boyer. Wanger had hired Ben Hecht and Charles MacArthur to write a screenplay, and these unruly, undeniably brilliant gadflies had created a script that excised the entire second generation of the story.*

The route from Walter Wanger to Sam Goldwyn was, depending on the source, either circuitous or direct. One source holds that Sylvia Sidney, convinced that both she and Boyer were wrong choices to play Cathy and Heathcliff, showed the script to Goldwyn. Another source maintains that Wanger took it to Goldwyn for his opinion. The result was the same in both cases: Goldwyn found it unfilmable, a tale much too gloomy and forbidding for the general public. There seems to be no doubt about his ultimate pronouncement: "I don't like stories with people dying in the end. It's a tragedy." He also disliked stories in which characters appeared "in period costumes and wrote with quill pens." The fate of *Wuthering Heights* (the movie) appeared to be as dark and gloomy as the story itself.

Evidently, William Wyler continued to harbor the hope that he would someday film *Wuthering Heights*. While making *Jezebel* at Warners with Bette Davis, he had shown her the Hecht-MacArthur script, and she had hurried to Jack Warner's office to urge him to buy it as her next vehicle. While Warner was reading it, Wyler telephoned Goldwyn and told him that Jack Warner was about to buy *Wuthering Heights* for Bette Davis. Goldwyn was suddenly interested in the property, especially when he was convinced by Wyler that Merle Oberon, who was on occasional loan from Alexander Korda, would have an ideal role in Cathy. Goldwyn added *Wuthering Heights* to his production schedule.

---

*Another version has it that Hecht and MacArthur wrote the screenplay purely on speculation at Alexander Woollcott's cottage, where they infuriated Woollcott by pretending to maul the famous story with what he regarded as their "insensitive hooligan touch." When none of the major studios wanted it, the writers took it to Wanger, who was looking for properties to release under his new deal with United Artists.

Lockwood (off camera) comes upon the grim residents of Wuthering Heights. Left to right: Isabella (Geraldine Fitzgerald), Heathcliff (Laurence Olivier), Joseph (Leo G. Carroll), and Nellie (Flora Robson). Gregg Toland's brooding, shadowed photography won an Academy Award.

According to Oberon's biographer Charles Higham, Oberon, and not Sylvia Sidney, had always been Walter Wanger's one choice to portray Cathy; he recognized that a passionate woman lay behind her cool, well-bred demeanor. When Wanger sold the package to Goldwyn, and Goldwyn immediately agreed to star her, the actress was elated. The novel had always been a favorite of hers, and she felt that no one else could play Cathy with the same fire and abandon. By that time, William Wyler was in Europe, but Oberon pleaded with Goldwyn to have him return to direct the film. She also insisted on Gregg Toland as cinematographer, knowing how attractively he had photographed her in other Goldwyn films, notably in *These Three*.

The overriding question was: Who would play Heathcliff to Oberon's Cathy? Once again, the stories vary, leading to Laurence Olivier by different routes. When Ronald Colman, Goldwyn's automatic first choice for any film with a period or English setting (and an extremely unlikely Heathcliff), proved to be unavailable, the next candidates were Douglas Fairbanks, Jr., whom Oberon wanted for the role, and British actor Robert Newton. When their tests displeased Goldwyn, he agreed reluctantly to cast Olivier, whom Wyler had always preferred. Another story holds that Olivier was brought directly to Goldwyn's attention by Charles MacArthur, who saw this "surly-looking guy" hanging around the Beverly Hills Tennis Club and thought that he looked ideal for

Laurence Olivier as the desolate Heathcliff, crying for his lost love Cathy.

Heathcliff and Cathy gaze in awe through a window of the Linton house at the lavish ball taking place within. Over the years, Oberon's performance has been criticized as lacking in passion, but in fact she succeeds quite well in suggesting Cathy's willful, quixotic nature.

Heathcliff. (He was surprised to learn that Olivier had appeared on the stage with Noël Coward and Katharine Cornell.) Yet another source claims that it was Ben Hecht who suggested Olivier for the role.

In any case, Olivier, at first, had not wanted to play Heathcliff, and when Wyler sent him a cablegram offering the role, his initial reaction was not favorable. His earlier experiences in Hollywood had been either unrewarding—he had roles in several minor films—or humiliating—after two days, he was replaced by John Gilbert as Greta Garbo's leading man in Rouben Mamoulian's production of *Queen Christina*. Olivier was also in the midst of a love affair with Vivien Leigh while they were both married to others; they were vacationing together in the south of France when he received the cablegram. He insisted that he would play Heathcliff only if Leigh was cast as Cathy. When they offered her the role of Isabella, Heathcliff's tormented wife, Leigh refused, and Olivier seemed inclined to reject Heathcliff once and for all. Constant entreaties from Wyler, and a comment from his friend and fellow actor Ralph Richardson, finally convinced him to accept. (Reportedly, Richardson, in his cryptic, eccentric style, merely said, "I should, old boy. Bit of fame. Good.") Six months later, after being told by Wyler that she would never get a better role than Isabella until she had made a name for herself, Leigh was cast as Scarlett O'Hara in *Gone With the Wind*.

David Niven presented another casting problem. Another Goldwyn contract player, he had been highly reluctant to play another milksop supporting role—he was one of Ruth Chatterton's diffident lovers in *Dodsworth*—and the reserved Edgar Linton seemed to offer few strong acting possibilities. He went to see Goldwyn, stating firmly that he would rather go on suspension than play Edgar, but Wyler persisted, certain that he was the ideal choice to play the role. It was a decision Niven would later regret whenever Wyler exploded with rage at his acting.* (Niven was not his only target.) Other roles in the film were aptly cast: Geraldine Fitzgerald, in her second American role, as Isabella; the distinguished actress Flora Robson as the maid Ellen; Leo G. Carroll as the pious servant Joseph; and Hugh Williams as Cathy's dissipated brother Hindley.

Now that the film was under way, Goldwyn spared no expense in creating a reasonably authentic production, that is, until the expense included the possibility of shooting on location in England, which Wyler wanted. When that idea was rejected, a California site was selected; 450 acres of desert in the San Fernando Valley of Ventura County were turned into a facsimile of the gloomy English countryside. Before any work was done, Goldwyn sent a camera crew

---

*Geraldine Fitzgerald recalls that Niven refused to cry onscreen and when Wyler insisted, he claimed to have a clause in his contract that stated he was not obliged to shed tears in front of the camera. Wyler demanded to see the contract, which, to his amazement, *did* have such a clause.

to England to film the Yorkshire moors so that they could be matched by scenic designer James Basevi. His extravagance extended to importing one thousand heather plants to serve as background for Cathy and Heathcliff's idyllic assignations on the moors.* He also had one thousand panes of hand-blown British glass imported for the interiors. One brouhaha occurred before production when it was revealed that the Hollywood animal trainer who provided ducks and geese for the barnyard scenes had cut their vocal chords to keep them from honking noisily during the filming. The uproar from animal lovers and antivivisection champions rumbled across the moors like a thunderstorm, then faded away.

Other of Goldwyn's decisions brought about drastic changes in the production. He insisted that the period of the movie be changed from the original Regency of the novel to the Georgian, advancing the time from 1801 to 1841 because he felt that the gowns would be more becoming to Oberon. He also demanded that the modest Linton home of the novel be turned into a lavish, beautifully appointed mansion complete with cavernous rooms and glittering chandeliers. Many of his early judgments had to be fought bitterly by Wyler. Seeking to "glamorize" the production, Goldwyn tried unsuccessfully to smother Oberon's face in modern-day cosmetics. He also objected strenuously to Olivier's appearance in filthy rags. Viewing the first takes of the actor, he screamed, "He's a mess: dirty, unkempt, stagy, hammy, and awful." Most astonishingly, he referred to Olivier, one of the handsomest men on the screen, as "that damn ugly actor," reacting, perhaps, to what Geraldine Fitzgerald calls Olivier's "dangerous" face, which, in addition to the dark, smoldering eyes, lacked the even contours of then-fashionable male stars such as Tyrone Power.

During the filming, the tensions on the set were palpable. Although Oberon and Olivier had worked together before (in *The Divorce of Lady X*), their relationship now was chilly since they both knew that neither had wanted the other in the roles. The extent of their acrimony may have been exaggerated over the years—stories about his spitting in her face during their love scenes and his uncomplimentary remarks after a blowup may well be apocryphal—but there were angry exchanges, followed by the usual walk-offs and reconciliations. (In addition, Oberon twisted her ankle on the set and Olivier limped from a swollen foot induced by gout and the too-tight shoes he was given by the costume department.) Niven's worst fears about working again under Wyler were being realized—the director's ceaseless verbal abuse left him furious and exhausted.

Apparently, Wyler's tyranny extended to the entire cast. A stern taskmaster widely known for his many takes—as many as sixty—on virtually every scene,

---

*According to some reports, the "imported" heather may have turned out to be a publicity gambit. To some observant eyes, the heather in the film seemed too tall and luxuriant to be real.

Bitten by one of the Linton dogs, Cathy is comforted by Heathcliff and a solicitous Edgar Linton (David Niven). At first, Niven balked at playing the genteel Edgar, but William Wyler insisted that he was the best choice for the role.

Wyler drove his actors relentlessly, often commenting vocally on their lack of ability. Olivier would later claim that Wyler taught him a great deal about film acting ("He made me a good film actor by teaching me in an extremely rough and insulting way."), but the director's constant badgering could not have been a pleasant experience. Oberon, too, suffered from Wyler's insistence on many takes. In the scene in which Cathy rushes out frantically into a storm, terrified that Heathcliff has left her forever, the dissatisfied Wyler had her rush over and over into the studio-induced downpour until he felt that she had fully expressed Cathy's anguish and passion. Oberon became ill, and the production was shut down temporarily. (She returned only on the condition that special heaters would be used to warm the wind that lashed her during the storm.)

Despite all the difficulties, the film was finally completed. When a rough cut was shown to Goldwyn, he expressed his satisfaction with everything but the ending. The idea of closing with Cathy dead in Heathcliff's arms appalled the producer: "I don't want to look at a corpse at the fadeout," he told Wyler. He insisted that a brief scene be added at the end showing Cathy and Heathcliff reunited in heaven. When Wyler refused adamantly, he was placed on suspension. It was not until the world premiere at the Pantages Theater in Hollywood on April 13, 1939, that the director realized what Goldwyn had done: Drawing on his own idea of heaven, he had added a double-exposure shot of Heathcliff and Cathy (played by doubles), seen from behind as they walk together on white clouds into an eternal future. To Wyler, it was "a horrible shot," but there was nothing he could do.

For all the turmoil that went into making *Wuthering Heights,* and for all the critical carping it has endured over the years, the film remains a commendable achievement and one of the screen's great love stories. (Long after the shouts and threats, Goldwyn acknowledged that it was his favorite movie.) Following the credits, shown to the accompaniment of Alfred Newman's lushly melodic if insistent musical score, the film plunges the viewer immediately into an atmosphere that seems more suitable for a horror melodrama than a passionate romance: On the bleak, storm-tossed Yorkshire moors, somewhere around 1840, the lone figure of Lockwood (Miles Mander) searches desperately for shelter. We half-expect him to find Dracula's castle; instead he comes upon the somber ruin of Wuthering Heights, where he is attacked by dogs, treated inhospitably by the surly master, Heathcliff (Olivier), and his worn wife, Isabella (Fitzgerald), and finally given a cold, cheerless room for the night. The tone changes from horror to the supernatural as Lockwood hears a woman crying on the moors and feels an icy, ghostly hand as he reaches through a broken window. When Heathcliff plunges madly into the storm, crying, "Cathy! Come back to me! Oh, my heart's darling!" it remains for the servant Ellen Dean (Robson) to relate the tragic tale of the doomed lovers. Gregg Toland photographed these early scenes with considerable artistry, giving them a chilling reality—bleak faces against stark backgrounds—that contrasts effectively with the later romantic, otherworldly sheen.

Returning twenty years in time, *Wuthering Heights* establishes the background for the strange, passionate relationship that develops between free-spirited Catherine Earnshaw and Heathcliff, the orphaned street waif from Liverpool who becomes a stableboy in the Earnshaw house. The death of kindly Mr. Earnshaw (Cecil Kellaway) paves the way for increased hostility between Heathcliff and Cathy's brother Hindley (Williams), who grows from a spiteful boy into a cruel, dissolute man. As young Heathcliff matures into a darkly glowering man, and young Cathy turns into a willful beauty, their intense, almost mystical feeling for each other becomes the film's catalyst, affecting all the events that follow. Many viewers retain vivid memories of their scenes together on Peniston Crag, the wind blowing through the heather as they declare their undying love.

As the story progresses, the central conflict develops with striking force: Cathy's romantic nature (her dreams of Heathcliff as a lost prince, her longing for "dancing and singing in a pretty world") remains constantly at war with her immutable bonding with Heathcliff, while Heathcliff, unable to suppress his

Haggard and wretchedly unhappy, Isabella pleads with Heathcliff to end his obsession with Cathy. Geraldine Fitzgerald received a well-deserved Oscar nomination for her performance as the unfortunate Isabella, capturing the desperation of a woman hopelessly in love with a haunted, doom-ridden man.

proud, volatile nature, suffers and rages at her every whim or capricious act. On the one hand, Cathy adores the lavish, decorous world of Edgar Linton (Niven) and his sister Isabella, a world that only inspires Heathcliff's curse ("I'll bring this house in ruins about your head!"). On the other, she remains Heathcliff's princess of Peniston Crag, and in a well-remembered love scene, she reaffirms her devotion to him ("No matter what I do or say, this is me! Heathcliff, fill my arms with heather! All I can hold!").

Cathy's dual nature emerges most strongly in one of the film's finest scenes, in which, bubbling with insincere joy, she tells Ellen, her housekeeper, about Edgar's proposal of marriage. What about Heathcliff? Ellen asks discreetly. "It would degrade me to marry him!" she cries, whereupon Heathcliff, listening behind the door, flees into the night. But Cathy continues, and in a well-rendered speech compounded of fear and self-discovery, she expresses her bond to Heathcliff: "He's more myself than I am. Ellen, I *am* Heathcliff! Everything he has suffered, I've suffered." When she realizes that Heathcliff has overheard her saying that marrying him would degrade her, she rushes after him into the storm.

The film moves into its next phase as Cathy, recovering from illness of body and soul, accepts Edgar's proposal and becomes the serene, gracious mistress of Thrushcross Grange. Yet years later, when Heathcliff returns, wealthy now and owner of Wuthering Heights, she again feels the helpless terror that binds her to him. When he expresses that bond ("You willed me here across the sea."), she pushes him away, and his fierce pride turns to revenge: With false ardor, he courts and proposes to Edgar's sister Isabella. In a superbly played scene, Cathy clashes with Isabella, accusing Heathcliff of being "something dark and horrible." (Oberon's acting here is reasonably persuasive, but Fitzgerald dominates the scene with her barely suppressed passion for Heathcliff.) Later, Heathcliff rejects Cathy's plea not to marry Isabella, cruelly blaming her for their plight: "You must destroy us with that weakness you call virtue. . . . You can think of me as Isabella's husband!" When Cathy importunes Edgar to prevent the marriage, he realizes the depth of her feelings for Heathcliff. Niven plays this scene with a delicacy and subtlety—pain barely reflected in his eyes—that may justify Wyler's relentless badgering.

As time passes, the story moves to its tragic climax. With Cathy gravely ill, Isabella, trapped for years in a loveless marriage, can finally voice her despair and resentment to Heathcliff. "If Cathy died, I might begin to live!" she tells him. She begs him, "Let love come into the house!" However, still lost in a dream of Cathy, he can only ask her, "Why isn't there the smell of heather in your hair? Why are your eyes always empty?" When he learns that Cathy is dying, he cannot be restrained by Isabella, who cries, "Let her die where she belongs—in Edgar's arms! Let her die!" Geraldine Fitzgerald, a consummate actress, performs with heartbreaking intensity.

One of the most memorable death scenes in American films, Cathy's final tryst with Heathcliff moves us with an unabashed romanticism that has virtually vanished from the screen. Heathcliff's tangle of wild emotions, in which he blames her ("You wandered off like a greedy, wanton child to break your heart and mine!"), then blames himself ("I killed you! Haunt me then! Haunt your murderer!"), erupts with passion in Olivier's mercurial performance. Cathy, on the other hand, has no more time for curses or regrets, and when she asks Heathcliff to take her to the window for one last look at the moors, she seems to have already left her body. Oberon emphasizes her virtual weightlessness, her fragility, as she whispers, "I'll wait for you . . . till you come," and dies. He carries her corpse to the bed, then kneels beside it, dismissing Ellen's pious belief that Cathy is in heaven by asking, "What do they know of heaven and hell, Cathy, who know nothing of life?"

Cathy's death: one of the most poignant and best remembered scenes in film history. "Haunt your murderer!" Heathcliff cries, as his beloved Cathy breathes her last. At her bedside are Edgar, Dr. Kenneth (Donald Crisp), and Nellie.

Returning to Ellen as she relates the story to Lockwood, the film moves to Heathcliff's final reunion in death with Cathy. Ellen explains that the figure Lockwood saw in the storm was not Cathy but "Cathy's love, stronger than time itself. Still sobbing for its unlived days and uneaten bread!" When Doctor Kenneth (Donald Crisp) reports finding Heathcliff dead on the moors, Ellen can affirm the mystical bond: "He's with her. They've only just begun to live! Goodbye, Heathcliff! Goodbye, my wild, sweet Cathy!" It is at this final point that the movie should have ended, without the "heavenly" coda insisted on by Goldwyn.

The performances in *Wuthering Heights* are all exemplary, with perhaps a special nod to Niven for being able to turn the pallid Edgar Linton into a sympathetic and even poignant character. Olivier showed, in his first major American film, that he was considerably more than a handsome juvenile, and Geraldine Fitzgerald won deserved praise and an Academy Award nomination for her incisive characterization of Isabella. Only Merle Oberon has been unjustly criticized over the years for portraying Cathy in too dainty or remote a fashion, without the wild passion the role requires. This familiar judgment needs to be re-evaluated. Although she cannot play with the tragic dimension of Garbo (and is also perhaps several years too old for the early scenes—she was in her late twenties), Oberon handles the most difficult scenes expertly, fluctuating persuasively between her romantic illusions and her passion for Heathcliff. As she dies, she appears to be already looking beyond her room to a place where she can at last find peace from her tormented emotions. As her strength ebbs, she can manage one last fleeting hope: "If I could only hold you until we were both dead!" Oberon plays this scene with an artistry that has been overlooked in the general praise for Olivier, Wyler, and even Goldwyn.

While the performances, especially Olivier's, contribute notably to the film's success, as does Wyler's expert direction, Gregg Toland's photography should not be minimized. Throughout the film, he alternates between a glowing romanticism—lingering shadows and diffused candlelight—and the forbidding chill of Gothicism: a crumbling house standing mutely in the darkness, mists swirling ominously around the moors. Aided by the shimmering sets of James Basevi and the lavish costumes of Omar Kiam, Toland's camera finds apt visual images for the dark and sometimes lyrical mood of the story: Lockwood, clutching his frozen fingers that had touched Cathy's ghostly hand in the swirling snow; Cathy and Heathcliff, racing ecstatically through the heather; Cathy, rushing desperately through the storm to bring Heathcliff back to her. Toland makes effective use of windows for dramatic contrast: Our first glimpse of the Linton house is through Cathy's enchanted eyes as the camera moves through the window to the lavish ball she watches in awe; much later, after Heathcliff has returned as a successful landowner to disrupt the lives of the Lintons, the camera retreats through the same window from the figures of Cathy and Edgar, now facing a threat to their placid marriage.

On the whole, the reviews for *Wuthering Heights* praised the film, although there were a number of reservations. Frank S. Nugent's review in *The New York Times* called the film "Goldwyn at his best" and "a strong and somber film, poetically written as the novel not always was, sinister and wild as it was meant to be, far more compact dramatically than Miss Brontë had made it." He concluded by hailing it as "one of the most distinguished pictures of the year, one of the finest ever produced by Mr. Goldwyn, and one you should decide to see." Although he complained that the people were "not in themselves twisted enough to make their actions and end inevitable," Otis Ferguson, writing in *The New Republic,* acclaimed it "among the best pictures made anywhere," with "a sustained mood of bleakness and sullen passions." John Mosher's review in *The New Yorker* asserted that "the Goldwyn production approximates the quality of the fierce, tempestuous story with a force one might never have expected. . . .

Seldom has the tone of a great novel been so faithfully reproduced by the movie people."

Other reviews at the time were less cordial. Suspecting (rightly, as it turned out) that the movie's "general somberness and psychological tragedy" would be "too heavy for general appeal," *Variety* considered it "more of an artistic success for the carriage trade." Graham Greene, writing in the London *Spectator*, found the film lacking in "carnality," maintaining that "a lot of reverence has gone into a picture which should have been as coarse as a sewer." He considered Olivier and Oberon unconvincing: "This Heathcliff would never have married for revenge (Mr. Olivier's nervous, breaking voice belongs to balconies and Verona and romantic love), and one cannot imagine the ghost of this Cathy weeping with balked passion outside the broken window." There was also some adverse criticism of Alfred Newman's score: While enthusiastic about the film, James Shelley Hamilton in *The National Board of Review*'s magazine called the music "particularly unfortunate, syrupy and banal and completely missing the feeling it should heighten." Business was disappointing; despite eight Academy Award nominations (only Gregg Toland won for his photography) and a citation by the New York Film Critics as the year's best film, audiences did not flock to attend it.

If contemporary audiences were surprisingly unresponsive, *Wuthering Heights* has succeeded in surviving the years as one of the screen's most beautiful love stories. By this time, it hardly matters if the heather was real; the plight of the storm-tossed lovers as they move inexorably to their doom continues to affect us deeply. Goldwyn's final shot of Heathcliff and Cathy may indeed be superfluous—an implication made unnecessarily literal—but there is nothing superfluous about the emotions their story arouses, or the memories it evokes, as they stand on Peniston Crag, together forever in a timeless world.

Wuthering Heights. A Samuel Goldwyn Production, released by United Artists. Directed by William Wyler. Screenplay by Ben Hecht and Charles MacArthur, from the novel by Emily Brontë. Photography by Gregg Toland. Music by Alfred Newman. Art direction by James Basevi. Costumes by Omar Kiam. Edited by Daniel Mandell. Cast: Merle Oberon, Laurence Olivier, David Niven, Geraldine Fitzgerald, Flora Robson, Hugh Williams, Leo G. Carroll, Miles Mander, and Cecil Kellaway. Remade by Luis Buñuel in 1953 as *Abismos de Pasión* (also known as *Cumbres Borrascosas*), as an Egyptian film, *El Gharib*, in 1955, and by Robert Fuest in a 1970 British version. Also several television versions.

Hedonistic heiress Judy Traherne (Bette Davis) is teased and intimidated by her horse trainer Michael O'Leary (Humphrey Bogart).

The Quiet Passing of Judith Traherne: Dark Victory

"Nothing can hurt us now. What we have can't be
destroyed. That's our victory. Our victory over the dark."
—Bette Davis to George Brent in *Dark Victory*

The ingredients that go into the making
of a film star are sometimes quite mystifying. Once we concede the need for at
least a modicum of acting ability (and sometimes we marvel at how minuscule
that modicum can be), we can add other requirements: an exceptionally pleasing
or striking personality, an air of mystery or a sense of secrets withheld (at least
before the days when stars revealed that they were like everyone else), and a
face that the camera loves to photograph. Stir in a talent for self-promotion, a
knack for choosing—or the luck to stumble upon—the best or showiest of roles,
and you have an actor whose name above the title on the marquee can attract
paying customers.

By these standards, Bette Davis would qualify as a likely film star in some
respects, and a most unlikely one in others. The first three years of her film
career, which started in 1931, were spent in mostly nondescript roles that tested
few of her resources; she also lacked conventional starlet prettiness. The closest
she came to the sort of edgy, flamboyant performances that would make her
reputation in the early years was as the come-hither Southern girl Madge Nor-
wood in *Cabin in the Cotton* (1932). ("Ah'd love to kiss you, but Ah just washed
mah hair!") Then in 1934, on loan to RKO from Warners, she played Leslie
Howard's vulgar, grasping nemesis in a film version of Somerset Maugham's
Of Human Bondage. It earned her audience attention and strong critical notices,
but when she returned to Warners, she found that she was back again on the
studio treadmill, playing mousy heroines in indifferent movies.

There were a few notable exceptions in which she was able to display her
talent for playing women with exposed nerve endings. In *Bordertown* (1935), her

At Judy's first examination, Dr. Steele (George Brent) notices her difficulty in lighting his cigarette, while Judy, edgy and frightened by her symptoms, pretends to be flippant. Davis gives one of her finest performances in this film, charged with a feeling and intensity that few screen actresses of the period could match.

Dr. Steele consoles Judy before her brain surgery. "When you get inside my head," she tells him, "see if you can find any sense there." Brent appeared opposite Davis in a number of films, usually giving reliable if unexciting performances. Offscreen, they were romantically involved for a time.

wanton Marie murders her oafish husband, implicates the man (Paul Muni) she covets in the crime, and ends up, babbling incoherently, on the witness stand at his trial. (Ida Lupino performed the same bravura turn in *They Drive by Night*, a partial remake released in 1940.) As possible compensation for not being nominated for her performance in *Of Human Bondage*, she was awarded an Oscar for playing alcoholic actress Joyce Heath in *Dangerous* (1935). In *Marked Woman* (1937), she gave one of her best performances in the thirties, as a hardened, knowing dance-hall "hostess" who turns on a kingpin mobster after her younger sister is murdered. Spewing her venom as her eyes blazed with vengeful fury, she vivified the screen with her intensity.

By 1939, Bette Davis was one of Warners' leading acresses. The year before, she had won her second Oscar as willful Southern belle Julie Marsden, who, in *Jezebel*, learned the two virtues required by Hollywood's "good" women: humility and self-sacrifice. Enormously successful, the film had given her the status that made her name a selling point among ticket buyers. Just ahead, however, was the movie that not only marked a peak in her career but also carried her to the top rank of film stardom. She had to die onscreen to receive this eminent position, but it was a brave and noble death that would flood the theaters with tears. The film was *Dark Victory*.

A film version of *Dark Victory* had been considered for a number of years. The original play by George Emerson Brewer, Jr., and Bertram Bloch had a brief run (fifty-one performances) on Broadway in 1934, with Tallulah Bankhead starring as the ill-fated heiress. Early in 1935, David O. Selznick, still a producer at MGM, wrote to Greta Garbo, asking her to consider *Dark Victory* as her next vehicle instead of *Anna Karenina*, which she was anxious to play. He and George Cukor felt that she needed a modern story rather than the heavy costume dramas in which she had been appearing. Garbo filmed *Anna Karenina* after all, but Selznick purchased the rights to the Brewer-Bloch play for his own production company. For the next few years, it was talked about as a possible vehicle for a number of leading actresses, including Merle Oberon, Janet Gaynor, and Carole Lombard, but it never reached production. At Warners, screenwriter Casey Robinson, who had known about *Dark Victory* for three years, urged the studio to buy it from Selznick for contract star Kay Francis, whose regal bearing and throaty voice had made her a natural choice for "women's" films. When Francis declined—apparently she was superstitious about playing a dying woman— Bette Davis, who had also known about the property, stepped up her vigorous campaign to get Jack Warner to buy it for her. Associate producer David Lewis and director Edmund Goulding joined her in the campaign. Warner was not enthusiastic—"Who wants to see a dame go blind?"—but he finally agreed to take it over from Selznick for $27,500. The shooting began in mid-1938.

Casting the crucial role of Frederick Steele, the doctor who diagnoses and falls in love with heroine Judith Traherne, had its interesting aspects. Casey Robinson, who wrote the screenplay, was anxious to have Spencer Tracy play the part—he wrote Warners' production head Hal Wallis, "I don't need to tell you what the combination of Bette Davis and Spencer Tracy on the marquee would do to the box office"—and Davis, who admired Tracy more than almost any other actor, approved of the choice. When Tracy proved to be unavailable, or perhaps Warner turned him down when he thought of the complex negotiations with MGM, the studio looked to its contract players. (Tracy later played the role opposite Davis in an abbreviated version on "Lux Radio Theater.") Basil Rathbone tested for the role but it turned out so badly for a number of reasons that Rathbone wrote a long letter to Warner, pleading with him to destroy the test. Finally George Brent, Warners' all-purpose leading man and an actor who made up in quiet dependability what he lacked in charisma, was assigned to play Dr. Steele. The part of Judith's secretary and best friend Ann King, which had not appeared in the play, had been wisely added to the script by Edmund Goulding so that Judith would not have to face the tragic devastation of her illness all by herself. This important role went to Irish-born actress Geraldine Fitzgerald, making her American film debut. Other roles were filled by Ronald Reagan as Judith's playboy friend Alec Hamin, Humphrey Bogart as her Irish horse trainer and would-be lover Michael O'Leary, and Henry Travers as kindly Dr. Parsons.

For Bette Davis, the early weeks of filming *Dark Victory* proved to be a difficult period. Shortly before the production began, her marriage to Harmon ("Ham") Nelson had collapsed, and she had recently experienced another trauma with the ending of her stormy relationship with director William Wyler, who wanted to marry her but married Margaret Tallichet instead when Davis failed to respond to his proposal. Her badly frayed nerves may account, if only in part, for the raw intensity of her acting in the scene in which she first learns of her illness in Dr. Steele's office, which was filmed before any other. At any rate, before the first month's shooting was completed, Davis wanted to leave the film, claiming that she identified so completely with the character that she was headed for a nervous breakdown and could no longer bear to talk or even think about illness and death. Hal Wallis coaxed her into returning, urging her to use her personal feelings creatively in her performance. For whatever reason, she finally took possession of the role, making the doomed Judith Traherne a fully rounded character of touching valor and quiet strength.

Davis dominates the film from the very start, investing every soap-operatic cliché of Casey Robinson's screenplay with conviction. Over the years, impressionists have exaggerated her mannerisms—the popping eyes, the clipped, staccato speech, and the swiveling walk—but here they work for the character,

Bitter at learning about her hopeless condition, Judy resumes her hedonistic bar-hopping with friends like Alec Hamin (Ronald Reagan). In the background, a singer renders "Oh, Give Me Time for Tenderness," with its ironic lyrics ("Oh, give me time for tenderness/oh, give me one little hour of each big day. . . .").

charging the screen with an electricity that grips a viewer's attention in every scene. When we meet Judy, she is living brazenly in the fast lane, driving too fast with her disapproving friend Ann and riding her horses with a careless disregard for her safety. It also becomes clear that she is ill, perhaps seriously. Riding her horse Challenger over the hurdles, she experiences double vision and falls off the horse. She dismisses any thought of illness—"I haven't any time for doctors"—but when she tumbles down the stairs, evasion is no longer possible. Through her worried family doctor (Travers), she goes to see Dr. Frederick Steele (Brent), who is about to retire his practice to carry out research on brain cells.

In her first scene with Dr. Steele, Judy plays the flippant, carefree young heiress, fully capable of self-awareness and bursting with plans for a rosy, comfortable future ("I'm well and strong and nothing can touch me!"). But there is a fear behind her eyes that Davis projects superbly in her performance of the scene, her voice a little too shrill, her hands moving nervously as she clutches her cigarette. George Brent plays against her intensity with calm assurance; quietly, his Dr. Steele notices the burns on her hands, the difficulty with her vision. Finally, she admits that she is frightened and blurts out all the symptoms that have been troubling her for months. Her face in close-up shows a growing resignation and respect for her doctor.

Judy goes into the hospital for surgery, confident that all will be well. The prognosis, however, turns out to be negative—a brain tumor will end her life within ten months, and nothing can be done to save her. She will experience no pain, only blindness in her last hours and then a peaceful death. The doctors elect to hide the truth, to allow her a measure of happiness during her last months. Believing that she is totally cured, an elated Judy expresses her gratitude to Steele ("Thank you for my life!"), which soon grows into love. After uttering the requisite cliché ("A girl so alive!"), an anguished Steele tells Ann the tragic truth about Judy's condition: Though she has perhaps less than a year to live, "she's not going to suffer anymore," and her quiet death will be "God's last small mercy."

As Judy's feelings for Dr. Steele deepen into love, Ann becomes increasingly alarmed (Fitzgerald acts with a perfectly balanced mixture of covert pity and concern), and she visits Steele to tell him about Judy. He concedes that he loves Judy as well but feels hopeless in the face of her fatal illness. "The main thing is for her to be happy," he tells Ann. And for a while, Judy is happy, especially after Steele admits to loving her. They plan to be married as soon as possible.

The severe blow comes when Judy learns the truth about her condition. Seeing her file in the doctor's office, she reads the words *prognosis negative* and a few questions to his nurse leads Judy to understand that she is dying. She reacts with bitterness and anguish, accusing Ann and Steele of lying to her ("My dearest friends!" she says, with mocking scorn). Resuming her playgirl life, but now with an edge of desperation, she haunts the nightclubs with her old friends, especially Alec (Reagan). Tipsy at a bar, she joins the lounge singer in a rendition of "Oh, Give Me Time for Tenderness," a song written for the film by Edmund Goulding and entertainer Elsie Janis. The words ("Oh, give me time to stop and bless the golden sunset of a summer day") are a poignant echo of her plight. Davis pulls out all stops for these scenes, with only her eyes reflecting the terror she is feeling behind the fake-hearty manner.

Before Judy can make peace with her illness and give herself fully to loving her gentle doctor, she has a strange interlude with her horse trainer Michael O'Leary (Bogart with an unconvincing, sporadic Irish brogue). In a scene re-dolent of D. H. Lawrence's Lady Chatterley and her lover, Judy and Michael exchange banal observations ("We only live once, Miss Judith") and equally banal questions ("Are you afraid to die, Michael?") that lead inevitably to an ardent kiss. We are not too surprised to learn that Michael has always been in love with her ("The nights I've laid awake thinkin' of you!"), but for Judy, their amorous moment is only the final straw. "I just can't go on this way," she tells

Weary and depressed, Judy tells Ann (Geraldine Fitzgerald) that the waiting is the hardest. "Would it be wrong," she asks, "if I made it happen?"

him. "Michael, I just can't die like this." She goes to Steele and begs him to forgive her and protect her. In one of her most touching scenes in the film, she reacts with joy to his sudden proposal of marriage:

> Marry? Oh, wouldn't it be marvelous if we could . . . have a real wedding and be given away . . . with church bells, and champagne, and a white frock and orange blossoms and a wedding cake. That's one thing I won't have missed, and you're giving it to me. I can never love you enough!

They marry, and for a while they are idyllically happy on his farm in Vermont. He conducts his research while she enjoys the simple pleasures of tending the house and garden. Ann comes to visit, and in reply to her unasked question, Steele tells her, "We just pretend that nothing's going to happen." But all too soon, the inevitable time of Judy's death is at hand. It is true that this long closing sequence of the film milks the tragic situation unabashedly, to the accompaniment of ear-assaulting Max Steiner music. Yet Davis and her fellow players act it with such restraint, such delicacy of feeling, that the scene remains one of the best-remembered from films of the period. It fairly begs for tears, and audiences wept without embarrassment at every viewing; but its tears are earned honestly.

Actually filmed at Malibu Lake, the sequence begins as the Steeles are preparing for a trip to Philadelphia. Ann is digging in the garden when Judy remarks, "It's getting darker by the minute. Funny, I can still feel the sun on my hands." Suddenly she gasps with the realization of what is happening to her, and a look of horror passes across Ann's face. She is sobbing in Judy's arms when Steele arrives, excited about a telegram summoning him to New York for a medical conference. As her eyesight dims, Judy decides to carry off her last deception and die alone, cleanly and beautifully, as he would want.* She declines to go to New York with him, hides her sudden blindness and imminent death, and reassures him that in any case she is not afraid. "When death comes," she tells him, "it will come as an old friend." In one of the most affecting moments she ever played, Davis brings stature to the dying Judy, who asks her beloved doctor to say, whenever he achieves something in his work, "That was for Judith, my wife!" With heartfelt pride, she affirms, "Nothing can hurt us now. What we have can't be destroyed. That's our victory. Our victory over the dark."

With her husband gone, Judy now confronts her final moments on earth. She insists on helping Ann to plant the hyacinths—"They're his favorite flowers"—and asks Ann to "take care of my doctor." As Ann gazes at her with sorrow, Judy tells her, "I must go in now. No one must be here . . . Ann, be my best friend. Go now, please." Ann hurries away in tears, and Judy moves into the house. She says goodbye to her dogs, walks up the stairs, and after praying at her bedside, lies down on the bed, staring sightlessly into the void as the scene fades. Many years later, commenting on Max Steiner's "heavenly chorus" in the background, Davis remarked with amusement that the composer had killed her off long before she actually expired.

The reason this scene works so well, apart from Geraldine Fitzgerald's able support, is that Davis plays the scene with restraint, without undue emphasis on the character's tragic demise. Apparently, this was the most difficult scene in the film for the actress. Her identification with the character was so complete that she could not keep herself from crying. "I don't know what's wrong with me," she told Goulding. "Dammit, I can't cry in this scene; it's all wrong!" After many takes, she played the scene most effectively, dry-eyed, subdued, and serene. Credit should also be given to Edmund Goulding, who allowed her to find the right approach, without the bullying tactics used by other directors.

---

*In an interview with *Life* magazine in April 1939, Davis remarked that her hardest task was to simulate loss of sight. She would drive home at dusk, pretending it was really daylight and that she was going blind. She noted, "I'd try to look as far as I could into the darkness."

Judy enjoys an idyllic period in Vermont with her new husband. At the end, with death approaching, Davis has one of her most touching moments when she urges him to go on with his experiments to find a cure for whatever is killing her. She tells him, "With each blow you strike, you can say, 'That was for Judith, my wife.'"

Goulding, a refined Englishman, had long been able to extract competent and even memorable performances from his leading ladies, including Joan Crawford, never more appealing than in *Grand Hotel* (1932), or the luminous Jane Bryan in *We Are Not Alone* (1939), which he directed later that year.

For Bette Davis, who won an Oscar nomination (as did the film and Max Steiner), *Dark Victory* was a landmark film. She would go on to give other memorable performances, including long-suffering spinster Charlotte Lovell in *The Old Maid* (filmed later in 1939), lying murderess Leslie Crosbie in *The Letter* (1940), and vulnerable stage star Margo Channing in *All About Eve* (1950). Yet much of her finest acting can still be found in Judith Traherne in *Dark Victory*,

Ann sobs in Judy's arms, knowing that her friend's dimming vision signals the beginning of the end for her. The actresses transcend bathos by playing the scene honestly and forthrightly, with a result that still has viewers weeping copiously.

as she moves from careless hedonism to bleakest despair and finally to a personal and heartbreaking "victory over the dark." Davis's virtuosic acting in this film would remain a shining beacon among the many great performances of 1939.

Dark Victory. Warner Bros. Produced by Hal Wallis and David Lewis. Directed by Edmund Goulding. Screenplay by Casey Robinson, from the play by George Emerson Brewer, Jr., and Bertram Bloch. Photography by Ernest Haller. Art direction by Robert Haas. Costumes by Orry-Kelly. Edited by William Holmes. Cast: Bette Davis, George Brent, Geraldine Fitzgerald, Humphrey Bogart, Ronald Reagan, Henry Travers, and Cora Witherspoon. Remade by Daniel Petrie in 1963 as *Stolen Hours*, and as a television film in 1976 under its original title.

Joe Louis knocks out "Two-Ton" Tony Galento . . . Pan American Airlines begins air service to Europe . . . The first local food-stamp program in America starts in Rochester, New York . . . The one millionth person enters the New York World's Fair . . . Barbara Stanwyck weds Robert Taylor . . . Byron Nelson wins the U.S. Open golf tournament . . . Hungary adopts anti-Jewish laws expected to expel 300,000 from the country . . . Germany and Italy sign a ten-year "Pact of Steel," which binds them militarily, economically, and politically . . . England's Viscount Halifax tells the Reich that his country is ready for war . . .

. . . and new films that add to the astonishing roster include *Young Mr. Lincoln, Goodbye, Mr. Chips,* and *Only Angels Have Wings* . . .

Flyer Geoff Carter (Cary Grant) and showgirl Bonnie Lee (Jean Arthur) share a scratchy but ultimately loving relationship.

High Flyers: Only Angels Have Wings

"Joe died flying, didn't he? That was his job. He
just wasn't good enough. That's why he got it!"
—Cary Grant to Jean Arthur in *Only Angels Have Wings*

If films such as *Dark Victory* were rele-
gated to the so-called "women's" audience, other films, such as *Gunga Din*,
appealed to the masculine ethos, with their emphasis on straightforward action
and brave men joining together, under a code of honor and duty, in a common
cause against the enemy. Romance and emotion were left behind as heroes with
swords or guns rode bravely into the fray, or soared boldly through the skies
in their flying machines. From the leaps of Douglas Fairbanks to the swash-
bucklings of Errol Flynn, the adventure film never claimed to be a profound
genre, but it was often exhilarating.

Some directors proved to be exceptionally adroit at handling the adventure
film. Usually burly, rough-hewn men with rugged backgrounds, they were able
to apply their life experiences to their work. Feisty and profane, Raoul Walsh
had worked as a sailor and Western wrangler before joining the film industry
in the silent years, directing Douglas Fairbanks in the spectacular *The Thief of
Bagdad* (1924) and bringing an earthy vigor to the film version of the war play
What Price Glory (1926). Early in his career, Henry Hathaway also specialized in
the area of action and adventure, giving pace, color, and visceral excitement to
his best films, especially *The Lives of a Bengal Lancer* (1935).

Another director who excelled in the adventure film, as well as other genres,
was Howard Hawks. Like Raoul Walsh, Hawks had enjoyed a rugged life before
entering films in the early twenties, working as a racing driver and as a pilot
with the Army Air Corps in World War I. His background not only helped him
develop a bluntly pragmatic attitude toward life but also a direct, unpretentious
style of filmmaking that scrupulously avoided the bravura touches of other

A panoramic view of the set for the dock in Barranca. The ship pulling into the dock is bringing Bonnie Lee, who will not only find romance but a new point of view in a man's world.

directors. His own flirting with danger made him deeply respect those who risked their lives daily, not necessarily for a Great Cause but because it was the right, the honorable thing to do. His greatest admiration went to the men who responded to perilous situations by banding together with unstated courage and resilience, without a shred of self-pity or sentimentality. It became the central theme of many of his movies.

Happily, Hawks was able to combine this theme with his lifelong interest in aviation in several of his best thirties films. In 1930, he directed the first version of the World War I aviation story *The Dawn Patrol*, in which a group of stiff-upper-lip British aviators participate in dangerous and sometimes fatal sky encounters with the enemy, while their leaders assume the lonely burden of command. Not one woman intruded into their male bastion of duty and responsibility. Five years later, he directed *Ceiling Zero* (1935), in which James Cagney played a cocky, irresponsible pilot who causes tragedy before he can learn the spirit of teamwork. Pat O'Brien, in another of his costarring roles with Cagney, played his irritated superior. The importance of the bonds between men in groups appeared as a recurring theme, even in Hawks films that strayed from the airfields. In his classic crime film *Scarface* (1932), loyalty to the gang

Kid (Thomas Mitchell) threatens to attack Bat McPherson (Richard Barthelmess), the flyer he holds responsible for his brother's death.

supersedes all other commitments; in the criminal code, treachery is more despicable than murder. In later years, Hawks would extend his theme to the Westerns, most notably *Rio Bravo* and its loose remakes, *El Dorado* (1967) and *Rio Lobo* (1970). Yet in order to present the theme in its purest, most concentrated form, Hawks returned to the world of aviation in his 1939 melodrama *Only Angels Have Wings*. It turned out to be one of his finest films.

Reportedly, *Only Angels Have Wings* got under way when Harry Cohn, head of Columbia Pictures, asked to see Hawks, who was visiting Frank Capra at the studio. He told Hawks that he needed a story for two stars (Cary Grant and Jean Arthur) who were ready to work. Obligingly, Hawks scribbled the film's story on ten pages of yellow paper, then submitted it to Cohn. He drew on many sources for his story: He recalled previous aviation films about men flying dangerous missions, not only a few of his own but also *Night Flight* (1933) and *Flight From Glory* (1937), both of which had plot elements similar to *Only Angels Have Wings*. No doubt he remembered the films in which a beautiful girl of the hard-knocks school invades an all-male domain, spraying perfume and trouble in every direction (the most notable example: *Red Dust*, 1932, with Jean Harlow and Clark Gable).* Hawks also claimed that he had also drawn on incidents in his personal experience, especially one in which a pilot had been blackballed

---

*The idea of a girl stranded among men in a tropical clime continually appealed to filmmakers. *Red Dust* was remade twice as *Congo Maisie* (1940) and *Mogambo* (1953), and the 1940 movie *Torrid Zone* had a plot line so similar to *Red Dust* it seemed almost like a remake.

for leaping out of his failing airplane, leaving his partner to crash and die. Hawks had watched the man jump and seen his partner's body on a slab in the morgue. Out of these various elements, Hawks had scenarist Jules Furthman construct the screenplay for the movie. Cohn liked the script and wanted Hawks to begin working in a few weeks to keep the stars from moving off to other commitments.

After Cary Grant and Jean Arthur were signed for the leads, Hawks sought to cast the remaining principal roles. To play Grant's mentor and best friend, he chose Thomas Mitchell, an actor adept at projecting pixieish Irish charm and warmth without resorting to excess. For the important role of the flyer who must redeem a cowardly act in his past, Hawks cast Richard Barthelmess, an actor who had been a major star in the silent years in such films as *Broken Blossoms* (1919), *Way Down East* (1920), and *Tol'able David* (1921). His strikingly handsome face and earnest manner made him especially ideal to play D. W. Griffith's innocent heroes. He failed to make the transition to sound, however, and began playing secondary roles in minor films. *Only Angels Have Wings* represented his attempt at a comeback—it was his first film in three years—but he made only three more movies in supporting roles, then retired from the screen.

To play his seductive wife, Harry Cohn asked Hawks to consider a beautiful auburn-haired actress named Rita Hayworth, who had been on the Columbia lot for several years, playing feminine leads in low-grade films. Her role in *Only Angels Have Wings* would be her most important to date, and at the time, stories were circulated about her relentless campaign to play Judy McPherson. Fan magazines gossiped about the night Hayworth, dressed in an expensive, form-fitting dress, went to the restaurant where Howard Hawks and Harry Cohn were having dinner. (*Photoplay* had her saying, "It was the beauty-jaded moguls of Hollywood I was trying to reach.") Apocryphal or not, her efforts won her a photographic test and then the role she coveted. Still unformed as an actress if not as a woman, she took her place among the cast's professionals, which included the ever-reliable Sig Rumann, Allyn Joslyn, and Noah Beery, Jr.

After a walled village was built on the Columbia lot in the San Fernando Valley, shooting the film proceeded smoothly under Hawks's assured direction. Many years later, he could only recall the special difficulties he had with Hayworth. Fully aware of the sexuality she exuded in her every movement, he had her enter the film at midpoint, going into a room of brawling men, who stop their fight to stare at her as the camera moves over her body. It was an easy and inevitable beginning for her role, but later in the filming, her insecurity created problems. Hawks remembered having to guide her through a scene in which she becomes slightly drunk: "I said, 'Cary, what's the matter with this thing?' He said, 'Howard, I don't know, she doesn't seem to know what I'm talking about.' So I sent the prop man for a big pitcher full of ice cubes and

Geoff and Judy (Rita Hayworth) rekindle their relationship. Hardly a polished actress at this point, Hayworth created a number of problems for director Howard Hawks.

water, put it behind the bar, and told Rita to go in there and make a misstep and knock something off the bar. 'Cary,' I said, 'when you feel that scene is dying, you just say, "You don't know what you're talking about, do you?" and grab her by the neck and pour this whole thing right over her head. She'll holler or scream or do something, and we'll dissolve. You put a towel over her head and be drying her hair and say, "What you want to know is this." You take her lines and your lines too.' She got quite a credit for playing a drunk scene and doing it well."* Hayworth's flashy role made audiences and studio executives sit up and take notice, but she played several more minor or supporting roles before achieving full-fledged stardom in the early forties.

Started on the day before Christmas, 1938, *Only Angels Have Wings* was ready for release in May of 1939. Although Jules Furthman's screenplay was not exactly freshly minted, and Hawks himself admitted that some of the elements of the plot were slightly frayed around the edges, the movie clearly derived its strength from the strong bonding between the characters, especially the flyers, who face daily life-or-death assignments. Watching this film a half-century after its release,

---

*Joseph McBride, *Hawks on Hawks* (Berkeley: University of California Press, 1982), p. 42.

a viewer is struck by the fact that it is a high-flying adventure with one crucial difference: There is not all that much high flying. Whereas *The Dawn Patrol* and *Ceiling Zero* (especially the former) had extended aerial sequences, *Only Angels Have Wings* confines a great deal of its footage to a run-down saloon, a few side rooms, and the small office of the central figure's ramshackle air mail and freight office. Nor is much attention paid to the film's exotic setting of the port town of Barranca in Ecuador. There are scenes of perilous flying, ably supervised by Paul Mantz, yet Hawks and his screenwriter (several others are uncredited) are more concerned with attitudes than with action. The central question is: What keeps these civilian pilots risking their lives by flying mail and freight high over the Andes?

During the course of the movie, Brooklyn's own Bonnie Lee (Arthur) not only learns the answer to this question but also finds romance with the flyers' stoic and steely boss Geoff Carter (Grant). A showgirl stranded without a job, Bonnie arrives in Barranca, where she is immediately spotted by Joe (Beery) and Les (Joslyn), two flyers for Geoff's company. Amiable Joe makes a play for her, and they go to the saloon owned by the Dutchman (Rumann), who is the all-purpose man in town. Before Joe can share a steak with Bonnie, Geoff orders him to go up on an assignment, despite the treacherous weather. There can be no question of fear, or shirking of duty: a fact understood by all the flyers, including Geoff's closest friend, Kid Dabb (Thomas Mitchell).

Joe insists on flying, but in a well-wrought scene, he crashes and is killed when he tries to land in a thick fog. (Tense, worried faces move in and out of the fog as Joe tries vainly to steer his plane to safety.) The reaction to Joe's death stuns Bonnie: no mourning, no word of grief is permitted; the accident was Joe's fault for being a "wise guy." Geoff, in particular, remains businesslike ("I'm running an airline"), and with seemingly cold directness, he states the professional's code that cannot allow for error: "Joe died flying, didn't he? That was his job. He just wasn't good enough. That's why he got it!" Fatalism is a state of mind that has no room for feelings: "What's the use of feeling bad about something that couldn't be helped?"

Shocked by everyone's apparent indifference, particularly Geoff's, Bonnie reacts hysterically, slapping Geoff and crying until he tells her, simply, "How do you think *we* feel?" Suddenly, Bonnie realizes what they have been doing: concealing the pain to keep on going. With this revelation, she becomes another ideal Hawksian woman, warm, supportive, and keenly aware of the true caring that lurks beneath the surface. She is there to provide comfort and occasionally love, and to take part, if allowed, in the rituals and rites of life and death. Hers is not a role to gladden the hearts of feminists in the 1980s, but in Hawks's world, it is more than enough. Fully converted, Bonnie can now ask, "Who's Joe?" and expect the response, "Never heard of him!" as she plays the piano

The film's high point: the stoical, understated demise of Kid Dabb. Quietly, Kid confronts the fate that often awaits those who face peril every day of their lives. In a single year, Thomas Mitchell displayed his wide range as an actor, giving solid performances in this film and in *Stagecoach*, *Mr. Smith Goes to Washington*, and *Gone With the Wind*.

for their sing-along. (Traditionally, in films of this kind, the sing-along signifies male camaraderie into which women are initiated.)

Like many other heroes in Hawks's films, Geoff regards women as both a hindrance and a pleasant interlude. Yet as she becomes increasingly attracted to him, Bonnie senses that one particular woman made him bitter ("Somebody must have given you an awful beating once."). In a moment of candor, Geoff admits that there was such a woman, one who left him with his present point of view: "No looking ahead. No tomorrows. Just today." Bonnie finds herself drawn to this fatalistic enigma. "I hardly know the man," she tells Kid, and he replies, "Sure. But you'll get over it." Bonnie decides to stay on, baffled by her feelings for Geoff and by his rough treatment of her. He treats her roughly. Oddly, their scenes together are never entirely successful. Arthur had spent the thirties building on her smart, perky "career girl" persona and her role here as a self-described "chump" who admires the flyers' "macho" image is not altogether believable. And too much Cary Grant charm seeps through Geoff's "man of steel" image to make him completely credible.

Enter the long, long arm of coincidence. A new flyer named Bat McPherson (Barthelmess) turns up to take Joe's place, and he turns out to be a man actually named Kilgallen, a notorious flyer who bailed out of his failing plane in terror, leaving his mechanic to crash and die. The mechanic was Kid's younger brother. The arm of coincidence stretches even further when it appears that McPherson's beautiful wife Judy (Hayworth) is the very same woman who deserted Geoff years ago, or, as one of the flyers might have put it, the old flame who burned a hole in Geoff's heart. Geoff's troubles—dealing with a detested flyer, facing a phantom from his past—are compounded when he has to ground Kid for poor eyesight. Thomas Mitchell, a first-rate character actor, makes Kid an appealing and touching character, a gentle man in a tough business. He handles, with consummate skill, the difficult scene in which he realizes that McPherson is the man responsible for his brother's death, and struggles to repress his murderous impulses.

In Howard Hawks's canon of professionalism, McPherson has committed the ultimate sins of cowardice and self-preservation, and now he must prove himself by taking the most difficult and dangerous assignments. At the same time, Bonnie becomes aware that Geoff and Judy were once lovers, but by this time she is completely in love with him. Again, she has turned herself into Hawks's ideal woman: self-effacing, undemanding, and willing to spend her life in fear of his perilous occupation. At one point, she tells Geoff, "You don't have to be afraid of me anymore. I'm not trying to tie you down. I don't want to plan. I don't want you to change anything." On the other hand, Judy is the worst kind of Hawksian woman: selfish, demanding, and unwilling to give her man the simplest trust. "You're no good, Judy, and never were!" Geoff tells her, and later, as she anxiously tries to learn about her husband's terrible past, she comes to agree: "I'm no good. I was only thinking of myself, not how to help him."

All these self-revelations and romantic crisscrossings necessarily cut into the film's adventure content. Yet Hawks does manage several of his usually proficient action scenes.* In one, Geoff is required to test a repaired plane, and when it veers out of control, he must desperately find a way to land. While Bonnie watches in terror, he narrowly escapes a fatal crash. However, Hawks reserves his largest guns for the film's climactic sequences. When an important flight is scheduled in truly dangerous weather, Geoff decides to take the assignment himself. Kid pleads to go up with him but he refuses. In a plot device that smacks of easy contrivance rather than logic, Bonnie, hysterical at the thought of Geoff flying through the storm, loses her acquired "cool" and accidentally shoots him in the arm. Contemptuously, Geoff consigns her to the waste bin of womanhood: "You're just like all the rest!"

Without Geoff's knowledge, Kid takes his place and goes up with McPherson. Flying under impossible conditions, they soon lose altitude. Refusing Geoff's frantic orders, they insist on trying to land the plane together. However, Kid is seriously wounded when a condor crashes into the cockpit window,

---

*Roy Davidson and Edwin C. Hahn received an Oscar nomination for their special effects in the flying sequences. This was the first time that the category of Special Effects was recognized by the Academy.

causing a piece of debris to strike him. Forced to attempt the landing by himself while Kid is laid low in the cockpit, McPherson survives a dangerous crash landing, but Kid's wound is fatal. His death scene, perhaps the best-remembered in the film, embodies the stoicism of the characters. As Kid praises McPherson's bravery ("Sat right there and took it like it was an ice-cream soda!"), Geoff quietly tells him the blunt truth: "Your neck's broken, Kid." For Kid, death is not an unexpected visitor, but he must welcome it by himself. "Get that bunch out of here—quick," he tells Geoff. He wants to go it alone—like his first solo. Their parting is swift, unemotional ("So long, Kid." "So long, Geoff."). Geoff exits, and a solitary Kid meets his maker.

Although McPherson has regained the trust of the group by his act of heroism, Geoff realizes that his air service must be shut down, while Bonnie understands that it is time to move on. Yet when she sees him crying over Kid's belongings—the welcome chink in his armor—she knows that she could never leave him. In an ending reminiscent of *The Front Page*, Geoff lets her know that he really wants her to stay. They will flip a coin, and if it turns up tails, she will leave, and if it turns up heads, she will be waiting for him when he returns. He leaves, and she sees that he has used a trick coin, with two heads! In his own left-handed way, Geoff has shown that he is unwilling to take a chance on losing her.

The triteness of the plot line of *Only Angels Have Wings* cannot be denied, and the leading roles might not be ideally cast: In his wide-brimmed hat and oddly cut trousers, Cary Grant cuts a faintly ludicrous figure, and Jean Arthur is nobody's idea of a showgirl. Yet perhaps more than any other film by Howard Hawks, this adventure tale offers an eloquent and moving statement of the director's feelings about courage and comradeship. Furthermore, in its portrayal of pioneering aviators, it dwelt on technology that would have had special fascination for audiences of the day. The camaraderie of the pilots, men bound together by the threat of imminent death, is still stirring. And in the farewell scene between Grant and Mitchell, Hawks created a moment of truth that has echoed down the years. Few films of any year can make that claim.

Only Angels Have Wings. Columbia. Produced and directed by Howard Hawks. Screenplay by Jules Furthman (uncredited, William Rankin and Eleanore Griffin), from a story by Howard Hawks. Photography by Joseph Walker and Elmer Dyer. Art direction by Lionel Banks. Costumes by Robert Kalloch. Edited by Viola Lawrence. Cast: Cary Grant, Jean Arthur, Richard Barthelmess, Thomas Mitchell, Rita Hayworth, Sig Rumann, Noah Beery, Jr., and Allyn Joslyn.

Mr. Chipping (Robert Donat) and some of the students at Brookfield School.

A Teacher's Lot: Goodbye, Mr. Chips

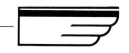

"I thought I heard you say, 'twas a pity I never had
any children. But I have . . . thousands of them
. . . and all boys."
—Robert Donat in *Goodbye, Mr. Chips*

During a foggy week in London in November 1933, a struggling young writer named James Hilton was finding it difficult to meet his deadline for a story for the Christmas issue of the *British Weekly*. He desperately needed the money, but no idea for the story was forthcoming. After a sleepless night, he went for a bicycle ride in the early morning and returned, refreshed and happy, with the idea. He wrote in longhand for four days, making only a few changes. The result was a short novel called *Goodbye, Mr. Chips,* concerning a gentle and much-loved schoolmaster who spends most of his life at a British public school. Published in the *British Weekly* to little notice, the sweetly sentimental story then crossed the ocean to appear in the April 1934 issue of *The Atlantic Monthly*, where it received wide acclaim. The Little, Brown edition of the book, published in June 1934, went through thirty-six printings. The enthusiasm for Hilton's novel extended to every walk of life; readers seemed to be able to recall a "Mr. Chips" whose wisdom, compassion, and reverence for learning had influenced their lives.

References to the novel and the character turned up everywhere. In Boston's Trinity Church, Bishop William A. Lawrence spoke of *Goodbye, Mr. Chips* in a sermon; in New Haven, William Lyon Phelps, Yale's most quoted professor, said the book "is a masterpiece and ought to be so regarded a hundred years from now." Alexander Woollcott, the publicly sentimental but privately acerbic critic known as radio's Town Crier, devoted an entire program to *Mr. Chips*, which he hailed as "the most profoundly moving story that has passed this way in several years." Since few critics of the period were as influential as Woollcott in affecting the reading habits of Americans, sales of the novel soared during

Mr. Chipping's beloved Brookfield School was actually the 382-year-old Repton School. It was chosen for the film mainly because its playing fields were flanked by a fourteenth-century church and fifteenth-century ruins.

the first year of its publication. James Hilton was astonished at the book's great success, especially since writing it had been such a painless chore. In his preface, he admitted, "I don't think I have ever written so quickly, easily, and with so much certitude that I needn't think twice about a word, a sentence, or a movement in the narrative."

Inevitably, the book's extraordinary success came to the attention of Hollywood filmmakers, especially MGM's Irving Thalberg, the frail but still active production head who had been the studio's wunderkind since the mid-twenties. It was not difficult to convince Louis B. Mayer, whose taste for genteel sentimentality was insatiable, to purchase the film rights to *Goodbye, Mr. Chips.* (After Thalberg died of pneumonia at age thirty-seven in 1936, an open letter of tribute from the principals involved was added to the film's opening credits.) MGM had recently opened a studio at Denham outside of London, where they had filmed much of *A Yank at Oxford* (1938) and *The Citadel* (1938), and it seemed logical to follow those films with another thoroughly English story. As a model and setting for the venerable but fictitious Brookfield School, the studio chose the 382-year-old Repton School, which not only had a playing field for the film's

Young Chipping meets with the headmaster, Dr. Wetherby (Lyn Harding), who tells him that "Our business is to mold men." He urges Chipping to have the "moral courage" to face his students again after they have mischievously disrupted his first class.

cricket match but which was also flanked by a fourteenth-century church and fifteenth-century ruins. Two hundred Repton boys were enlisted for a week of their holiday to serve as extras in the film, and the school's headmaster, equipped with sideburns and an old-fashioned topper, even played a small role.

Since the film covered roughly sixty years, costuming presented special problems. In order to create costumes for the 153 speaking roles, many of which required several changes of wardrobe, the designers had to pore over old files of illustrated magazines, fashion books, and family albums to find authentic styles. Yellowing photographs of school groups were studied to see exactly what clothing the students would wear. Masters' caps and gowns over the six decades also had to be devised, while khaki uniforms and mess jackets were needed for the sequences during World War I.

To play "Chips," MGM first considered Charles Laughton (how he would have twinkled and harrumphed!), then selected British actor Robert Donat, who had excelled in such movies as *The Count of Monte Cristo* (1934), *The 39 Steps* (1935), and *The Citadel*. His dignified bearing and mellifluous voice had made his characters-in-distress all the more affecting, and he seemed (as he proved to be) an ideal choice to portray the fussy, repressed but compassionate Mr. Chipping. The central role of Chipping's wife Katherine was cast with a beautiful British actress named Greer Garson, whom Mayer had seen during his trip to

Denham in 1937. She had been appearing in a play called *Old Music,* and Mayer had nearly leaped out of his seat at the sight of her auburn hair and lovely face. He met her for supper at the Savoy that evening, and ordered a screen test within the next few days. It was made with the greatest of care, and she was signed to a contract. After a long wait in Hollywood with no role (she was about to return to England), Sam Wood decided to use her in the film version of *Goodbye, Mr. Chips.* Within a few years, she would be established as the screen's foremost representative of English fortitude and reserve. Other roles in the film were strictly supportive, although Austrian actor Paul von Hernried (later Paul Henreid) made a brief impression as an Austrian-born instructor at Brookfield. The film's handling was entrusted to Sam Wood, MGM's versatile and craftsmanlike director who had demonstrated his stamina by surviving the Marx Brothers in two of their best films, *A Night at the Opera* (1935) and *A Day at the Races* (1937). By comparison, *Goodbye, Mr. Chips* would surely prove to be an almost restful change from the hectic pace of the Marxes. Indeed, the entire tone of the film is gentle, reflective.

From the start, *Goodbye, Mr. Chips* sets a leisurely pace, allowing every turning point in the life of the protagonist Mr. Chipping to unfold naturally, without the usual dramatic peaks and valleys of a conventional narrative. The episodic screenplay, credited to R. C. Sherriff, Claudine West, and Eric Maschwitz, scrupulously avoids dramatic confrontations and crises, maintaining the discreet and careful tone Chips himself would have wanted. Even in the very first sequence, the emotions lie in expressions and attitudes rather than actions. We meet Mr. Chipping in old age, long retired but still living near the school as a revered relic of the past. The year is 1928, and as Chips moves about the grounds of Brookfield School, he is greeted warmly. His mind, however, is somewhere else. When he hears the school song, he pauses to reflect, mouthing the words to himself. Already, through Robert Donat's artful acting, we feel that we know this eighty-three-year-old codger.

As he half-dozes alone in his quarters, his thoughts move back to the beginning, when he first arrived at Brookfield fifty-eight years earlier, an eager young man. On the train to the school with rowdy returning and first-time students, he appears awkward, uncertain, and an easy mark for their pranks. In the classroom, the boys provoke him deliberately, to test the stamina of their new instructor, Mr. Chipping, soon to be known as Chips. The headmaster (Lyn Harding) intercedes with a threat of caning the culprits, informing Chips that "our business is to mold men." Discipline, he tells Chips, is very important. Curiously, little attention is paid throughout the film to such matters as learning or academic standards. The film emphasizes the role of the school in developing moral courage and authority, or achieving the team spirit that comes with playing cricket. Classes are occasionally shown but have a secondary role. In a sense,

Chips addresses his students in the classroom he will occupy for fifty-eight years in Brookfield. The novel and film established the character as the model of the beloved teacher whose reputation depends more on his compassion and wisdom than on his abilities as an instructor.

Brookfield School resembles Shangri-La in Hilton's *Lost Horizon*, in which conflict is muted or avoided to make way for a reassuring (and also numbing) sense of decency and "rightness."

For a while, we see Chips failing to win the trust or affection of his students, especially when he insists on keeping the school's top cricket players in class at the time of a crucial match. (One of the angriest students, Peter Colley, is the first in a succession of Colleys taught by Chips.) As time passes, he becomes a lonely and withdrawn man, deserted at holiday time and passed over for the housemaster position he craves. Then, on a walking tour of Europe with his fellow teacher Staefel (Paul von Hernried), Chips's life is drastically altered. In the Austrian Alps—England's Lake District in the novel—he meets and, to his own astonishment, falls in love with a young woman named Katherine Ellis (Greer Garson). Chips finds himself thoroughly taken with her charm and beauty and exhilarated by the fact that she actually finds him, of all people, appealing. Their scenes of dawning love and genteel courtship may well be the best in the film: Chips's fuddy-duddy infatuation is amiably portrayed by Donat, and in her debut role, Garson radiates cheerful common sense without becoming the rather boring pillar of virtue of her later movies.

Chips's marriage to Katherine humanizes him for a while, and her none-too-profound homilies ("Believe in yourself. You can go as far as your dreams.") help to make him a more popular schoolmaster at Brookfield. Adored by everyone, Katherine is evidently too good for this world, and with surprising abruptness, she dies in childbirth. In keeping with the film's scrupulous avoidance of overt drama, Garson is given no deathbed scene; no lifeless arm drops to the side of her bed. Donat has no anguished speech to deliver. Instead, the screenplay opts for a somewhat subtler approach: In his classroom, Chips's boys fall silent and tearful at the news of Katherine's death, while in his mind Chips recalls their dancing to the strains of "The Blue Danube" in a Vienna ballroom.

Once Katherine has left the scene, the film slackens slightly into an over-the-years account of Chips's evolution from well-loved teacher to revered institution. Years later, we see him resisting retirement and shrugging off any changes in education. "I have seen the old traditions dying," he tells the current headmaster. "Grace, dignity, feeling for the past . . . Modern methods—poppycock!" Only Donat's convincing portrayal of the aging Chips keeps the moment palatable—we are being asked, after all, to admire and agree with a pedagogue who, in the name of "tradition," would summarily dismiss any advance in education since 1870. Naturally, Chips's students are indignant at the very thought of his being forced to retire, but five years later, "Chips of Brookfield" is himself finally ready to give up his post. At his retirement ceremony, Chips makes a farewell speech certain to draw tears from students and film audiences. "I will never forget your faces," he tells the assembled youngsters. "In my mind, you remain boys. Remember me sometimes. I shall always remember you."

Life changes for Brookfield and Chips when the First World War begins. The scenes involving the war years have an extra edge of poignancy considering that England, in 1939, was on the verge of entering the Second World War, but they are also unsurprising. We are moved when the solemn headmaster intones the names of the fallen students, yet we know that one of these dead will inevitably be the youngster who was most eager to get into the fray. When the newest Colley (young John Mills) becomes friends with the new recruit who was once his sworn enemy when they were boys, we are instantly aware that one of the two will be killed in battle. It turns out to be Colley. Nor are we terribly surprised when Chips insists on keeping his lecture going during a bombing raid, his white mustache fairly bristling with British resolve and fortitude. "We shall never again take our happiness for granted," he tells his students. There is a touching moment when Chips is named temporary headmaster during the war years and tells the spirit of Katherine, "You were right, my dear."

When the war ends, Chips drifts back into his private world, an amiable symbol of times past. In a warm scene, he meets briefly with the son of the Colley killed in action, played by Terry Kilburn, who appeared as all the other young Colleys. As the boy leaves, he turns to say, "Goodbye, Mr. Chips." His words turn out to be valedictory, since a few minutes later, old Chips is breathing his last. On his deathbed, he hears the current headmaster speaking about him:

Not long before her death in childbirth, Chips's adored wife Katherine (Greer Garson) tells her adoring husband, "You have all sorts of unexpected gifts and qualities . . . Believe in yourself. You can go as far as your dreams."

"Pity he never had any children." Chips rouses himself long enough to refute the remark: "I thought I heard you say, 'twas a pity I never had any children. But I have . . . thousands of them . . . thousands of them . . . and all boys." As the words "Goodbye, Mr. Chips, goodbye . . ." continue to resound in his ears, he passes gently from life.

Enormously popular with critics and audiences, *Goodbye, Mr. Chips* received Academy Award nominations for Best Picture, Best Actor, Best Director, Best Screenplay, Best Sound Recording, and Best Film Editing, but only Robert Donat won. His performance is truly the centerpiece of the film, and although his characterization inclines toward cuteness, especially in Chips's later years, it also resists numerous opportunities to overstress the sentimentality. As excellent as his performance is, however, it should be noted that Peter O'Toole succeeded in bringing greater subtlety and variety to the same role in Herbert Ross's rather dreary 1969 musical remake of the film, never leaning too heavily on the "lovable old codger" aspects of the character. The movie advanced the time span from

At the start of World War I, Chips enjoys a spot of tea with his boys, who are eager to serve. Young Forrester (Nigel Stock, standing at Chips's right) is one of the first to die in the fighting.

Eighty-three-year-old Chips dreams of the past, especially of his beloved Katherine. Donat's fully rounded and engaging performance won him the year's Academy Award as Best Actor.

1928 to 1969, added a number of terrible songs, and turned Katherine into an actress (Petula Clark) who is killed in a World War II London air raid.

As a rose-colored view of the British public school system, *Goodbye, Mr. Chips* makes an interesting contrast with a later film that deals with another teacher of classical languages. Terence Rattigan's 1951 film version of his play, *The Browning Version*, offered no lovable, twinkly Mr. Chipping but a dry, pedantic, and hopelessly ineffectual schoolmaster (Michael Redgrave) who must bear the contempt of his students, the calculating insensitivity of his colleagues, and the infidelity of his crass and brutal wife (Jean Kent). Rattigan's screenplay, completely at odds with the gentility and sentiment of *Goodbye, Mr. Chips*, allows Andrew Crocker-Harris only one crack in his veneer, his breaking down at the gift from one of his students of a rare Browning edition. Even then, his contemptuous wife takes pleasure in exposing the ulterior motive for the gift, shattering his pleasure and leaving him totally bereft. In almost every instance, *The Browning Version* contradicts the easy pieties of *Goodbye, Mr. Chips*. This public school generates snobbishness rather than moral fiber; students and faculty either detest or ignore Crocker-Harris's stultifyingly academic attitude rather than revering it, and instead of leaving the school with a heartfelt tribute to his "boys," Crocker-Harris apologizes for having failed them. "I am sorry," he tells them, as they sit in mortified silence. For Crocker-Harris, there is no idyllic interlude with an understanding wife; he is doomed to a life of humiliation with a woman who despises him. *The Browning Version*, although slight and attenuated, shows England's public school system without the blinders, whereas *Goodbye, Mr. Chips* keeps its rose-colored glasses firmly in place.

Yet any viewer can readily understand and appreciate the vast popularity of *Goodbye, Mr. Chips*, both novel and film. In the mid-thirties, the book was a gentle ode to venerable tradition. By 1939, when that tradition seemed threatened, it was a comforting reminder of a quieter, more gracious time. In the long run, *Goodbye, Mr. Chips* may have no more substance than flowers pressed between the pages of a book, and like a comfortable old overcoat, it may not fit as well as it once did. But the image of old Chips, rushing to class with his tattered robes flying behind him, is not so easily forgotten.

Goodbye, Mr. Chips. Metro-Goldwyn-Mayer. Produced by Victor Saville. Directed by Sam Wood. Screenplay by R. C. Sherriff, Claudine West, and Eric Maschwitz, from the novel by James Hilton. Photography by F. A. Young. Art direction by Alfred Junge. Costumes by Julie Harris. Edited by Charles Frend. Cast: Robert Donat, Greer Garson, Terry Kilburn, John Mills, Paul von Hernried (Paul Henreid), and Lyn Harding. Remade as a musical in 1969, under the same title.

Abe stands contemplatively on the steps of the Sangamo County jail after preventing the lynching of the Clay boys with his calm, reasoned address to the mob. In his next two films, Henry Fonda continued as an exemplary member of John Ford's company of players, giving memorable performances in *Drums Along the Mohawk* and especially *The Grapes of Wrath*.

The Man in the Stovepipe Hat: Young Mr. Lincoln

"I think I'll go on a piece. Maybe to the top of that hill."
—Henry Fonda as Abraham Lincoln in *Young Mr. Lincoln*

In the thirties, the biographical film seemed to find special favor with movie audiences. Apparently, viewers found it edifying and reasonably entertaining to learn about the tribulations and triumphs of celebrated people from all eras and all walks of life. With audience approval at the box office, the studios were willing to give their "true" stories elaborate productions, and to assign the leading roles to their most important actors. At Warner Brothers, Paul Muni, an actor so prestigious that his name was usually preceded with a lofty "Mr.," appeared as the famous French novelist in *The Life of Emile Zola* (1937). (Actually, the movie was not about his life but about his passionate involvement with the notorious Dreyfus case.) Muni also brought dignity to the role of scientist Louis Pasteur in *The Story of Louis Pasteur* (1936), also for Warners. The studio continued its scientific bent into the next decade with *Dr. Ehrlich's Magic Bullet* (1940), in which Edward G. Robinson starred as the doctor who found a cure for syphilis.

During the same period, other studios offered their share of biographical films, some of them far from serious-minded or instructive. Always eclectic in its taste (provided the film could lend itself to lavish production values), MGM ran the gamut from a tribute to theatrical entrepreneur Florenz Ziegfeld in *The Great Ziegfeld* (1936) to an account of the nineteenth-century Irish leader *Parnell* (1937). (Early in the forties, the studio would add to the scientific mode with the stories of *Edison the Man*, 1940, and *Madame Curie*, 1943.) Fox also ran the gamut, ranging in its biographical subjects from Ferdinand de Lesseps, the French architect who built the Suez Canal (*Suez*, 1938), to Alexander Graham Bell, the inventor of the telephone (*The Story of Alexander Graham Bell*, 1939),

Abe pores over the law book he bought from Mrs. Clay. Later he tells Ann Rutledge about his intellectual curiosity: "My brain gets to itchin' inside sometimes. I gotta scratch it."

·from Western bandit Jesse James (*Jesse James*, 1939) to turn-of-the-century musical star Lillian Russell (*Lillian Russell*, 1940).

In addition to its biographical films, Fox appeared to have a penchant for what might be called "down home" films: gentle and flavorsome accounts of small-town American life in which benign oldsters and resourceful youngsters dispensed wisdom and solved problems. With directors such as John Ford and Henry King on its payroll, men whose work had demonstrated a fondness for American values and traditions, it was inevitable that the studio would often lean to rustic or bucolic themes. Fox also had two suitable stars for its homespun films: the shrewd, easygoing, and enormously popular Will Rogers, and everyone's favorite child, Shirley Temple. Throughout the thirties, Fox had produced such low-keyed pieces of Americana as *Steamboat 'Round the Bend* (1935), *The Little Colonel* (1935), *The Farmer Takes a Wife* (1935), and *Banjo on My Knee* (1936). It seemed inevitable that by the end of the decade, Fox would combine the biographical film with a detailed view of life in folksy nineteenth-century America. The opportunity came in the long, lean form and melancholy visage of the nation's sixteenth president, Abraham Lincoln.

As usual, it all began with the word. Lamar Trotti, a Fox screenwriter and former journalist who had been turning out scripts (alone or in collaboration with Dudley Nichols) since the early thirties, had written a screenplay about the early years of Abraham Lincoln, when the Great Emancipator was a gawky, ambitious young lawyer in Springfield, Illinois. Although the script (originally titled "Lawyer of the West") had gathered dust for a while, Fox head Darryl Zanuck became interested in making the film after Robert E. Sherwood's play *Abe Lincoln in Illinois* scored a success on Broadway in October 1938. He assigned Kenneth MacGowan to produce the film and asked John Ford to direct. Ford's deep affinity for American themes, his reverence for the ties of family and community, and his brilliant directorial style that combined sweeping images with economy of expression had already been demonstrated in such movies as *Judge Priest* (1934) and *Steamboat 'Round the Bend*, and he had just finished revitalizing the Western genre with *Stagecoach*. (The more somber, brooding side of his "black Irish" personality had appeared in *The Informer*, 1935, and *The Prisoner of Shark Island*, 1936.)

At first, Ford was reluctant to take the assignment. He was not only exhausted from making *Stagecoach* but he also felt that the subject of Lincoln had been "worked to death." He changed his mind, however, when he read Lamar Trotti's screenplay. Trotti, who had collaborated on the script for *Steamboat 'Round the Bend* with Dudley Nichols, had written a literate and moving scenario that was an authentic piece of Americana and a fully rounded portrait of a man who was, to all appearances, a modest backwoods lawyer but who bore the mark of future greatness in his manner and bearing. Based partly on an actual trial in which Lincoln had been involved, and partly on Trotti's own experiences as a reporter in the South, the screenplay succeeded in turning the cold marble of a memorial into a thinking and feeling (albeit young and unformed) human being. It was a commendable achievement, and given John Ford's predilections, it would have been difficult for him to reject the assignment.

The inevitable, and larger, question was: Who would play Abraham Lincoln? Until then, Lincoln had appeared as the central character in only one major sound film, D. W. Griffith's unsuccessful *Abraham Lincoln* (1930), which took Lincoln (Walter Huston) from gangling youth to martyred president in a series of episodes. Usually, Lincoln appeared as a shadowy figure in staged historical events, as in *The Birth of a Nation* (1914), or as a deus ex machina who resolves a conflict, as in Clarence Brown's *Of Human Hearts* (1938). *Young Mr. Lincoln* required an actor who could be convincing as a homespun, cracker-barrel type, yet suggest a native shrewdness and wisdom blended with compassion and an underlying sadness. This tall order called for a rising actor named Henry Fonda.

The Nebraska-born actor had made his film debut only four years earlier in *The Farmer Takes a Wife*, in which he repeated his stage role, and within a few years, in such movies as *You Only Live Once* (1937) and *Jezebel* (1938), he had achieved some popularity for his honest, emotionally direct performances. By 1939, he was on the verge of superstardom. Over the years, there have been

Shy Abe converses with Ann Rutledge (Pauline Moore), whose death soon afterward affects him deeply. Alfred Newman's haunting theme for Ann recurs at various points throughout the film.

several versions of how Fonda came to the role of Lincoln, including one from Fonda himself. In his autobiography, the actor wrote that Lamar Trotti and Kenneth MacGowan came to him with the idea. At first excited by the prospect, Fonda claimed to be "a Lincoln nut" who had read "three-quarters of the books" written about him. Yet after hearing the script read aloud by its author, he changed his mind. He told them frankly, "Lincoln's too big a man. Not only too big in history, but too big in everyone's heart and affections. I'm not ready for a part like that." MacGowan urged him at least to go down to the studio and test for the role, and Fonda agreed, reluctantly.

Many years later, Fonda remembered, "I went through the three hours in the make-up chair while they put on the long nose, the mole, and all the rest, and when I looked in the mirror, wow! I got on the sound stage and we did a scene from some play—not from the script. I don't remember why. I went to the rushes of the test, saw this guy on the screen and thought, 'That's Lincoln!' Then I started to talk and—no, boys. I'm sorry, I can't stand it. I said no, and they gave up." Luckily, Fonda failed to reckon with the blunt force and tenacity of director John Ford, who summoned him to his office for their first meeting. There, Fonda encountered the feisty, irascible "Pappy" Ford, wearing a slouch hat and clothes that "looked like they came from the Salvation Army, too large for him, too ragged for anybody. He had either a pipe in his mouth or a hand-kerchief all of the time."

Abe Lincoln rides into Springfield to pursue his career as a lawyer. A bystander asks him, "What do *you* know about the law?" Abe replies, "Not enough to hurt me."

Trotting out his most profane words for the occasion, Ford fired both barrels at the actor. "What the ——— is all this ——— about you not wanting to do this picture?" he growled. "You think Lincoln's a great ——— Emancipator, huh? He's a young jack-legged lawyer from Springfield, for Christ sake!" Fonda recalls, "He was full of the words you don't use in polite society. He talked that way naturally, but for God to sit there and talk to me like that was awesome. What happened was he was trying to shame me into playing Young Lincoln, and that was the point he made. He *wasn't* the Great Emancipator. He *was* a young jack-legged lawyer from Springfield. We don't know at the end of the movie what's going to happen to this guy. That's not it. It's a good movie about a young lawyer in 1830. Anyway, Ford shamed me into it. I agreed, and I did the film."*

Once Ford had his Lincoln, casting the remaining roles was not especially difficult. To play the pivotal part of the Widow Clay, the simple farm mother who is asked to make a terrible choice at the trial of her accused sons, Ford chose Alice Brady, a notable stage actress (*Mourning Becomes Electra* and other

---

*Henry Fonda, *Fonda: My Life,* as told to Howard Teichmann (New York: New American Library, 1982), p. 127.

The Grand Parade on Independence Day in Springfield. The film's cinematographer, Bert Glennon, worked with Ford on a number of other movies, including *The Hurricane* (1937), *Stagecoach*, and *Drums Along the Mohawk*, Ford's first venture into Technicolor.

plays), who had appeared onscreen mainly as flighty society dowagers until her Oscar-winning role in *In Old Chicago* (1938), in which she played the Mrs. O'Leary whose cow reputedly started the Great Chicago Fire. Other roles went to actors who would soon become familiar figures in John Ford's loose "stock company" of players—Ward Bond as roughneck Palmer Cass; Francis Ford (John's brother) as the town drunk—and to players who could embody the colorful characters in the story: Donald Meek as the bombastic prosecutor Felder; Eddie Collins as Abe's friend Eph; and Spencer Charters as Judge Bell. Characteristically for Ford, the young female roles were blandly written and acted: Marjorie Weaver as a pallid Mary Todd; Pauline Moore as the ill-fated Ann Rutledge. (Ford reserved his greatest admiration for the nation's matriarchs, such as Ma Joad in *The Grapes of Wrath* and Mrs. Morgan in *How Green Was My Valley.*)

Before the film could get under way, Fox faced a legal problem with the property. Claiming that *Young Mr. Lincoln* infringed on their play *Abe Lincoln in Illinois*, which was running successfully on Broadway, the Playwrights Company and author Robert E. Sherwood sued the studio for unfair trade competition. The suit insisted that there had been no public interest in Lincoln until their play, and that previously produced plays and films had no box-office value before *Abe Lincoln in Illinois* appeared on the scene. They also demanded that any title infringement be enjoined and that Fox's movie carry a caption stating that it was not based on the Sherwood play. In January 1940, months after *Young Mr. Lincoln* was released, the suit was dismissed with the dictum that since the source of the Playwrights Company and Sherwood's material belonged to the public domain, "no exclusive right to the use thereof can be acquired, even though they were the first to discover its value as a medium to awaken public interest." The decision made a point of chastising the complainants: "As only the unbelievably ignorant and unsophisticated could possibly confuse the defendant's photoplay with Sherwood's drama and inasmuch as the title *Young Mr. Lincoln* fails to conflict with *Abe Lincoln in Illinois,* the court cannot determine the defendant guilty of unfair competition."

As filming began, Ford soon found himself in contention with Darryl Zanuck. He had determined from the start that the subject and the mood of the film called for a deliberate, elegiac pace, while Zanuck as studio head urged him to move more quickly. Knowing that he would have to move on immediately to another project, leaving the editing in other hands, he decided to ensure the way the film would be cut by editing in the camera, setting up slow dissolves, and destroying the negatives of all the takes except the ones he wanted. Zanuck continued to harass Ford about the slow pace, and he even managed to cut one scene that Ford prized. The director later described the scene to Peter Bogdanovich: "I had a lovely scene in which Lincoln rode into town on a mule, passed

Widow Clay (Alice Brady) listens as Abe reads her a letter from her jailed son Adam. A veteran stage actress, Brady played many light-headed dowagers in films until winning a supporting Oscar for *In Old Chicago* (1938). Her moving performance as Mrs. Clay should have earned her another nomination.

by a theatre and stopped to see what was playing, and it was the Booth family doing *Hamlet*: we had a typical old-fashioned poster up. Here was a poor shabby country lawyer wishing he had enough money to go see *Hamlet* when a very handsome young boy with dark hair—you knew he was a member of the Booth family—fresh, snobbish kid, all beautifully dressed—just walked out to the edge of the plank walk and looked at Lincoln. He looked at this funny, incongruous man in a tall hat riding a mule, and you knew there was some connection there."* Ford regretted the loss of the scene, but one has to wonder whether so obvious a touch might have induced winces rather than the shock of premonition.

Initially, Fonda had some difficulty with the role. As he rehearsed the part, he found that he had a tendency to make every gesture, every word seem characteristic of the sort of man he knew Lincoln would become. Of course, he recognized that Lincoln himself would not have known—or been impressed by—what the future held in store for him, yet he was such as indelible part of American history that Fonda was awed by the responsibility of impersonating

*Peter Bogdanovich, *John Ford* (Berkeley: University of California Press, 1968), pp. 72–73.

Mary Todd (Marjorie Weaver) gazes at Abe, who is lost in a memory of Ann Rutledge. Mary, later Mrs. Lincoln, is not a major character in the film, but her interest in Abe is apparent.

him. Working on the problem with Ford, he found that whenever he lapsed into playing the mature Lincoln rather than the young man starting his law practice in Springfield, it helped to swap Lincoln yarns and jokes with the director. By laughing together at the homespun stories, he could remove the character out from under the cloud of destiny. By the time he completed the film, Fonda was able to flesh out a many-faceted character that emerged, alive and well, from the dusty pages of history.

From the moment Lincoln appears on the screen, we feel that we know this man, and not from the formal portraits that hang in school auditoriums. The film begins in New Salem, Illinois, in 1832, when John T. Stewart, campaigning for the "great and incorruptible" Whig Party against Andrew Jackson, introduces a local storekeeper who has been asked to run for the legislature. As Alfred Newman's haunting theme is heard, Lincoln lifts his gangling frame from a chair to address the crowd. "Gentlemen and fellow citizens, I presume you know who I am," he tells the people. "I'm plain Abraham Lincoln." His statement of principles is brief, direct, and uncluttered by bombast or pomposity ("My politics are short and sweet, like the old woman's dance."), but something deeper shines through the "good old country boy" manner. When he meets the Widow Clay (Alice Brady) and her family, Abe's face brightens when he learns that they can give him books, especially law books, in exchange for some clothing material. Later, sprawled beside a tree, with his feet planted firmly against the trunk, he pores over one of the books, murmuring the word *law* with reverence.

Abe's reverie is interrupted by young Ann Rutledge (Pauline Moore), who becomes the focal point of one of the film's finest sequences. As they walk together by the banks of the river in a long tracking shot, talking about his ambitions and his popularity in the community, it is clear that he loves her but can only tell her obliquely ("I love red hair"). After she leaves him, he throws a stone into the water, and the ripples dissolve into a view of the river, now covered with ice floes in the dead of winter. A saddened Abe appears to plant flowers at Ann's grave and to talk to her about his confused aspirations. (In later films, most notably *She Wore a Yellow Ribbon*, Ford used the device of a graveside "conversation" to express a character's thoughts.)* Should he study the law? Abe asks Ann. The answer will be decided by the way a stick falls (either on or away from her gravestone), but when the decision is made in favor of the law, he wonders whether he might have tipped the stick Ann's way "just a little." The sequence remains a model of economical and effective editing and filmmaking, with each image, each frame, carefully chosen to cover Lincoln's tragic idyll in the briefest possible screen time.

We next see Lincoln in 1837, riding into Springfield to practice law. (Our first view is memorable: Lincoln in his stovepipe hat, seated atop a small mule, with his long legs nearly scraping the ground.) His quiet way of settling disputes with simple wisdom is demonstrated when he convinces two battling men to make concessions that will satisfy them both. The primary intention, however, of these early Springfield scenes is to show Lincoln as an active and popular member of the community, an integral part of the frontier life he always cherished. Ford also gets the opportunity to display his abiding affection for the folkways and traditions of American community life. In an extended, beautifully staged sequence at the town's Fourth of July celebration, we watch Abe participating in a rail-splitting contest and a tug o' war, and serving as judge in a pie competition. Bert Glennon's camera captures all the fun and excitement of the day in flavorsome detail.

Unfortunately, the holiday festivities are shattered that evening by a violent incident. When Abigail Clay's two sons Matt (Richard Cromwell) and Adam (Eddie Quillan) get into a fight with the town bullies, Palmer Cass (Ward Bond) and Scrub White (Fred Kohler, Jr.), Scrub is shot dead. It appears that not only

---

*In the documentary film *Directed by John Ford*, Henry Fonda recalls that Ford "loved graveyard scenes. He loved a man coming to the graveyard, all alone, talking to the person. I've done that in two or three pictures for Ford."

The principals, the jury, and the townspeople assemble for the trial of Adam and Matt Clay (Eddie Quillan and Richard Cromwell, in the front row). Behind them are Carrie Sue (Judith Dickens), Mrs. Clay, and Hannah (Arleen Whelan).

did one of the Clay boys fire the fatal bullet but also that Mrs. Clay witnessed the incident from only yards away and can identify the son who committed the crime. When the Clay boys are jailed, an angry mob forms with the intention of lynching them. Abe confronts the mob and with low-key but persuasive eloquence, he succeeds in keeping the angry crowd at bay. Fonda's performance in this sequence, as he addresses the mob in measured tones, prefigures the many men of decency and conscience he would later play in his career. He tells them:

> Maybe these boys do deserve to hang. All I'm askin' is that we have it done with some legal pomp and show. . . . Trouble is, when men start takin' the law into their own hands, it's just as apt in all the confusion and fun to start hangin' somebody who's *not* a murderer as somebody who is. . . . The next thing you know they're hangin' one another just for *fun*. We seem to lose our heads in times like this. We do things together that we'd be mighty ashamed to do by ourselves.

Before the trial of the Clays begins, *Young Mr. Lincoln* pauses for some quieter, more reflective scenes. (Ford's deliberately slow pace must have continued to anger Zanuck.) Abe attends a lavish party at the invitation of Mary Todd (Marjorie Weaver), who finds him both fascinating and puzzling. She wonders about the look of melancholy that crosses his face as he gazes out at the river, remembering Ann Rutledge. Abe also spends time at the Clays' farm, where he recalls his own childhood and early farm life ("You folks are just like my folks.").

As always, his memories are tinged with sorrow over irretrievable losses. Gently, he tries to get Mrs. Clay to name the son who fired the fatal shot but she refuses. Alice Brady's acting in this scene is exemplary; the racking anguish with which she expresses her inability to speak out makes one regret the years in which her skill was wasted in addled dowager roles.

Clearly, Ford enjoyed filming the long trial sequence that makes up the centerpiece of *Young Mr. Lincoln*. The camera catches the rowdy, disorderly atmosphere of a frontier trail, as Judge Bell (Charters) looks down with satisfaction on the throng of noisy citizens ("Mighty big crowd here today!"). Mr. Felder (Meek), the prosecuting attorney, hurls fire and brimstone at the heads of the hapless Clay boys, as Lincoln stands calmly at the center of the storm. In the process of jury selection, Lincoln approves of Frank (Ford), the town sot, who freely admits to lying, laziness, and hard drinking ("You're just the kind of honest man we want on this jury!"). A succession of damaging witnesses, led by Palmer Cass, makes it seem as if Matt and Adam Clay have little chance to avoid being hanged. Brought to the stand by the prosecution, Abigail Clay again refuses to single out one son as the killer ("I can't tell you . . . and you can't make me!"). Lincoln offers a stirring defense of her position, calling her "a simple, ordinary country woman." "I've seen hundreds of women just like her," he tells the court. "Women who say nothing but do much." By means of Lamar Trotti's screenplay, Ford appears to be expressing, once again, his veneration for America's resilient pioneer women and matriarchs.

The trial's climax, while nicely melodramatic, is also not unexpected and is rather perfunctory. Brought back to the witness stand, Palmer Cass suddenly claims to be an eyewitness to the killing, identifying Matt as the culprit. It would appear that all is lost for the Clays, but then Lincoln, in a reexamination of Cass, catches him in a simple lie that might have occurred to others before this time. Cass's testimony that he saw Matt kill Scrub White from a distance because the night was "moon bright" is disproved when Abe brings forth an almanac showing that the moon had already set by the time of the incident. Abe badgers Cass into confessing the crime.

Abe is now the town hero, and in one of the film's indelible moments, he is summoned to speak to the cheering crowd of citizens. His admirers include Mary Todd and future opponent Stephen Douglas (Milburn Stone), who promises "never to underestimate" Lincoln again. In a visual equivalent of his looming greatness, Lincoln moves forward into the frame, finally filling it with his strong presence, then removes his hat to address the people. The final moments reinforce this perception of momentous history in the making, a sense that the movie until now has largely avoided. Abe says goodbye to the happy Clay family, then remarks, "I think I'll go on a piece. Maybe to the top of that hill." As he climbs up the hill, a tiny figure against a vast and darkening sky, we see the

Clay wagon growing ever smaller in the distance. A chorus sings "The Battle Hymn of the Republic" as the rain begins to fall, and the film ends with a shot of the face of the President-to-be in the brooding expression of the Lincoln Memorial statue.

Appropriately, the world premiere of *Young Mr. Lincoln* was held on Memorial Day, 1939, at the Fox-Lincoln Theatre in Springfield, Illinois. Newscaster Lowell Thomas acted as master of ceremonies for the opening festivities, which brought forth a number of Hollywood celebrities, including some of the film's principal actors as well as a large group of newspaper writers from Eastern and Midwestern cities. During the day, the visitors were squired around the town to spots of historic interest, and in the evening, a huge crowd assembled for the premiere, which was broadcast over national radio. According to Bosley Crowther's report in *The New York Times*, "Marian Anderson, the Negro soprano, was imported to sing at the opening ceremonies" and "a couple of eminent Lincoln students were on hand to lend the academic touch." He reported that the people of Springfield apparently enjoyed it as "a novel and exciting festival."

More of a fable suggested by fact than an authentic re-creation of history, *Young Mr. Lincoln* should be looked on as John Ford's glowing and affectionate tribute to the American past and to the formation of an American legend. (The following year, in *The Grapes of Wrath*, he would show the dark side of the American present.) The film also marked the first collaboration of Ford and Henry Fonda, a director-actor teaming that would produce a number of notable movies. In his book on Ford, Lindsay Anderson aptly described the essence of their work together:

> In Fonda as in Ford, there is the same combination of sensibility with authority, gentleness with strength; the same openness of feeling; and the same compulsive integrity that reveals itself with a directness so seemingly simple that it is easy to overlook the artistry that such revelation, such simplicity demand.*

Young Mr. Lincoln marked the beginning of their cinematic journey. With Henry Fonda as his ideal spokesman and surrogate, John Ford made a film that, half a century after its release, can still be watched with pleasure.

Young Mr. Lincoln. Twentieth Century-Fox. Produced by Kenneth MacGowan. Directed by John Ford. Screenplay by Lamar Trotti. Photography by Bert Glennon. Art direction by Richard Day and Mark-Lee Kirk. Edited by Walter Thompson. Cast: Henry Fonda, Alice Brady, Marjorie Weaver, Arleen Whelan, Richard Cromwell, Ward Bond, Donald Meek, Francis Ford, Eddie Collins, Spencer Charters, and Pauline Moore.

---

*Lindsay Anderson, *About John Ford* (New York: McGraw-Hill Book Company, 1981), p. 100.

JULY/AUGUST, 1939

Bobby Riggs and Alice Marble win the tennis tournament at Wimbledon . . . The Yankee Clipper arrives in London, completing the first passenger flight over the Atlantic . . . The New York World's Fair sets a daily attendance record on August 27 . . . Lou Gehrig makes his emotional farewell to baseball at Yankee Stadium before nearly 62,000 fans . . . Albert Einstein writes to President Roosevelt, suggesting that an atomic bomb is feasible . . . Americans fearing a European war crowd aboard the *Normandie* ocean liner bound for the U.S. . . . The Nazis threaten to invade the hotly disputed and strategic city of Danzig in Poland, prompting France and England to issue a warning that such an action would provoke war . . .

. . . while moviegoers are shedding tears of sympathy for *The Old Maid*, or marching down the Yellow Brick Road to find *The Wizard of Oz* . . .

Miriam Hopkins and Bette Davis as cousins Charlotte and Delia Lovell. The rivalry of the characters in the story extended to the actresses off the set.

"Tonight, just tonight, she belongs to me! Tonight,
I want her to call me Mommy!"
—Bette Davis to Miriam Hopkins in *The Old Maid*

Following her triumph as dying heiress Judith Traherne in *Dark Victory*, Bette Davis, now the reigning queen on the Warners lot, had played the Empress Carlotta, ill-fated wife of the equally ill-fated Archduke Maximilian, in William Dieterle's historical drama *Juarez* (1939). It was a showy role, climaxed by a scene of staring madness as her duped husband, a pawn in the Mexican Revolution of the 1860s, faces the firing squad. It was not, however, a truly starring role, nor the sort of film that would give her the opportunity to display a wide range of emotions. She had enjoyed working with director Edmund Goulding on *Dark Victory*, and wanted a vehicle that would bring them together again. She found it in a property that Warners had purchased for her after it had gathered dust on Paramount's shelf for several years: an adaptation of Zoë Akins's play *The Old Maid*, which, in turn, had been derived from a novella by Edith Wharton.

The play, a period drama concerning Charlotte and Delia Lovell, two strong-willed cousins who wage a long, impassioned battle over a child that one has borne out of wedlock and the other has raised as her own, had opened during New Year's week in 1935 to mostly negative reviews. Starring Judith Anderson and Helen Menken as the warring women, the play was judged to be a rather musty curio that, in the words of the *New York Evening Journal* reviewer John Anderson, contained "everything except interest, drama, and life." Brooks Atkinson, in *The New York Times*, found it severely disappointing: "It is difficult to decide whether the uneven acting or the truncated narrative is the main source of disintegration. Whatever the source, *The Old Maid* leaves no single impression." Gilbert Gabriel's review in *The New York American* called it "another cos-

At the railroad depot, Charlotte and Delia bid farewell to Clem Spender (George Brent), who is going off to fight in the Civil War. Brent replaced Humphrey Bogart in the role after Bogart was deemed inadequate by the producer and director.

tume drama that is more costume than drama." Although several notices were favorable, the chances for a run seemed nil. Yet with women crowding the matinees, the play ran through the spring for 305 performances.

To nearly everyone's surprise, and to the outrage of many, *The Old Maid* was awarded the Pulitzer Prize as the year's best. Having lost several members of the play jury the previous year in a heated argument over the caliber of the selections, the trustees and advisory board of Columbia University, who bestowed the award, retreated into silence and refused, at first, even to identify the new jury members. They also refused to issue any comment on the storm of controversy that began to rage over the selection of *The Old Maid*. Such reputable critics as George Jean Nathan and John Mason Brown assailed the choice as "absurd" and "incredible," while other critics raced into print to have their say, ranging from Brooks Atkinson's rather temperate disapproval in the *Times* to Richard Lockridge's scathing condemnation in the *Sun*. Many theatrical producers who did not win the prize joined in the chorus of protest. A number of people wondered whether the elimination of Lillian Hellman's *The Children's*

Hour, a more likely choice for the 1934–35 season, was due to its "unpleasant" subject of lesbianism.

By the time Warners purchased *The Old Maid* from Paramount, the controversy over its selection had long simmered down, and the studio now considered it a worthy vehicle for their leading star, with the added cachet of its Pulitzer Prize as a potent selling tool. Bette Davis was not only pleased to be reunited with Edmund Goulding but also gratified that the play would benefit from a new adaptation by Casey Robinson, who had showcased her so brilliantly in *Dark Victory*. An able craftsman, Robinson worked to stress the complex relationship through jealousy that develops between the two women, rather than the events that turn Charlotte Lovell into an old maid.

To play the costarring role of Delia opposite Davis's Charlotte, the studio selected Miriam Hopkins, a capable if sometimes overemphatic actress who had appeared in films since 1930, often as brittle, sophisticated women (*Trouble in Paradise*, 1932; *Design for Living*, 1933), and notably as Fredric March's hapless victim in *Dr. Jekyll and Mr. Hyde* (1932). A decade earlier, Hopkins and Davis had worked together briefly in George Cukor's stock company in Rochester, New York, where Hopkins was a visiting guest star and Davis the resident ingenue. They were acquaintances but far from friends, and with good reason. A notoriously difficult actress, Hopkins apparently drove many a director to the brink of despair by trying to upstage every other player in the cast. According to all reports, she found a worthy adversary in Davis, who fought her for every minute of screen time. Since the two characters dominated the story and shared many scenes, the set of *The Old Maid* could be likened to a battleground in which the soldiers-in-crinoline clashed in furious contention.

Casting the major supporting roles (Jane Bryan as Davis's daughter Tina; Donald Crisp as a sympathetic doctor; Louise Fazenda as a devoted maid) caused few problems, except in the case of the pivotal character of Clem Spender, the man both women love. At first, in a blatant case of miscasting, Humphrey Bogart, then a contract player at Warners, was signed to play the part. Within a few weeks, after shooting a few scenes in which he appeared decidedly unromantic, the studio realized its error and decided to replace him, first with Alan Marshal and then with the ever-reliable George Brent, who had worked well with Davis in *Dark Victory*. In a memorandum to Hal Wallis, the studio's head of production, Edmund Goulding wrote: "I do feel that the picture needs George—because, as we all agreed, the picture is based on the two girls falling in love with a man. That man must be important both in name, performance, and appearance. He must be someone to remember throughout the play."*

---

*Quoted in Rudy Behlmer, *Inside Warner Bros.* (New York: Viking Press, 1982), p. 87. Brent performs competently in the role, but when he is described as "crazy" and "impulsive" by other characters in the story, a baffled audience can see nothing but the actor's bland persona.

Delia comes to visit Charlotte at her nursery for war orphans. When the melody of "Clementine" is heard on the soundtrack—the same melody used for Charlotte and Clem's brief idyll—the audience can have little doubt about the true identity of the child Tina (Marlene Burnett).

With Hopkins causing problems at every opportunity, the production of *The Old Maid* proceeded on its bumpy course. To Davis's annoyance, Hopkins continually asked to have dialogue rewritten, or attempted to place herself in the most favorable camera positions, spoiling many shots by moving arbitrarily. Other days she would fail to turn up on the set, claiming to be ill or otherwise indisposed. Well into the filming, she created a predicament by insisting on wearing long false eyelashes so that she would appear younger in her later scenes with Davis. (For her scenes as the older Charlotte, Davis used no eye makeup or lipstick, only a pale, ashen base.) Soon, the film's makeup man, Perc Westmore, was instructed to return Hopkins's makeup to the way it had been approved by the producer. Hopkins's cardinal sin, however, was not her makeup. Resolutely determined to make her character more sympathetic, the Georgia-born actress played many scenes with a molasses-sweet demureness that went against the grain of the self-centered Delia. Many years later, Davis remarked, "Miriam is a perfectly charming woman, socially. Working with her is another story." Four years after *The Old Maid*, when the actresses were reteamed for *Old Acquaintance* (1943), the rivalry continued, causing many "in-the-know" viewers to wonder whether the furious shaking an exasperated Davis gives to Hopkins in the climactic scene extended beyond the character she was playing.

Young Tina (Jane Bryan) with the man she loves, Lanning Halsey (William Lundigan). Bryan, an exceptionally talented actress with a fresh and winning quality, retired early from films.

Another problem arose during the filming of *The Old Maid*, but this concerned credits for the screenplay rather than on-the-set shenanigans. The question came up as to whether the author of the unproduced version of the play, written at Paramount before the property was sold to Warners, should receive screen credit with scenarist Casey Robinson. Robinson argued that his approach to the story was greatly different from that of the Paramount version and that he had, in fact, strengthened the motives of jealousy and hatred that consumed the two principal characters, motives that were underdeveloped in the original play. Robinson maintained that it was his conception of the story that persuaded Davis and Hopkins to appear in the film. As a result, he received sole credit for his adaptation of the play and Edith Wharton's novella.

In spite of the Sturm und Drang that undoubtedly rattled the set of *The Old Maid* the completed film betrayed little of the ongoing tension and, in fact, the real-life infighting may have added a few crackles of electricity to the onscreen clashes of the two leading characters. From the start, cousins Charlotte (Davis) and Delia (Hopkins) Lovell dominate the story with their ardent impulses, abandoning their maidenly restraint to behave either unwisely or vindictively out of their passion for the same man. On the day of Delia's wedding, at the time of the Civil War, her former lover, Clem Spender (Brent), returns after two years to claim her. Cousin Charlotte tells Clem about Delia's marriage, but, loving him herself, and in an effort to assuage his anger and bitterness, she gives herself to him.* Clem is killed in the war, and as the years pass, Charlotte hides Tina, the daughter of their union, among the war orphans for whom she cares. Delia becomes a widow with two children.

All this early exposition moves by so quickly that it is not until Charlotte plans to marry Delia's brother-in-law, Joe Ralston (Jerome Cowan), that the film pauses to catch its breath and to examine the subtler motives of the characters. When Delia learns the truth about Tina's identity, she wrecks Charlotte's chance for happiness by telling Joe that Charlotte is much too "sick" to marry anyone. Out of her own vanity and pride, knowing that Clem loved Charlotte and not her, Delia has committed an unforgivable act. When Charlotte realizes what Delia has done, the two women have the first of their bitter, angry confrontations. Her words spilling out with unbridled passion and anger, Charlotte accuses Delia of betraying her: "It was wicked of you! You hated me!" Davis's pyrotechnic display of acting tends to overshadow Hopkins, who tempers her character's selfishness with a degree of charm probably unintended in the screenplay. Later, in a calmer moment, Charlotte realizes that Tina must never know that she is her mother. She agrees to have Tina live with Delia and to pose as the girl's maiden "Aunt" Charlotte.

With the passing years, Charlotte, fearful that Tina will learn the truth, willfully turns herself into a prim, testy old maid, the sort of disapproving relative young girls would prefer not to have around. It is at this point that the film acquires a measure of depth and subtlety that raises it above the level of smoothly rendered soap opera. Although the character is perhaps primmer and testier than absolutely necessary, Davis nevertheless succeeds in making her a sympathetic, understandable woman whose life has congealed in memories of bitter regret. In makeup that, from today's viewpoint, has her looking distractingly like Mrs. Vale, the tyrannical dowager mother of another Charlotte the actress would later play in *Now, Voyager* (1942), Davis is given a number of privileged acting moments that rank with her very best work. One occurs after Tina (Jane Bryan), angry at Charlotte's disapproval of the dancing at the wedding of Delia's daughter, cries, "Just because *she* doesn't dance! Just because she's *never* danced!" Alone, Charlotte begins moving to the sound of a nostalgic waltz floating into the room, for a moment happily transported back to her unrecoverable past. Her back to the camera, she stops suddenly, aware of her lonely fate, then falls back onto the sofa, crying, "Oh, Clem!"

---

*In the fashion of the day, Charlotte's offscreen surrender to Clem Spender is so discreetly handled that only our knowledge of movie "shorthand" (she goes away for a while to cure "lung fever") tells us what actually happened.

Only thirty-one at the time of filming, Bette Davis was entirely convincing as the sixty-year-old spinster with a lifetime of bitter memories and regrets. Considering the rivalry between them, she and Miriam Hopkins handled the emotional climactic sequence with enormous skill, with no evidence of upstaging under Edmund Goulding's direction.

Heedlessly, Tina continues to berate "Aunt" Charlotte, until Delia offers Charlotte her pity. "You needn't pity me," Charlotte tells her, "because she's really mine. And if she considers me an old maid, it's because I've deliberately made myself one in her eyes. I've done it from the beginning so that she wouldn't have the least suspicion." And again, we see the price this effort has cost her when she sits alone and addresses an absent Tina, first as a caring, loving mother ("my darling little girl") and then as a querulous maiden aunt, only to begin crying heartbrokenly at the bleakness of her life. Davis's bravura acting in this scene as she moves from daydream to despair marks a peak in her long career.

Afraid that Tina has inherited her wild and impulsive nature, Charlotte opposes her love affair with well-to-do young Lanning Halsey (William Lundigan), leading to Tina's cruelest outburst of all. "She's just a sour old maid," she tells Delia, "who hates me because I'm young and attractive and in love, while she's old and hideous and dried up and has never known anything about love." Unable to bear the deception—or Tina's hatred—any longer, Charlotte wants to tell her daughter the truth and take her away, but Delia persuades her that it would be cruel, not only to Tina but to herself as well. She offers to adopt Tina legally, so that there can be no opposition to her marrying Lanning because she is a "foundling" with no family. Charlotte refuses at first, then consents for the sake of Tina's happiness.

The evening before Tina's wedding precipitates the key scene in the film, one in which the two women finally come to grips with their tangled relationship and confront a lifetime of jealousy and resentment. For Charlotte, the time has come to strip away the hardened veneer of the old maid and to speak with Tina as the mother she has always longed to be. ("Tonight, just tonight, she belongs to me! Tonight, I want her to call me mommy!") With passionate intensity, she accuses Delia of taking her revenge on her for loving Clem Spender, of taking her child away out of bitter jealousy: "I never could have done to you what you've done to me. You made me an old maid!" For her part, Delia finally admits to her long-suppressed feelings: "Clem didn't love you. He loved me. I loved him. She should have been ours. I am her mother!" Although this long emotional scene has its basis in a romantic soap-operatic conceit—women never forget the men they have loved—Davis and Hopkins play it with professional dexterity and aplomb, bringing conviction to some ripe dialogue.

Despite the fierceness of their climactic encounter, it comes as no surprise when Charlotte realizes that she cannot bring herself to reveal the truth to Tina, certainly not before her wedding. "She never belonged to me," she finally tells Delia, "perhaps because her father never belonged to me, either. . . . After all, she *was* mine when she was little." On a properly sentimental note, Delia asks Tina to bestow her last kiss on "Aunt" Charlotte as she leaves on her honeymoon with Lanning. Tina obliges, and the look of surprised delight that passes across Charlotte's face is genuinely touching. The two women return to the house, having found a kind of peace and understanding at last. Yet there is an intimation, expressed earlier by Delia, that the shadows of the past can never be entirely dispelled: "From tomorrow on, until death comes for one of us, we'll be sitting here alone together, beside the same lamp, in an empty house, with heaven knows what thoughts to keep us company."

The Old Maid may stand at some distance from cinematic art. Like the play and story from which it is adapted, its tale of two women locked in a lifetime rivalry has no more urgency or depth than a faded nosegay pressed in the pages of a dust-laden book. Too often its dialogue is punctuated with exclamation marks, and its scenes of confrontation are spaced as neatly and arbitrarily as plums in a pudding. Yet it remains one of the superior examples of filmmaking in that year of 1939. Handsomely designed by Robert Haas and photographed by Tony Gaudio with a keen appreciation of light and shadow, the film uses its principal setting—Delia's well-appointed but stifling, overdecorated home—as an ironic contrast to the heated passions that seethe within its walls. Casey Robinson's dialogue, by way of Zoë Akins, rings some interesting variations on the themes of mother love and sacrifice, and Edmund Goulding directs with a sure hand.

Above all, *The Old Maid* attests to the power of star acting. Only thirty-one when she made the film, Bette Davis manages to be entirely convincing as she goes from the girlish, impulsive Charlotte, fairly consumed by her passion, to the aging spinster, eyebrows raised in permanent disapproval. She is most affecting when the youthful Charlotte breaks through the old maid's mask, as when, late in the movie, Tina praises Charlotte's hair, more as a polite remark than as a genuine compliment. For a fleeting moment, Charlotte smiles and pats her hair, lost in memory. A lesser actress, Hopkins succeeds in keeping up with her costar, trading blow for blow in their feverish encounters. She is most persuasive in the scene with Dr. Lanskell, in which she confesses to having paid the price for her selfishness by being forced to endure the years of Charlotte's harshness and silent recriminations.

The Old Maid won no awards that year, yet its substantial merits should not be overlooked, and it marks an impressive achievement among Bette Davis's credits. Its style may be long out of fashion, but the sentiment it evokes is no less genuine for being part of a vanished era.

The Old Maid. Warner Bros. Produced by Henry Blanke. Directed by Edmund Goulding. Screenplay by Casey Robinson, from the play by Zoë Akins and the novella by Edith Wharton. Photography by Tony Gaudio. Art direction by Robert Haas. Edited by George Amy. Cast: Bette Davis, Miriam Hopkins, George Brent, Jane Bryan, Donald Crisp, Louise Fazenda, Jerome Cowan, and William Lundigan.

Dorothy and her friends arrive at the gate of Oz, where the gatekeeper declines to admit them.

Away Above the Chimney Tops: The Wizard of Oz

"Toto, I have the feeling we're not in Kansas anymore."
—Judy Garland in *The Wizard of Oz*

Is any film more cherished than *The Wizard of Oz*? Has any other movie so captured the hearts of every generation, spreading its joy and its simple message across half a century? In numerous showings on television, the merry old Land of Oz has been among the most popular destinations for those seeking fantastic adventure and fun. This is one movie that endures. Beyond the countless stories about its trouble-plagued production, beyond the special charisma and poignancy it has gained from its gifted but unstable star, beyond the feeble attempts to re-create the magic in new and more contemporary versions, the 1939 *Wizard of Oz* lives on.

The movie's acknowledged status as a beloved classic makes it all the more astonishing to note that when it was originally released in August of 1939, many of the reviews were unfavorable. A number of reputable critics were not at all delighted. In his notice in the New York *Herald Tribune*, Howard Barnes wrote, "Stunning as it may be pictorially, it strikes me that the show misses a great many of the fabulous accents of the original. . . . It is dedicated to the young in heart, but I think that its principal appeal will be simply the young. . . . It never quite makes one accept its fantastic assumptions. . . . It has a tendency to be definitely mundane when it might have been engagingly chimerical." Critic Eileen Creelman, writing in the New York *Sun*, asserted that the movie "lacks the spontaneity which is the spirit of all great fantasy. The production is overelaborate, its nonsense a trifle stilted, and it is surprisingly short on comedy." The reviewer for *Time* magazine, while acknowledging the virtues of its "whimsy and magic," found that "When it descends to earth, it collapses like a scarecrow in a cloudburst." Even *The New York Times*'s Frank S. Nugent, who admired the

Dorothy (Judy Garland) arrives in Munchkinland, where she is welcomed by the Good Witch (Billie Burke) and the tiny residents.

film greatly, complained, in a follow-up column, that the score was "neither as zestful or as tuneful as the occasion warranted," and maintained that "a really good libretto, with a frolicsome camera beating time to it, might have been the most valuable wizardry of all." In *The New Republic*, Otis Ferguson summed up the adverse comments by saying that the movie "weighs like a pound of fruit-cake, soaking wet."

Many of the other reviews were, of course, highly enthusiastic, and from the first, audiences flocked to see the film, lining up for blocks. MGM's apprehensive executives were pleased but not overjoyed. Filmed over twenty-two weeks at a total cost of $2,777,000, it was one of the studio's most expensive productions, and despite the large box-office receipts, it was not expected to make money. In fact, it took *The Wizard of Oz* twenty years to earn back its cost. Still, the studio was gratified by the reception, since fantasy was seldom a salable commodity on the screen. For the film's producer, Mervyn LeRoy, and his associate Arthur Freed, it was at least partial vindication for a project that had known stormy weather since its inception in the fall of 1937.

The story of Production #1060 has been told in detail in Aljean Harmetz's excellent book, *The Making of the Wizard of Oz* (Alfred A. Knopf, Inc., New York,

1977).* Yet it is such a representative story of the vicissitudes of Hollywood filmmaking in its "golden" period that the salient details are worth repeating. Even now, it is not clear who persuaded Louis B. Mayer to purchase the rights to L. Frank Baum's *Oz* stories from Sam Goldwyn.† Mervyn LeRoy, brought to MGM as a producer after years as one of Warners' most prolific directors, always maintained with some irritation that Mayer bought the material for *him*, while Arthur Freed, in an account shortly before his death, insisted that it was *he* who began negotiations with Goldwyn for the property, feeling that it would make a good musical. A songwriter on the lot for a number of years, Freed had ambitions to be a producer and would have liked *Oz* to be his first production. Whoever launched the idea, it was Mayer who agreed to purchase the rights. He assigned LeRoy as producer, rejecting his proposal to direct as well, and made Freed his associate.

With the production under way, attention turned to the screenplay. The first of the ten writers who would eventually work on the script was the brilliant, acerbically witty Herman J. Mankiewicz, whose alcoholism and compulsive gambling had cost him many assignments. (Two years later, he would achieve his greatest credit as co-author of the screenplay for *Citizen Kane*.) When Mankiewicz's adaptation, which seems to have had many eccentric, tongue-in-cheek aspects, was judged inadequate, two other writers, humorous poet Ogden Nash and an English playwright named Noel Langley, were assigned to the project. Nash lasted only a short time, but Langley's extensive treatment contained many of the elements of the completed film. He also retained as much of the Baum book as possible. By the time he had finished his three-month assignment, he had handed in four different scripts.**

After other writers, including Samuel Hoffenstein, a well-known author of light verse, were given a turn at the elusive screenplay, two MGM house writers, Florence Ryerson and Edgar Allan Woolf, were added to the growing list. They made numerous contributions to the final script, including greater use of the Wizard—they suggested placing him earlier in the story as Professor Marvel—and much stronger use of the Wicked Witch's menace, giving her a more threatening presence throughout the story. They also added emotional weight by stressing Dorothy's desire to get home to Kansas. At this point, the chain of

---

* Also in Doug McClelland's *Down the Yellow Brick Road* (New York: Pyramid Books, 1976).

† Lyman Frank Baum had written his *Oz* stories from 1900 until his death in 1919. The first, *The Wonderful Wizard of Oz*, was turned into a Broadway musical in 1903, with Fred Stone and Dave Montgomery, and two silent films had been made in 1910 and 1925, the latter starring Oliver Hardy. Baum himself, a resident of Hollywood, made three Land-of-Oz films between 1913 and 1915.

** Langley's sharp tongue eventually cost him his job at MGM. His remark about Louis B. Mayer—"Every time Mayer smiles at me, I feel a snake has crawled over my foot"—was overheard and reached Mayer. He was fired and also blackballed from the film industry until 1942, when MGM rehired him.

events becomes somewhat cloudy. Apparently, the Ryerson-Woolf version infuriated Noel Langley, who had an ardent champion in "Yip" Harburg. Harburg went to Arthur Freed, who reassigned Noel Langley to the film. By the time the movie went into production, a few more writers had worked on the script, but the final credits went to Langley, Ryerson, and Woolf (with uncredited input from Harburg).

Casting the film proved to have considerable obstacles as well. To play twelve-year-old Dorothy, LeRoy had first considered Shirley Temple, still the country's most popular child star, and when she was unavailable, his thoughts turned briefly to Universal's young new sensation, Deanna Durbin. Universal, which had returned to solvency because of Durbin, would not consider it. And so the role went to the MGM contract player who was always Arthur Freed's first choice. A plump and rather ungainly sixteen, Judy Garland had signed with the studio in 1935 after a sensational audition at which her vibrant voice shook the walls. Not certain what to do with her, even after the usual ministrations (capped teeth, strenuous dieting), MGM had loaned her to Fox for a single film, *Pigskin Parade,* and then gave her a role in *Broadway Melody of 1938* (1937), where her rendition of "Dear Mr. Gable," complete with heartfelt recitative, had been the film's highlight. Now Freed convinced Mayer to cast her as Dorothy Gale in *The Wizard of Oz.*

The other major roles were filled after several rounds of musical chairs. Bert Lahr was always the first choice for the Cowardly Lion (he was signed after lengthy negotiations), but the original choice for the Scarecrow was Buddy Ebsen, a gawky dancer who had appeared prominently in several MGM musicals, and Ray Bolger was scheduled to play the Tin Woodman. When Bolger, a lithe and rubber-limbed dancer, objected strenuously to being confined to a metal suit, the roles were switched. When Ebsen became ill by inhaling the aluminum facial dust sprayed over his clown-white base makeup, he was replaced by Jack Haley. The role of the Wizard had first been offered to Ed Wynn and W. C. Fields, who turned it down for different reasons, and Wallace Beery, then a major MGM star, also made a test. (The mind boggles at the idea of this actor, whose trademark was a combination of vulgarity and sentimentality, playing the role.) The part finally went (wisely) to Frank Morgan, a contract player adept at portraying lovable but befuddled characters. After several false starts, the roles of the Good Witch and the Wicked Witch went, respectively, to Billie Burke and Margaret Hamilton.

The Wizard of Oz being a fantasy, special casting problems had to be considered, none more troublesome than filling the tiny shoes of the Munchkins, the little people Dorothy meets when she arrives in Oz. To find 200 midgets for the movie—at the end there were 124—the studio hired Leo Singer, the proprietor of Singer's Midgets, who found and trained his midgets in Germany and

An indelible moment in movie history: Judy Garland's Dorothy longs to fly "Over the Rainbow." The now-legendary song was nearly excised from the movie, but Arthur Freed insisted that it remain in the score.

Austria. Working with studio scouts, actors' agents, and many other sources, Singer was able to find no more than a hundred midgets, and Major Doyle, a midget entertainer himself, was hired to find the rest. Doyle refused to work directly with Singer, who he claimed had refused him jobs in the past. The midgets, who eventually mingled with some child performers in Munchkinland, turned out to be a wildly unruly and raunchy lot who constantly held up the production with their antics. According to all reports, they drank heavily, often propositioned members of the cast (including Judy Garland), and fought among themselves continually. Garland remembered that they "had to scoop them up in butterfly nets," and Bert Lahr recalled the day when a drunken midget, called the Count, fell into the latrine and couldn't get himself out.

However, most of this disruption lay ahead as the film continued to take shape. As the screenplay moved through its many changes and ramifications, the thought turned next to the musical score, which became Arthur Freed's responsibility. His first choice was his friend Jerome Kern, who was interested, but the assignment finally went in May 1938 to composer Harold Arlen and lyricist E. Y. ("Yip") Harburg, whose work for the theater had the sort of impudent, lighthearted, and fanciful touch the score for Oz required. (Others also mentioned were lyricist Dorothy Fields and composer Nacio Herb Brown.) For Arlen and Harburg, it was a welcome chance to write music that would grow out of the characters rather than being imposed on them. Harburg later remembered, "I loved the idea of having the freedom to do lyrics that were not just songs but *scenes*. That was our own idea, to take some of the book and do some

Down the Yellow Brick Road with the Scarecrow (Ray Bolger), Dorothy, and the Tin Man (Jack Haley), with Toto leading the way. To get the right color for the road, all kinds of paints and dyes were used, until Mervyn LeRoy suggested that they try some cheap yellow fence paint. It worked beautifully.

Dorothy dries the tears of the Cowardly Lion (Bert Lahr), while the Tin Man and the Scarecrow show their disapproval of the Lion's blubbering. A hugely gifted and hilarious clown, Lahr gave a glorious performance as the Lion, but sadly, he was never used well in his other films.

The Tin Man, the Scarecrow, Dorothy, and the Lion scamper happily through the poppy field, after being awakened from a sleep induced by the Wicked Witch. The poppy field covered over an acre of sound stage and contained 40,000 red poppies with two-foot wire stems.

of the scenes in complete verse, such as the scenes in Munchkinland."* It was an idea that foreshadowed the later integrated musicals such as *Meet Me in St. Louis* and *Gigi*.

By now the story of "Over the Rainbow" has become part of Hollywood legend, and as with all legends, some details remain amorphous. Apparently, it was written, almost as an afterthought, at Arthur Freed's request, to balance the lighter comic songs that punctuated the story. According to Arlen, the melody came to him while he was driving to Grauman's Chinese Theatre with his wife. At first Harburg thought the melody was too powerful for a young farm girl to sing and he scaled down its "symphonic" sound with simple, childlike words. Everyone connected with the film was enchanted by the song, and at the recording session, Garland gave it her uniquely full-throated and sensitive rendition.

Then a furious controversy got under way. At the first preview of the film, studio executives insisted that the song was slowing down the movie and had to be removed. Others joined in the clamor to delete the song, including the executive producer of the studio's musical division. (The whole score, he maintained, "was above the heads of children.") Stories vary about the defense of the song—LeRoy and Freed each claimed that *he* knew its value and refused to cut it. Freed continued to demand that the song stay in the score, and each time the film was previewed without it, he stormed into Mayer's office to protest. Finally, he offered an ultimatum: "The song stays—or I go." Mayer decided to keep the song, and it went on to win the Academy Award as the year's best song.†

With the script, score, and cast in place, the obvious question remained: Who would direct the film? By the time the movie was completed, four directors had worked on it for varying lengths of time. Although Norman Taurog, a director noted for his handling of such budding young actors as Deanna Durbin and Mickey Rooney, seems to have been a first choice, the assignment went initially to Richard Thorpe, a workmanlike and indefatigable studio director whose most notable MGM film to date was a thriller entitled *Night Must Fall* (1937). After two weeks of apparent confusion and dissatisfaction, he was replaced with George Cukor, who lasted only two days but who had enough prescience to suggest that Judy Garland's flowing blond wig be replaced with a more natural look. (He also encouraged her to act more naturally.) A bemused

---

*Quoted in Max Wilk, *They're Playing Our Song* (New York: Atheneum, 1973), p. 234.

†It should be noted that Herbert Stothart, one of the studio's house composers, also won an Oscar for his score for the film, which combined original material with fragments from classical composers. Today, he probably would have shared the award with Arlen and Harburg. Other composers and arrangers worked on the score, notably Ken Darby, who created the voices for the Munchkins and the Winkies, who were the Witch's guards.

player in this game of musical chairs, Cukor left a fanciful Oz for the burning Atlanta of *Gone With the Wind*. When he was fired from that film, he was assigned to *The Women*.

The next director seemed an odd choice for a children's fantasy. A burly, rough-hewn man whose films included such lusty stories as *Red Dust* (1932) and *Captains Courageous* (1937), Victor Fleming seemed more suitable for a Clark Gable adventure than the whimsy of *Oz*. After accepting the assignment reluctantly, Fleming first turned to a writer, John Lee Mahin, who had worked with him on four previous films. Mahin's main contribution was to rewrite the first scene, making Dorothy apprehensive about Miss Gulch and giving Auntie Em and Uncle Henry a better reason (a broken egg incubator) other than meanness for not listening to her. Fleming worked on the film for four months, during which time his behavior seems to have ranged from "understanding, sensitive, kind" (Jack Haley) to "very sarcastic" (Margaret Hamilton). When he left to take over the direction of *Gone With the Wind*,* he was replaced by King Vidor, who was responsible primarily for filming the Kansas sequences that frame the story.

Creating Hollywood magic always requires prodigious effort, and as *The Wizard of Oz* got under way, a virtual army of skilled technicians was enlisted for the task. Cedric Gibbons and his art department built sixty-five different sets on all of MGM's twenty-nine sound stages. Jack Dawn created the astonishing makeup for the residents of Oz, and Adrian designed their flamboyant costumes. Perhaps most wondrous were the special effects developed by Arnold ("Buddy") Gillespie and his staff. How do you make monkeys fly? You make scores of miniature monkeys out of rubber and suspend them from a moving trolley on piano wires. How do you show "a horse of a different color"? You paint a number of horses with various flavors of Jell-O. And how do you melt a witch? You have her stand atop a hydraulic elevator, with dry ice attached to the inside of her cloak and her costume fastened to the floor. As the elevator was lowered, the dry-ice vapors gave the illusion of melting, and nothing remained onstage but the costume.

From all reports, making *The Wizard of Oz* was an ordeal for most of the actors. The elaborate costumes and makeup caused them nearly to suffocate in the intense heat generated by the powerful incandescent lights. Many of the actors also faced their own excruciating difficulties. Jack Haley was unable to sit or lie down in his Tin Woodman costume; he could only lean against a reclining board. In his Lion's costume, Bert Lahr was unable to eat solid food and could only ingest liquids. Ray Bolger had trouble going to the bathroom

---

* After ten weeks on *Gone With the Wind*, Fleming collapsed and was replaced for a while by Sam Wood. The consensus on Fleming is that he was more disagreeable than not, a rather difficult and contentious man.

because of the straw stuffed into his costume. And Margaret Hamilton's skin acquired a green tinge from her makeup, which took months to disappear. She was also the victim of a nearly fatal accident while filming the scene in which she vanishes in a puff of red smoke in Munchkinland. By a miscalculation, the smoke and flames that were meant to disguise her disappearance came too soon, and her hat and broom were set on fire. Parts of her face and one hand were seriously burned, and she was hospitalized for weeks.

Somehow surviving accidents, illnesses, changing personnel, and the normal vicissitudes of filmmaking, the production of *The Wizard of Oz* persisted, until principal photography was completed in March 1939. Within a few days, the sets had disappeared, and the making of the film was a memory. The film itself still required considerable work before its first preview in June. Ahead were the years that transformed it from Production #1060 to a durable movie legend.

How does one approach from a fresh point of view a film seen countless times? Probably only a child could do that, rediscovering its enchantment each time, like a fairy tale heard many times over at bedtime. Yet each adult re-viewing brings its own rewards and its own discoveries, some of them surprising, others perfectly trivial but, in a sense, revealing. Thus, we observe the credits, knowing by this time that the names cited for the writers, cast members, and director are the end result of many changes and reversals, and a few squabbles. We also see that Judy Garland receives top featured billing, but her name is of equal size with Charley Grapewin, who appears only in the sepia sections at the beginning and the end of the movie as Dorothy's Uncle Henry. Fame for Garland arrived with *Oz* but was acknowledged when she costarred with Mickey Rooney in her next film, *Babes in Arms*.

The first scenes show us a Kansas that is flatter, grayer, and drearier than even the state's worst enemy could imagine, but we accept it because it's so obviously fake and because we know (even at a first-time viewing) that a fantastical Oz must lie ahead. An apprehensive Dorothy tries to warn everyone about the approach of the dreaded Miss Gulch, but Auntie Em and Uncle Henry are too worried about the chickens, and farmhands Zeke (Lahr), Hunk (Bolger), and Hickory (Haley) are too busy establishing their basic characters. (An offhand question: How can such a small farm employ three farmhands?)

Rebuffed and ignored, a forlorn Dorothy longs for "some place where there isn't any trouble . . . behind the moon, beyond the rain. . . ." Garland's rendition of "Over the Rainbow" now belongs to the ages, of course, and each time we hear it, it has a sweetness and wistful longing, even if we separate it from the emotional weight it has been given over the years by Garland's unhappy life. Two things are inconceivable: one, that MGM could ever have considered removing it from the score; the other, that Shirley Temple, for all her enormous talent, could have ever brought the same poignant quality to the song.*

Dorothy, of course, is destined to travel "over the rainbow," courtesy of a Kansas twister, but first she must cope with the nasty Miss Gulch (Hamilton), who wants her dog Toto destroyed. Margaret Hamilton found a kind of immortality with the role of Miss Gulch and the Wicked Witch, but she had been playing testy, gossipy spinsters and housekeepers ever since her debut in 1933, when she repeated her stage role in *Another Language*. Here, her hatchet-faced Miss Gulch has a shrill voice and wonderfully sour countenance that make her transformation into the Witch all the more convincing. Before Dorothy can travel to Oz, she must also meet Professor Marvel (Morgan), the genial traveling medicine man who sends her back to the farm after she runs away. A longtime screen veteran—he had made his film debut back in 1916—Morgan brought his trademarked bumbling, good-natured style to his Professor-Wizard, making it difficult to imagine anyone else (W. C. Fields?) in the role.

Caught up in the cyclone, with the farmhouse whirling and twisting in the wind, Dorothy lands with a heavy thump and opens her bedroom door into one of the screen's most magical first views: a brightly Technicolored Munchkinland in the county of Oz. To the strains of "Over the Rainbow," she confirms what we already suspect, telling Toto, "I have the feeling we're not in Kansas anymore." Soon she meets Glinda (Billie Burke), the Good Witch of the North, who arrives in a large pink bubble and introduces Dorothy to the twittering little Munchkins. It seems that Dorothy has become their heroine by inadvertently dropping the farmhouse on the Wicked Witch of the East. (Although her singing voice was dubbed by Lorraine Bridges, Burke makes a pleasing Glinda, adding a touch of the light-headedness she brought to her many dowager roles.)

While the Munchkinland set is appropriately elaborate and colorful, this early section of the movie is, in some ways, the least appealing. Most of the fault lies with the Munchkins themselves, who are a rather off-putting lot with their wizened faces and grating voices altered in the recording studio. (Some of the Munchkins, notably the little girls who are members of the Lullaby League, are clearly children and not midgets.) Most of the sequence's charm comes from the songs ("Ding-Dong! The Witch Is Dead," "Follow the Yellow Brick Road"), which are delivered with brio and enthusiasm by professional singers dubbing for the Munchkins. (None of the midgets could carry a tune.) By the time the Wicked Witch turns up, furious at her sister's death and cackling her baleful

---

*Garland sang "Over the Rainbow" so many times in her career that she grew heartily sick of it, possibly resenting the personal connotations it was given by many of her overwrought fans. Even after her death, some writers could not resist saying that she had finally gone "over the rainbow."

The Tin Woodman relies on the Lion's tail for support as they climb up the cliff to the Witch's castle. After Jack Haley's predecessor Buddy Ebsen became ill from inhaling aluminum dust sprayed on his face over a clown-white base, makeup chief Jack Dawn devised a paste of the dust (tinted with household bluing) that caused no difficulties.

threats, we are grateful for the intrusion. We are also delighted to follow Dorothy as she leads the Munchkins down the Yellow Brick Road, headed for the Emerald City and home.

Dorothy's first encounter with the Scarecrow, the Tin Woodman, and the Cowardly Lion constitutes one of the best sections of *The Wizard of Oz*, and for three good reasons named Ray Bolger, Jack Haley, and Bert Lahr. Summoning up all the expertise and professionalism gleaned from many years of theater experience, they give performances that are not only funny and endearing but also happily shine through the many pounds of cumbersome makeup they were obliged to wear. Bolger's eccentric dancing style had made him a popular entertainer in Broadway shows, and he had made his film debut in *The Great*

Ziegfeld (1936). A veteran of the stage and vaudeville, Haley had settled in Hollywood in the thirties, where he appeared mainly as a likable boob in comedies and musicals. Lahr, another theater veteran, with a brash manner and a comical face that drew laughs before a word was spoken, had appeared sporadically (and unmemorably) in a handful of movies. Given variations of "Yip" Harburg's lyrics for "If I Only Had a Brain/ a Heart, the Nerve," the three comics succeeded in creating characters that were, paradoxically, both human and fantastic.* If there is one image everyone retains from the movie, it is surely that of Dorothy and her friends marching down the road to the bouncy melody of "We're Off to See the Wizard."

While all three actors are splendid, Bert Lahr warrants special praise. From the moment we meet him, snarling ferociously at Dorothy and her new friends ("Put 'em up! Put 'em up!"), we know that we are in the presence of a performer with a boundless gift for low comedy, a buffoon who is also an artist. Behind the lion's makeup, we can see his features crumble along with his bravado. "What did ya do *that* for? I didn't bite him!" he says, sobbing as spunky Dorothy slaps him for chasing Toto. This pitiful creature is terrified by everything—he's even spent many sleepless nights because he's afraid of the sheep he has to count! Bellowing "I could show my prowess/ Be a lion, not a mow-ess!" Lahr gives the outrageous Harburgian rhyme an extra surge of trouper's energy.

Of course, all is not jollity along the Yellow Brick Road, as Dorothy and her friends turn up fresh obstacles at every turn, including apple trees that resent being picked and that throw their fruit at intruders. The Witch also makes an appearance, warning the Scarecrow and the Tin Woodman to "stay away" from Dorothy and tossing a lighted match at the terrified Scarecrow. In retrospect, isolated moments such as this seem inappropriate for a lighthearted fantasy—although he is a fantastic creation, the Scarecrow is not an animated figure who can spring back to life after being burned to a crisp, and his terror is too genuine to be amusing. At any rate, the Witch has other hindrances for the travelers, especially a field of poppies coated with a poison that will put them to sleep. Contemplating her wicked deed, the Witch enunciates key words with a special relish: "Something with poi-son in it. . . . Poppies to put them to sleep. Now they'll sle-ee-p." Fortunately, Glinda appears to wake up the sleeping group with a light dusting of snow and send them on their way to the Emerald City. The accompanying song, a lively little tune known as "Optimistic Voices" ("You're out of the woods, you're out of the dark"), was written by Arlen, Harburg, and Herbert Stothart and sung by a group called the Rhythmettes.

---

*Part of Ray Bolger's dance and his final chorus of "If I Only Had a Brain" were deleted from the release print. The dance could later be seen in MGM's compilation film *That's Dancing!* (1985).

While the Witch's cohorts and Dorothy's friends look on, the Witch melts away, leaving only a pile of clothes. Margaret Hamilton replaced Mervyn LeRoy's first choice, Gale Sondergaard, who would have played a glamorous, subtly wicked Witch.

Arriving at the gate of the Emerald City, the group is stopped by the gate-keeper (Frank Morgan in the first of a number of incarnations), who capitulates only when he sees Dorothy's ruby slippers. They enter the city, where a cockney-sounding coachman (Morgan again) drives them about, pulled by a white horse that keeps changing color. (The coachman explains that this is the proverbial "horse of a different color.") To the tune of "In the Merry Old Land of Oz," the travelers get the royal treatment: Dorothy and the Lion are given permanents, the Tin Woodman gets a buffing, and the Scarecrow is given new straw. Every-one is deliriously happy until the Wicked Witch appears to skywrite SURRENDER DOROTHY with her broom.

As they wait nervously for an audience with the Wizard, the Lion gets to render the film's brightest and most amusing number, "If I Were King of the Forest." ("Not queen, not duke, not prince.") The number is a triumph in every respect, combining Lahr's outsize personality (usually too large to be contained on the screen) with Arlen's bombastic melody and Harburg's clever lyrics, brimming with impudent rhymes and wordplay. ("What makes the Hottentot so hot? . . . Courage!") Lahr's rendition reaches a peak of hilarity as he struts royally in a rug placed on his shoulders by his adoring subjects, his newly permed hair crowned with a broken flower pot. Naturally, his bravado deserts him when he must join the others at the altar of the Wizard, who appears to them as a giant head emerging out of roaring flames. The Wizard's thundered order: Bring him the broomstick of the Wicked Witch and he will grant them their wishes.

Off the four friends go on the final leg of their adventure. Moving through the eerie Haunted Forest with a giant wrench, a net, and a spray gun of Witch Remover, they come upon a sign that reads: I'D TURN BACK IF I WERE YOU. The Lion nods in agreement and tries to make a complete turn, only to be stopped by his friends.* The Witch is ready for them, sending her squadron of Winged Monkeys to capture Dorothy and Toto. This sequence is more than a little unsettling: Not only are the monkeys unusually grotesque but they also manage to tear the Scarecrow apart in the struggle. The Tin Woodman's gag line, "That's you all over!" as he stuffs straw back into the Scarecrow's body does not help to alleviate a fleeting moment of dismemberment.

In the Witch's Castle, the story moves briskly to its climax. While the Witch frightens Dorothy with imminent destruction, Toto escapes to summon the Scarecrow, the Tin Woodman, and the Cowardly Lion. In their rescue effort, the Lion's tail provides much of the fun: The others cling to it as they climb up a mountain, and when they disguise themselves in uniforms purloined from the Witch's guards, his tail juts out hilariously as they march with the guards. When they are trapped by the Witch and all seems lost, Dorothy accidentally throws a pail of water on her, causing her to dissolve before their eyes. "I'm melting! I'm melting!" the Witch screams, adding, "What a world! What a world! Who could have thought a good little girl like you could destroy my beautiful wickedness?" Even as she vanishes, leaving a pile of clothes and nothing more, the Witch bemoans a society that refuses to understand the efficacy—indeed, the necessity—of evil.

Returning to the Wizard with the Witch's broom, the quartet discovers one of the first and saddest disillusionments of childhood, that wizardry and magic can be a sham based on trickery and sleight of hand. The Wizard, however, is prepared to help them with simple truths that satisfy their needs. The Scarecrow gets a diploma that makes him Doctor of Thinkology, and the Lion is given a medal that makes him a member of the Legion of Courage. For the Tin Woodman, the Wizard has a testimonial—a clock shaped like a red heart. "Remember,

---

*Originally, on the way to the Witch's Castle, the group performed a major musical number called "The Jitter Bug." In the number, which was produced and then deleted, they are attacked by pink and blue mosquitoes called Jitter Bugs, sent by the Witch to stop them.

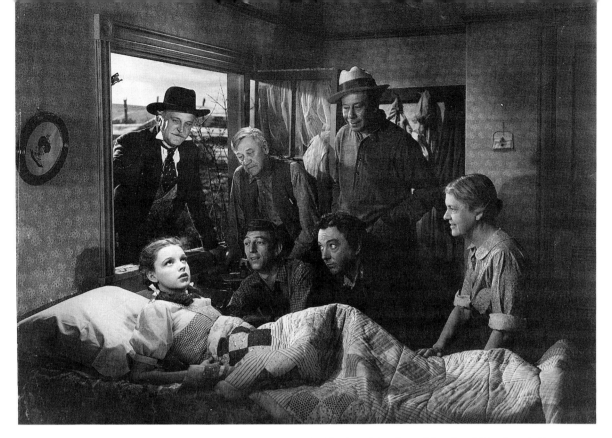

Back home again in Kansas, Dorothy is surrounded by her friends and family. "Oh, Auntie Em, there's *no* place like home!" became one of the best-loved, best-remembered lines in film history, and *The Wizard of Oz* took its rightful place among the screen's most cherished movies.

my sentimental friend," the Wizard says, "you will be judged not by how much you love, but by how much you are loved." The Wizard also promises to take Dorothy back to Kansas in a balloon.

In the Emerald City's square, with a huge crowd waiting to bid farewell to Dorothy and the Wizard, the balloon suddenly ascends without Dorothy, leaving her stranded in Oz. Once again, Glinda comes to her rescue, telling her that she always had the power to return to Kansas by using her ruby slippers and saying "There's no place like home!" But now Dorothy must say goodbye to her dear friends in a scene that has reduced several generations to tears. "Now I know I have a heart," the Tin Woodman tells her, "because it's breaking." She whispers to the Scarecrow, "I think I'll miss you most of all." Yet through all the sadness, the experience has taught her a lesson: "If I ever go looking for my heart's desire again, I won't look any further than my own backyard, because if it isn't there, I never really lost it to begin with." Tapping her heels together, she suddenly finds herself back in the simple black-and-white of her Kansas bedroom, with Auntie Em, Uncle Henry, and the farmhands. Even Professor Marvel stops by to see "how the little girl is doing." "Oh, Auntie Em," Dorothy cries, "there's *no* place like home!"

Opening on August 15 in Los Angeles and on August 17 in New York City, *The Wizard of Oz* attracted large audiences from the start. And yet by the time all the costs were tallied, MGM had lost nearly a million dollars on the production. Apparently, a part of the reason for the loss was that so many members of the audience were children who were admitted at reduced prices. It was not until the rerelease in 1948 that the film moved into the profit column, and it only became truly profitable after it was leased to television.

Clearly, the television showing could reach infinitely more viewers than the film could in its original release to theaters. Yet this cannot account in full for the special mystique this movie has acquired. It may be that its simple message of the happiness in our own backyards found a stronger response in audiences who had experienced a world war than in those who were emerging from the Depression into a false optimism. It may also be that, paradoxically, the small television screen gave Dorothy's adventure in Oz a touching immediacy and an impact that the large screen could not duplicate. (How many parents share this author's memory of a small child sobbing inconsolably before the television set as Dorothy bids farewell to her Oz friends?)

No matter. *The Wizard of Oz* will take us forever on a recurring journey to that land "over the rainbow." It seems to be one journey we are never tired of making.

The Wizard of Oz. Metro-Goldwyn-Mayer. Produced by Mervyn LeRoy. Directed by Victor Fleming. Screenplay by Noel Langley, Florence Ryerson, and Edgar Allan Woolf, from the book by L. Frank Baum. Photography by Harold Rosson. Music by Harold Arlen and E. Y. Harburg. Musical adaptation by Herbert Stothart. Art direction by Cedric Gibbons and William A. Horning. Costumes by Adrian. Special effects by Arnold Gillespie. Character makeup by Jack Dawn. Cast: Judy Garland, Frank Morgan, Ray Bolger, Bert Lahr, Jack Haley, Billie Burke, Margaret Hamilton, Charley Grapewin, Clara Blandick, Terry (as Toto), and the Munchkins. Oscars went to Arlen and Harburg for Best Original Song ("Over the Rainbow") and to Herbert Stothart for Best Original Score. Judy Garland received a special award for her outstanding performance as a screen juvenile.

Other sound films based on the Baum book have included: *Journey Back to Oz* (1974), an animated film with the voices of Liza Minnelli, Milton Berle, Ethel Merman, Mickey Rooney, and Margaret Hamilton (as Auntie Em); *The Wiz* (1978), a lifeless extravaganza adapted from the all-black Broadway musical version, with Diana Ross as a too-old Dorothy; and *The Return to Oz* (1985), a large-scale but rather depressing version in which Dorothy escapes from a sanitarium to return to her beloved land.

Jack Haley as the Tin Woodman

Billie Burke as the Good Witch of the North

Dorothy's boon companions, in disguise

Bert Lahr in his memorable role as the Cowardly Lion

Vivien Leigh, the final choice for Scarlett O'Hara after a highly publicized search.

One of the lavish scenes that helped make *Gone With the Wind* the most expensive and most popular movie of its day.

Atlanta in flames

Tara, from afar

GUNGA DIN

2 WOMEN ON A DESPERATE JOURNEY WITH 7 STRANGE MEN . . . . .

NINE ODDLY ASSORTED STRANGERS start out by stagecoach for Lordsburg, New Mexico. Each has his own personal reasons for wanting to get there. Then strange things begin to happen. The telegraph is mysteriously cut . . . the way station burned to the ground. Danger grows steadily more menacing

. . . UNTIL . . .

As conventions break down, the lives of the travelers are tangled together . . . you live with them this strange adventure . . . tense, full of action . . . deeply moving . . .

STAGECOACH

A WALTER WANGER Production • Directed by JOHN FORD

with CLAIRE TREVOR • JOHN WAYNE

Andy DEVINE • John CARRADINE • Thomas MITCHELL • Louise PLATT • George BANCROFT • Donald MEEK • Berton CHURCHILL • Tim HO...
RELEASED THRU UNITED ARTISTS

Mickey gives some hot licks on the cello as Judy and Betty Jaynes show the "old folks" their idea of a show!

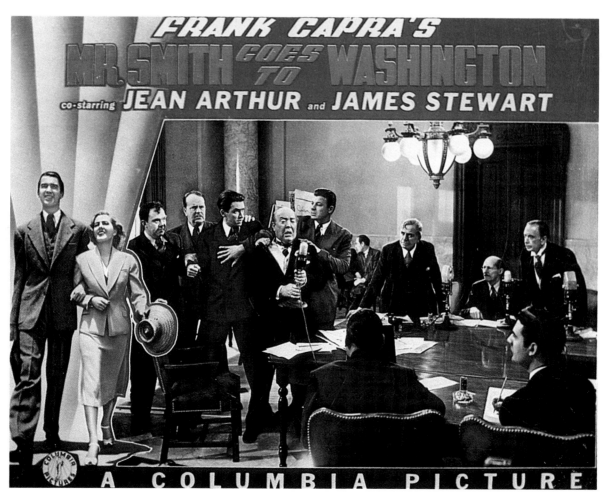

FRANK CAPRA'S
MR. SMITH GOES TO WASHINGTON
co-starring JEAN ARTHUR and JAMES STEWART

A COLUMBIA PICTURE

GRETA GARBO

"Let us dance! Everything is so wonderful!"

NINOTCHKA

Metro-Goldwyn-Mayer PICTURE

MARLENE DIETRICH · JAMES STEWART

DESTRY RIDES AGAIN

A NEW UNIVERSAL PICTURE

Copyright 1939 Universal Pictures Company, Inc. — Country of Origin U. S.

Sigmund Freud dies at age eighty-two . . . The Yankees win the World Series against the Reds . . . New York's North Beach Airport is renamed LaGuardia Airport, with the colorful mayor in attendance for the dedication . . . In his first encyclical, Pope Pius XII denounces dictators, treaty violators, and racists . . . A German U-boat and two German tankers are sighted off the Florida coast . . . Stocks soar as investors predict a war boom . . . The British government publishes eyewitness accounts of atrocities against Jews in Nazi camps . . . and 1.25 million German soldiers storm the Polish border, precipitating declarations of war from France and England . . . On radio, Charles A. Lindbergh urges America to avoid becoming involved in the war . . .

. . . and Hollywood lightens the mood with the release of the wickedly funny comedy *The Women* and the sprightly musical *Babes in Arms* . . . In October, *Mr. Smith Goes to Washington* and lifts the spirits of all Americans . . .

Dressed in their finery, the principal women meet in the powder room of the Casino Roof for a final baring of their "Jungle Red" nails.

Five-Letter Females: The Women

"I've had two years to grow claws! [She holds up
her hands to show her new nail polish.] Jungle Red!"
—Norma Shearer in *The Women*

On the evening of December 26, 1936,
in the post-Christmas glow of good cheer and fellowship, a play called *The Women*
opened on Broadway and immediately curdled the milk of human kindness.
Written by Clare Boothe, a former managing editor of *Vanity Fair* and the new
wife of magazine publisher Henry Luce, the play was only the second of her
five plays to reach Broadway, but its impact reverberated far beyond the walls
of the Ethel Barrymore Theatre. A vitriolic assault on the smart women of Man-
hattan, the play sprayed a poisonous mist over their arrantly bitchy behavior
as it moved through a cyclorama of bridge clubs, fitting rooms, maternity wards,
and nightclub powder rooms. The play's witty, acid-drenched dialogue was
well-delivered by an all-woman cast that included Margalo Gillmore, Ilka Chase,
Audrey Christie, Phyllis Povah, and Marjorie Main. (Arlene Francis also appeared in two small roles.)

Although the play received generally strong notices, there were rumblings
of dissatisfaction from some of the major critics. While acknowledging the bril-
liance of the production and the first-rate acting, *The New York Times*'s reviewer
Brooks Atkinson found the experience distasteful, put off by its "stingingly
detailed pictures of some of the most odious harpies ever collected in one play."
Richard Watts, Jr., writing in the New York *Herald Tribune*, was also troubled
by the nasty tone and objected to the insufferable nobility of the heroine: "Mrs.
Stephen Haines is so pure, so game, so heroic and so given to a stiff upper lip
that it isn't long before you are inclined to join the innumerable villainesses of
the work in an inclination towards mayhem." He acknowledged, however, that
the play "will make a million dollars for its author and producers." His prognosis

proved correct; audiences flocked to the play like ancient Romans hurrying for a day of sport at the arena.

Inevitably, Metro-Goldwyn-Mayer, with its glittering stars and expensive production values, bought *The Women* for the screen, planning to film it early in 1939. Just as inevitably, Norma Shearer, who had seen the play in New York and wanted to do it, was signed to play the leading role of Mary Haines, the long-suffering wife who loses her husband to a predatory gold digger. Neither particularly beautiful nor especially gifted as an actress, Shearer had reigned for a number of years as pampered queen of the MGM lot, mainly by virtue of her offscreen role as the wife of Irving Thalberg, MGM's young and powerful head of production. After Thalberg's premature death, Shearer's status at the studio was not affected. Yet she needed a strong role to counteract the poor impression she had made as a bogus Russian countess in *Idiot's Delight* (1939). As the center of the action, surrounded by a score of essentially supporting actresses, Mary Haines seemed an ideal choice.

To direct *The Women*, producer Hunt Stromberg originally signed Ernst Lubitsch, whose elegant, sophisticated style would appear to be at odds with the play's rather coarse approach. However, when George Cukor became available after being fired from *Gone With the Wind*, the studio wisely assigned him to *The Women*, leaving Lubitsch free to direct Greta Garbo in *Ninotchka*. Although Cukor had directed many exemplary performances by actors, he was widely known and respected as a director of actresses, including the studio's most difficult star, Greta Garbo. At a news conference, Cukor told reporters that he was prepared to have the time of his life, directing the all-women cast of *The Women*. Various writers tried their hand at writing the screenplay—reputedly, they included F. Scott Fitzgerald and Donald Ogden Stewart—but the final writing credits went to Anita Loos and Jane Murfin.

With virtually every actress at the studio coveting a role in *The Women*, casting the film proved to be exceptionally difficult, a battleground littered with mines waiting to explode. The story's second most important character, venal gold digger Crystal Allen, required an actress who could project vulgarity and brazen sexuality covered with a thin veneer of smooth-as-silk refinement. The Culver City walls nearly shook when Joan Crawford announced that she wanted to play Crystal. Now a major MGM star, Crawford had developed from the wild "dancing daughter" of her silent years to the glamorous clotheshorse who suffered at the hands of no-good men, then found belated contentment with the decent hero. Feeling that her career needed a boost, Crawford was convinced that Crystal, actually a large supporting role, would stand out amid all the haughty society women who populated the screenplay.

Predictably, everyone was appalled by the idea. Louis B. Mayer, who thought of Crawford as one of his own daughters, insisted that the role could harm her

Having learned about Stephen Haines's philandering, Sylvia Fowler (Rosalind Russell) telephones her friend Edith Potter to spread the news. Russell, a contract player at MGM since 1934, campaigned to play the role of the vicious and outrageous Sylvia. Here, she barely conceals her glee at Mary's misfortune.

career and was also unworthy of her star stature. (According to movie lore, Crawford responded, ''The woman who steals Norma Shearer's husband, Mr. Mayer, can't be played by a nobody.'') Hunt Stromberg still retained the image of Crawford from her silent days as a wild, jazz-mad ''flapper.'' There was also the crucial matter of the long-standing antagonism between Shearer and Crawford. Their mutual dislike had been building for many years, with Shearer regarding Crawford as an ambitious upstart and Crawford bitterly resenting the many times she had been given roles rejected by Shearer. Dauntless as always, Crawford persisted in her campaign, with Cukor's support, and the studio finally consented.*

---

*In his book on Norma Shearer (*Norma*, St. Martin's Press, 1988), Lawrence J. Quirk reports that he was told by Anita Loos that Shearer actually initiated the choice of Crawford for the role. According to Loos, Shearer placed the good of the picture above her personal feelings.

The ladies gather at Mary's house for lunch. Left to right: Edith Potter (Phyllis Povah), Sylvia Fowler, Mary Haines, Peggy Day (Joan Fontaine), and Nancy Blake (Florence Nash). Only Phyllis Povah appeared in the original stage production in 1936.

Unable to restrain their curiosity, Edith and Sylvia confront Crystal Allen (Joan Crawford) at the perfume counter in Black's Department Store. Sylvia's cattiness ("A pretty girl like you . . . with all the rich men that float in here . . .") is matched by Crystal's knowing retorts ("Goodbye, Mrs. *Prowler* . . .").

Another central role, that of vicious gossip Sylvia Fowler, was won by Rosalind Russell after a hard-fought battle. The part had been played brilliantly on the stage by Ilka Chase, and George Cukor, who was a friend of Chase's, wanted her to repeat Sylvia on the screen. Russell, who had spent years at the studio playing lofty, genteel, and boring ladies, wanted the chance to show her skill for playing comedy. As with Crawford, everyone was opposed to giving her the chance. Stromberg told her that she was "too beautiful" for the part and also a "wonderful dramatic actress." Reluctantly, Cukor agreed to test her, asking her to play a scene in ways ranging from realistic to wildly exaggerated. The day after the test, Russell was signed for the role that gave her career a new direction. Her larger-than-life performance as the venomous, outrageous, and garishly garbed Sylvia stole the film from under the noses of all the other actresses.

Other roles in the film were well cast. To play Peggy, the meekest and mousiest of the women, Cukor selected Joan Fontaine, a young actress (and the sister of Olivia de Havilland) whose blond prettiness and demure manner had made a mild impression in a number of RKO films, including *Gunga Din*. Long afterward, Fontaine acknowledged that Cukor's direction helped her to understand what it truly meant to be an actress: "I learned more about acting from one sentence of George Cukor's than from all my years of acting lessons. His advice was simply this, 'Think and feel, and the rest will take care of itself.' " Her big scene in which she reconciles with her estranged husband over the telephone shows evidence that she was learning to project some genuine emotion, and in fact, the following year, she won stardom playing the beleaguered heroine in Alfred Hitchcock's *Rebecca*.

The role of Miriam, the frank, knowing showgirl who steals Sylvia's husband, went to Paulette Goddard, a beautiful but limited actress whose best previous role had been as the spunky waif befriended by the Little Tramp in Charlie Chaplin's 1936 *Modern Times*. (They were married that year, or possibly earlier.) Mary Boland, the effervescent stage and screen actress who had been typecast for years as a scatterbrained matron, was signed to play one of the juiciest roles, the much-married Countess de Lave. Two of the roles were filled with the actresses who had played them on the stage: Phyllis Povah as the continually pregnant Edith Potter, and Marjorie Main as Lucy, the Reno ranch cook with no illusions about men. Other parts in the large cast of actresses (not a man in sight) included Lucile Watson as Mary Haines's sensible mother; Virginia Weidler as her young daughter Little Mary; Florence Nash as sardonic novelist Nancy Blake; and Dennie Moore as the gossipy manicurist Olga, who starts all the trouble.

Considering the animosity between the movie's two leading ladies, filming *The Women* must have been equivalent to a long walk on eggs, wearing army

Mistress Crystal Allen confronts wife Mary Haines in a dressing room. Since both actresses were not exactly fond of each other, this classic confrontation between the two reigning queens on the MGM lot was approached with great trepidation.

boots. Shearer and Crawford had only one scene together, but it sparked an incident that has been variously reported. During one rehearsal, Crawford sat on the sidelines, feeding cues to Shearer in the usual manner. Apparently, this time Crawford chose to knit with huge needles that clacked together noisily, distracting Shearer who, contrary to her air of self-confidence, was actually a high-strung actress. When Shearer complained, Crawford seemed not to hear, and the needles grew louder. According to one version, Shearer said with icy control, ''I think that Miss Crawford can go home now and you can give me her lines.'' An angry Cukor berated Crawford for her rudeness, insisting that he would not allow such unprofessional behavior on his set. He asked her to apologize but instead Crawford sent Shearer a telegram that spewed forth her years of resentment. The atmosphere on the set the following day was decidedly frigid. Later, Cukor remarked, ''I liked Joan very much, except when she was behaving in this idiotic fashion." At any rate, the key scene between the warring ladies was completed as everyone held their collective breath.

Despite the tension that lingered in the air much of the time, the filming of *The Women* went smoothly enough. Louis B. Mayer, however, was unhappy with having one of his major stars playing the "heavy," and at his insistence, the producer tried to make Crystal more sympathetic. When the results at the film's sneak preview were disastrous, Anita Loos received a frantic cable in New York, asking her to suggest alternative dialogue for Crystal's exit that would induce audience laughter but keep her "bitchy" status intact. After a few false starts ("Well, it looks like I'm going back to Black's Fifth Avenue. But you'd better come and see me because a little perfume wouldn't do you ladies any harm"), the final version had Crystal saying, "By the way, ladies, there's a name for you ladies, but it isn't used in high society—outside of a kennel."

Five weeks into the production, another problem arose, this one involving Rosalind Russell rather than her sparring costars. Insisting on top billing with Shearer and Crawford (there were strong indications that she was stealing the picture), Russell decided to get "sick" when her demand was refused. Shearer, who had graciously consented to share costarring status with Crawford, had balked at adding yet another name above the title. While the production shot around her, Russell "recuperated" in her garden. Eventually, an MGM troubleshooter visited her to announce that Shearer, feeling that Russell was so good in the movie, would consent to her receiving star billing. It was only a partial victory for Russell. In the credits, her name appears in much smaller letters than either Shearer's or Crawford's.

In her autobiography *Life Is a Banquet*, Russell cites several instances of the imaginative touches that George Cukor added to intensify the already extreme character of Sylvia Fowler. In a scene with Norma Shearer, Cukor had Russell knitting furiously and chewing gum while she rattled off her inane dialogue. Shearer objected to this obviously scene-stealing ploy, but Cukor kept it in. In a scene in a confined dressing room, in which Russell buzzes at Shearer like some demented bee, Cukor surrounded Russell with four full-length mirrors, giving the impression that four Sylvias instead of one were badgering poor Mary Haines. It worked effectively to heighten Sylvia's outlandish personality. Russell remarks, "The only thing I take credit for is keeping my mouth shut because I knew the break I was getting."

In a real sense, *The Women* proved to be not only a break for Russell but also a boon for Crawford, who showed that her instincts were sound by giving a smoothly persuasive performance. It also proved to be a reasonable career move for Shearer, who was always in her element playing noble, sophisticated women. All the actresses, in fact, seemed to thrive in Clare Boothe's atmosphere of mingled perfume and poison. If the screenplay intensified the perfume and

The start of one of the film's most famous scenes. Syliva Fowler is about to realize that Miriam Aarons is her soon-to-be-ex-husband's latest romance. The revelation leads to an hilarious, no-holds-barred catfight between the two ladies. On the sidelines are Peggy, Mary, and the Countess.

diluted the poison, there was still enough venom left to satisfy any diehard misogynists in the audience. The concept of life inside a female jungle is advanced in the clever opening credits, in which the stars are seen as animals: Norma Shearer as a fawn, Rosalind Russell as a panther, Joan Crawford as a leopard, Paulette Goddard as a fox, Joan Fontaine as a lamb, Mary Boland as a chimpanzee, Lucile Watson as an owl, and Virginia Weidler as a doe. The movie even begins inside the lair of a woman's salon, where manicurist Olga (Moore) sets the plot in motion by telling all-ears Sylvia Fowler (Russell) about the cheating of her friend Mary Haines's husband, Stephen.

We now meet Mary Haines (Shearer), the film's principal character and Number One Star, who is such a model of wifely and motherly behavior that one wonders fleetingly how she came to be friends with such spiteful harridans as Sylvia and Edith. At her bridge party, Mary rises to the bait when Sylvia suggests that she visit manicurist Olga to have her nails done. Distraught when she learns that her husband is indeed carrying on with a scheming minx of a salesgirl named Crystal Allen, Mary talks with her mother (Watson), who tries to explain Stephen's indiscretion with an argument that many a straying male has used to justify his peccadilloes: "He's tired of himself. A man has only one escape from his old self, to see a different self in the mirror of another woman's eyes." Mary responds with a view that sounds surprisingly feminist for the time: "Stephen and I are equals. I won't qualify that relationship now. It's wrong, shockingly wrong!"

The film moves inevitably to the confrontation of Mary with her archrival Crystal, pausing for one hilarious scene in which Sylvia and Edith seek out Crystal (Crawford) at her counter in Black's Fifth Avenue. Crystal, it turns out, has her act well in order: a mixture of sleek sexuality and cooing helplessness toward the men in her life, and ice-cold hardness to anyone who stands in her way. Crawford plays the role perfectly—she was always best when that honeyed voice was used for selfish rather than self-sacrificial reasons. When she finally meets Mary in a salon dressing room, she has only scorn for Mary's high-mindedness ("You noble wives and mothers bore the brains out of me!"), while Mary recognizes Crystal's essential cheapness and vulgarity. ("Stephen couldn't love a girl like you!") As they parry and thrust, a viewer has the inescapable feeling that fragments of reality have been mixed in with the make-believe: Crawford, the coarse, aspiring, up-from-the-ranks working girl contending with Shearer, the lofty, highborn widow of the boss.*

When Edith Potter blurts out the story of Mary and Crystal's meeting to a gossip columnist, embellishing it with Sylvia's malicious lies, the affair becomes

---

*The confrontation of the two ladies is preceded by a brief and intrusive fashion show (filmed in Technicolor) in which models display a succession of rather outlandish women's wear.

front-page news (would a war or plague have pushed it back to page three?), sending a humiliated and defeated Mary on her way to Reno. After a few scenes with Mary and her daughter, the movie brightens considerably when Mary meets the light-headed Countess de Lave (Boland), who remains cheerful from divorce to divorce, and Miriam Aarons (Goddard), a showgirl with her eye on the main prize. The ladies all converge on a Reno ranch run by Lucy (Main), a salty woman who has seen it all. In a matter of weeks, the Countess has found an (unseen) cowboy suitor named Buck Winston, while Mary waits sadly for some word of reconciliation from Stephen. ("You have the Reno jumpsie-wumpsies!" the Countess tells her.) It also turns out that Miriam expects to marry Sylvia's about-to-be ex-husband, Howard.

Enter Sylvia, braying as usual, and indignant at having to go through the ordeal of a divorce. In one of the movie's best-remembered sequences, she suddenly realizes that Miriam is the girl linked with her husband in the gossip columns. In the ensuing cat fight, the ladies tear at each other with the zeal and ferocity of Roman gladiators. Miriam has the last word about Howard Fowler: "I made him pay for what he wants. You made him pay for what he doesn't want!" Probably encouraged by George Cukor, Russell plays this scene with such hysterical abandon that she appears to be having more of a nervous breakdown than a temper tantrum. The result at certain moments is more unnerving than funny. Soon afterward, a distraught Mary learns that Stephen has married Crystal Allen.

As time passes, Crystal settles into luxury as the new Mrs. Stephen Haines, affording Crawford her best scene in the film. In her preposterously ornate bathroom, Crystal soaks in a tub, her vulgarity and bad temper rampant as she barks at her maid. A telephone conversation tells us that Crystal is brazenly cheating on Stephen with Buck Winston, the radio star and the Countess de Lave's latest husband. A garishly dressed Sylvia comes to visit, brandishing her weapons of malice and deceit and delighted to learn about Crystal's clandestine affair. Throughout this scene, Joan Crawford acts with steely authority, alternating between hard-edged brassiness and silken seductiveness, and never lapsing into caricature.

Two years after Mary's divorce, the women gather at Mary's house for a dinner party, where the Countess is given a memorable line: "Isn't it wonderful to see all our lives so settled . . . temporarily." Later, however, she admits that her life with Buck is far from settled; he no longer loves her and seldom sees her. Mary appears to be resigned to her single lot, until her daughter innocently tells her that not only is Stephen unhappy in his marriage to Crystal but also that Crystal seems to have a secret boyfriend. Suddenly, it becomes clear to Mary that if she is to win Stephen back, she must resort to the same conniving and trickery as her "friends." Armed with her knowledge about Stephen and

With evident distaste, Mary's daughter, Little Mary (Virginia Weidler), hands a sponge to her stepmother, Crystal. Over the years, Hollywood delighted in placing its glamorous stars in bathtubs, discreetly covered with bubbles or suds. Weidler, a popular juvenile of the thirties and forties, was unable to build a career after adolescence.

Crystal, she hurries off to the Casino Roof, where everyone has gathered, telling her astonished mother, "I've had two years to grow claws!" She holds up her hands, indicating a new nail polish: "Jungle Red!"

Mary's last-minute switch from tear-streaked nobility to well-armed aggression occurs in one of the film's most extravagant sets, the powder room of the Casino Roof, where all the women have gathered, dressed to the nines or possibly tens. As Sylvia marches in with Crystal, Mary trots out all her ammunition, turning one woman against the other with scandalous revelations eagerly lapped up by gossip columnist Dolly de Peyster, played by famed real-life gossip columnist Hedda Hopper. Soon, chaos ensues offscreen as marriages and relationships dissolve in a welter of accusations and counteraccusations. All the women turn on Crystal, who takes her defeat philosophically and heads back for the perfume counter at Black's Fifth Avenue. Joyfully, Mary rushes toward an unseen Stephen with open arms. Love, or at least a love worth fighting for, has triumphed over foolish pride.

In transferring *The Women* to the screen, MGM had sacrificed some of the play's acerbic and malicious edge to the glitter and glamour of the studio's usual production values, and to the slightly overstated sentimentality of its star Norma Shearer. Still, the film version retained enough of the original material to make it a surprisingly jaundiced and bitter-flavored look at one slice of life. There are only a few characters in this distaff bestiary who warrant our respect or admiration; most of them are vicious harpies and gossip-mongers, scheming minxes, or bubble-headed fools, and they are surrounded by a host of sycophantic, backbiting women who serve their needs. Even in its diluted form, *The Women* is no paean to womanhood but, rather, a vitriolic assault on its single-minded attitudes (spiteful) and concerns (men).*

What prevents the high acidic content from eating a hole in the film's fabric is the hilarity these ladies generate as they go about their wicked business. One cannot help but laugh at their vanity, their duplicity, and their unbridled nastiness as they sharpen their claws on each other. Many of their barbs have a sting that surprises viewers into laughter. (In the beauty salon, one woman says to another, "I hate to tell you, dear, but your skin makes the Rocky Mountains look like chiffon velvet!") Even the less aggressive women make us smile with their unabashed self-awareness. "L'amour! L'amour!" the much-married Countess de Lave intones. "Where love leads, I always follow!" Mary's spinster friend Nancy tells her, "I'm what nature abhors. An old maid. A frozen asset."

Admittedly, from the vantage point of the eighties, one can take strong issue with *The Women* for reinforcing negative images about the feminine gender. Women, it seems to be saying, are defined almost entirely by their men. They struggle to keep themselves alluring to men, scheme to hold them, and weep at their loss. Crystal Allen, the one character motivated by greed—any rich man will do—is viewed as a vulgar monster. The only major character who seems entirely content with her lot is Edith Potter, who is little more than a breeding sow. And high-minded Mary Haines, who refuses to forgive her husband's infidelity, descends to the level of her "friends" to win him back.

Yet in spite of its dubious point of view, *The Women* can still be regarded as one of MGM's most diverting films of the period in its lavishly appointed production and cluster of star performances, as well as its often funny dialogue. Its ladies may not be ladies at all, but they are certainly enjoyable to visit.

---

*In 1956, *The Women* was further diluted in a musical remake entitled *The Opposite Sex*, directed by David Miller. June Allyson played Mary (here called Kay); Joan Collins was Crystal; and Dolores Gray appeared as Sylvia. Others in the cast, which included men, were Ann Sheridan, Ann Miller, Joan Blondell, Agnes Moorehead, Charlotte Greenwood, Leslie Nielsen, and Jeff Richards. The play also had a brief (sixty-three performances) revival in 1973 with a cast headed by Alexis Smith, Rhonda Fleming, Dorothy Loudon, Kim Hunter, and Myrna Loy.

A publicity pose of the film's cast, with director George Cukor at the center. Cukor was widely admired for his special skill with actresses.

The Women. Metro-Goldwyn-Mayer. Produced by Hunt Stromberg. Directed by George Cukor. Screenplay by Anita Loos and Jane Murfin, from the play by Clare Boothe. Photography by Oliver T. Marsh and Joseph Ruttenberg. Art direction by Cedric Gibbons. Costumes by Adrian. Edited by Robert J. Kerns. Cast: Norma Shearer, Joan Crawford, Rosalind Russell, Mary Boland, Paulette Goddard, Joan Fontaine, Lucile Watson, Phyllis Povah, Florence Nash, Virginia Weidler, Ruth Hussey, Marjorie Main, Dennie Moore, and Hedda Hopper. Remade as musical *The Opposite Sex* in 1956.

Judy Garland and Mickey Rooney pooled their considerable talents to become one of the most popular teams in movie history.

Mickey and Judy:
Babes in Arms

"Our time has come!"
—Mickey Rooney in *Babes in Arms*

Judy Garland's triumph in *The Wizard of Oz* made it abundantly clear to MGM that it had a new star personality in the sixteen-year-old singer. Although her snub nose and wide, questioning eyes had undeniable appeal, she was not conventionally pretty, and her weight was inclined to fluctuate. She was also under the thumb of a classically aggressive stage mother. But her piquant, tremulous manner and throbbing voice had attracted audiences and made them want to comfort and protect her. (In her last years, when her life was crumbling, the devotion of her fans became a smothering blanket.) A new film was needed to ride the crest of her popularity. One morning, producer Arthur Freed offered Louis B. Mayer an idea for that film. In New York he had seen the hit stage musical *Babes in Arms,* by Richard Rodgers and Lorenz Hart, with a cast headed by Mitzi Green, Ray Heatherton, Wynn Murray, and Alfred Drake.* Its story of a group of talented youngsters, the children of vaudevillians, who band together to help their struggling parents, was greatly bolstered by one of Rodgers and Hart's best scores, which included "Where or When," "My Funny Valentine," and the title song. Freed suggested *Babes in Arms* as a vehicle to reteam Garland and Mickey Rooney, who had appeared together in several of the Hardy family films and in a modest racetrack story entitled *Thoroughbreds Don't Cry.* Rooney, an energetic, multitalented favorite with moviegoers, would sing and dance onscreen for the first time. Mayer

---

*The stage musical had opened in April 1937 to generally enthusiastic notices: "A genial and buoyant show"—Brooks Atkinson, *The New York Times.* "A gay, tuneful and ingenious score"—Richard Watts, Jr., New York *Herald Tribune.* "A zestful, tuneful and brilliantly danced affair"—John Mason Brown, *New York Post.*

liked the idea and had Freed buy the property for $21,000. Given his first pro-
ducing assignment, Freed launched an auspicious career that made him arguably
the single most important influence on the development of the movie musical.

Work began on the screenplay for *Babes in Arms*. Originally, it was assigned
by Freed to Florence Ryerson and Edgar Allan Woolf, who (with Noel Langley)
had been credited with the final script for *The Wizard of Oz*. Their version turned
out to be disappointing to Freed, who gave the job to John (Jack) McGowan, a
writer (and former actor) on the MGM staff since 1936. By the time the final
draft had been approved, various other writers, including Anita Loos, Noel
Langley, and Sid Silvers, had also worked on the screenplay. Eventually, yet
another writer, Kay Van Riper, polished up the script, and she and McGowan
were given final screen credit. The principal difference between the stage and
film versions was the addition of the older generation, the fading performers
who could no longer work after the death of vaudeville. They were used as a
contrast to the vibrant, energetic offspring (headed by Rooney and Garland)
who made up the heart of the movie. By the time the elements were added to
the script to accommodate the stars, there was little similarity between the two
versions.

To direct the movie, Freed chose Busby Berkeley, signing him to a one-
picture contract. Berkeley had achieved fame at Warners, where his lavish,
kaleidoscopic musical numbers in such films as *42nd Street* (1933) and *Gold Diggers
of 1933* (1933) had revitalized the musical genre in the early thirties. Later in the
decade, however, the musical films emphasized romance and comedy rather
than gargantuan production numbers, and Berkeley's special gifts were less in
demand. After directing one nonmusical film, *They Made Me a Criminal*, Berkeley
decided not to renew his contract with Warners and accepted the offer from
MGM to direct *Babes in Arms*. It was a new challenge for him; instead of creating
self-contained musical numbers that would fit into a backstage plot, Berkeley
now had to integrate the music into the story and deal with characters who had
stronger emotional needs and feelings than the gold-digging chorines of his
Warners musicals. He also had to cope with a smaller budget and more modest
production values than he was accustomed to at Warners. He could no longer
place scores of Berkeley girls against the background of a gigantic waterfall, or
have them whirling in bizarre hoop skirts as they played neon-lighted violins.

Judy Garland presented a different sort of problem for Berkeley. Even at
her young age, Garland's nerve endings were frayed, and it is possible that she
was already taking the combination of diet and pep pills that made her hyper-
active one moment and lethargic the next. She was also exhausted from filming
The Wizard of Oz and traveling cross-country to promote that film. Keeping up
with Mickey Rooney's high energy level was a formidable task for her, and in
addition, she clashed continually with Busby Berkeley, whose temperament

Mickey (Mickey Rooney) and Patsy (Judy Garland) dream of fame and fortune in the ice cream parlor. In these films, Garland was usually required to idolize Rooney beyond all reason. Here she tells him, "Sometimes I think being a great Broadway producer isn't going to be big enough for you."

could also be volatile. There were some anchors to keep the production from foundering. Rooney, already a show business veteran of many years, could be counted on to provide professional support, and the cast included other solidly experienced performers who could also help to keep things on an even keel. Charles Winninger, a headlined vaudeville performer and Broadway actor for many years, played Rooney's father, and Guy Kibbee, like Berkeley, a veteran of the years at Warners, appeared as a sympathetic judge. Winninger's wife was played by Grace Hayes, mother of comedian Peter Lind Hayes, and herself an old-time performer on the vaudeville circuit.

In the Hollywood "never leave well enough alone" tradition, most of the original Rodgers and Hart score was discarded to make way for musical numbers that would serve better as showcase for the stars. Only two of the original songs were retained—the rousing title song and the wistful "Where or When"—while others were considered and then dropped (the witty and brilliantly rhymed "I Wish I Were in Love Again"); used only as background music ("The Lady Is a Tramp"); or not considered at all ("My Funny Valentine," "Johnny One Note," and others). A new song called "Good Morning" was written by Arthur Freed and Nacio Herb Brown for Rooney and Garland, and for Garland's requisite torch song, Freed chose the standard "I Cried for You," adding the sort of plaintive recitative that she had performed for her famous "Dear Mr. Gable" number in *Broadway Melody of 1938*. The film's finale was given over to Harold Arlen and E. Y. (Yip) Harburg's "God's Country," which had originally appeared in comedian Ed Wynn's 1937 stage musical, *Hooray for What!*

Completed in two hectic, nerve-racking months, *Babes in Arms* turned out to be the first in a series of popular films that came to be known as the "Mickey-Judy" musicals. It set the pattern for those that followed, focusing on Rooney as the young, brash, live-wire entertainer, the catalyst who brings together all the other entertainers for the requisite show, and Garland as the winsome, self-effacing girl who worships him and longs only to please him. From their very first scene together, we can clearly see the form their relationship would take in this and subsequent films. As they dream of the future, Mickey expresses his longing to "make it" in the theater ("I want success!"), while Judy is asked to play the role of the humble, adoring fan who hails him as a genius at every opportunity ("I'll work hard for you, Mickey. Honest I will!") She fairly swoons when he kisses her, and as the movie progresses, the fact that he scarcely notices her until he has almost lost her rarely interferes with her dogged devotion.

As always in a "Mickey-Judy" musical, the plot of *Babes in Arms* mixes a sizable helping of high spirits with a large dollop of rather sticky sentiment. In this case, the movie retained the basic framework of the stage show, centering on the children of a group of old-time entertainers who have settled down to genteel poverty after the demise of vaudeville. Chips off the old blocks, the kids want to prove their worth and their talent to a disbelieving world. Rooney plays Mickey Moran, the son of vaudeville headliners Joe and Flossie Moran (Winninger and Hayes), and an aspiring songwriter who is determined to achieve stardom. Garland is Patsy Barton, his faithful pal. When a local busybody (Margaret Hamilton) strives to have Mickey and his "wild" friends placed in a work school, the parents try vainly to return to their old two-a-day routines. Just when things look bleakest, the youngsters come together under Mickey's leadership to put on their very own show. There are setbacks along the way, both personal and professional, but eventually the kids triumph.

Although much of the dialogue accompanying these non-epic tribulations is a little too sappy for modern tastes, *Babes in Arms* contains more than enough lively musical numbers as compensation, and with the energy of Rooney and Garland sparking the proceedings, the movie seldom sags. Their first number takes place in a music publisher's office, where ever-eager Mickey, accompanied by Patsy, auditions one of his tunes. Since Mickey seems to be driven by his own nonstop engine, and Patsy's full-throated voice exudes joie de vivre, their

Mickey rehearses a dance number for his show. Rooney's energetic performance called on him to sing, dance, or emote virtually every minute, and it so impressed his peers that they nominated him for an Academy Award for Best Actor.

rendition of "Good Morning" has an ebullience that makes the publisher (and the audience) sit up and take notice.

Despite her subsidiary role, Garland is given several chances to excel musically, and the first occurs when she shares a number with Mickey's young sister Molly (Betty Jaynes). To demonstrate that they have the talent to accompany their parents on a tour, the kids improvise a number in the Moran living room. The highlight of the number contrasts the singing styles of Patsy, who loves the "up" tempo of "swing," and Molly, who prefers opera. The number is reminiscent of Garland's first appearance on film in the musical short *Every Sunday* (1936), in which she has a friendly "jazz-vs.-opera" competition with young Deanna Durbin. Here, Garland's exuberant singing and pert demeanor shine all the brighter next to Betty Jaynes's stiff, formal soprano voice and coy manner.

The youngsters work hard to entertain, but when they are turned down, Mickey, upset and angry, comes up with his own plan: "Our time has come!" he proclaims. They will put on their own show and prove to their families that they can earn their own way. His enthusiasm leads to a lavishly produced version of the title song. Led by Mickey, Patsy, and Don (played by a stolid young baritone named Douglas McPhail), the boys and girls rally their forces, striding through the streets and singing "Babes in Arms" to express their determination.

Busby Berkeley stages the sequence adroitly, matching the players' youthful enthusiasm with his own giddily spinning camera.

As the show gets under way, the problems mount for Mickey and Patsy. Mickey's personal dilemma takes the form of Baby Rosalie (June Preisser), a former child star searching for a "comeback" role. She enters to the melody of "The Lady Is a Tramp," yet another of the many misinterpretations of that excellent song in which the "lady," wittily mocking the foibles of society, tells us that she definitely is *not* a "tramp." For a while, Mickey is too worried about his parents' failure on the road and the fate of his friends to notice the vamping Rosalie. But when she accepts the leading role in his show, he is wildly elated, while a tentatively jealous Patsy is underwhelmed.

Mickey's rehearsals of the show tend to leave the movie both dramatically and musically becalmed. Dramatically, the script does little but concentrate on poor Patsy's predicament, asking her to stifle her jealousy over Mickey's attentions to Baby Rosalie, and to behave with tearful gallantry when she is asked to relinquish the leading role "for the good of the show." Garland reacts to the bad news with the trembling lips and quavering voice she would bring to many similar ordeals in the next few years. Musically, this rehearsal period merely affords Garland the chance to prove what every viewer must realize by this time, that she is the most talented member of the cast. After Don and Molly render their flat, juiceless version of "Where or When," Garland reprises the song, demonstrating the phrasing and the feeling that elude the junior league Eddy and MacDonald.

In the canon of "Mickey-Judy" musicals, Garland must remain forlorn until the triumphant last reel. Here, she hurries off to visit her mother, on tour in Schenectady, convinced that she has lost Mickey forever to Baby Rosalie. Enroute, seated on the bus, she gets her big moment. She sings a plaintive, expressive version of the standard "I Cried for You," adding a monologue in which she admits she's "no glamour girl" and in the "ugly duckling" stage. "You go your way and I'll go mine!" she tells an absent Mickey. The premise is, of course, absurd: Garland, at this point, was a pertly appealing if slightly thick-waisted teenager, and certainly the most radiant actress in the cast. Yet the studio felt it necessary (here and in later musicals until *Meet Me in St. Louis*) to emphasize her feelings of worthlessness.

This being a musical and not a weighty domestic drama, all problems are resolved in not too long a time. Patsy's mother exhorts her to return to the show; Baby Rosalie is ousted from the leading role by her irate father; and faithful Patsy resumes the lead. All that remains is the problem of Mickey's downtrodden father, convinced that he has been a failure to his family but too proud to seek help. Secretly, Mickey arranges with his show's producer (Henry Hull)—an old friend of his father's—to take Dad on as a veteran advisor. It is interesting to

In their big minstrel show, blackfaced Mickey and Judy cavort to "I'm Just Wild About Harry (Mandy)." Today, this number would not be likely to make it to the screen, but it passed muster in a more innocent era.

note that while young Rooney plays these sentimental scenes rather strenuously, the seasoned Winninger gives the father's role a pathos and a genuine feeling that are never excessive.

When the youngsters' show finally gets on, it proves to be something of a mixed bag. One now-painful blackface minstrel number, in which Mickey and Judy perform a brace of standard songs ("Oh, Susanna," "On Moonlight Bay," "Ida"), has Judy wearing unconvincing dark-colored makeup as she sings a lively version of "I'm Just Wild About Harry." (A thunderstorm wrecks the performance of this number, probably not a moment too soon.) Afterward, when the show has been discovered, reorganized, and restaged on Broadway the film skips to the elaborate final number, "God's Country." A flag-waving celebration of America's ethnic diversity and democratic ways, the number has Mickey, Judy, and the performers marching down the aisle of the theater, cavorting in various costumes, and, in general, behaving with a patriotic fervor that could make an American Legionnaire blush. Curiously, the song—as it appeared in *Hooray for What!*—was inspired by the erection of a munitions factory. With

A moment of triumph as Mickey leads the orchestra in the overture to his show, *Babes in Arms*. With all that energy and dedication, could anyone doubt that he would succeed?

revised lyrics, it now served as an orgy of self-congratulation with which to end the movie.

The triumph of Rooney and Garland as fresh, exuberant young film stars was apparent with the release of *Babes in Arms*.* Whatever trouble had occurred during the filming seemed irrelevant beside the praise for their talent and for the infectious spirit of the movie. It was a new kind of movie musical—light, breezy, and modestly scaled in comparison with the extravaganzas of the early thirties. The milieu was still "show business," but the setting was a backyard rather than backstage. Appropriately, the transition from one kind of musical to another was made by Busby Berkeley, the man who directed both kinds. If,

---

*Rooney's hyperenergetic performance impressed the members of the Academy of Motion Picture Arts and Sciences, who awarded him with a nomination as Best Actor. Competing against such actors as Clark Gable (*Gone With the Wind*), Laurence Olivier (*Wuthering Heights*), and James Stewart (*Mr. Smith Goes to Washington*), who all lost to Robert Donat (*Goodbye, Mr. Chips*), Rooney was hardly in the running, but he must have been flattered to be in such good company.

with *Babes in Arms*, he had difficulty diluting the high sugar content of the story, he was certainly able to master the intimate and easy charm of the musical numbers. It seemed inevitable that he would be assigned to direct the next two "Mickey-Judy" musicals, *Strike Up the Band* (1940) and *Babes on Broadway* (1942). Although neither was as diverting as the original, audiences flocked to see Mickey and Judy perform with their customary zest.

Although far from being a landmark musical film, or even an especially good one, *Babes in Arms* reflected a significant transition away from the escapist fantasy musicals of the early thirties, shows that buoyed the spirits of Depression-era moviegoers. The beleaguered musical producers of *42nd Street* and *Footlight Parade* dream of creating spectacle; Mickey only wants to sell his songs, help his family become solvent, and keep his friends out of work school. Ahead were changes for Mickey and Judy: Rooney continued to play variations of Andy Hardy long after it was still becoming, and he moved eventually into character roles and a long-starring stint in the stage musical *Sugar Babies;* Garland strengthened her standing with several exemplary performances, notably *Meet Me in St. Louis, The Clock,* and *A Star Is Born,* and matured into a durable legend.

For a brief few years, in movies that started with *Babes in Arms* and ended with *Girl Crazy* (1943), Mickey Rooney and Judy Garland brightened the screen with the kind of youthful joy and hope that cannot be duplicated. Rooney and Garland made one last appearance together in *Words and Music* (1948), finally getting to perform "I Wish I Were in Love Again," the Rodgers and Hart song that was deleted from *Babes in Arms*. Universal tried to emulate the "Mickey-Judy" musicals with a series of low-budget movies starring their own teenage contingent, Donald O'Connor, Peggy Ryan, and Gloria Jean, but at best they were thin, pale echoes of the original. *Babes in Arms* shows the team at its best—and watching the sheer performing pleasure they exude as they perform "Good Morning" early in the film, we know that they will cheerfully ride over the opposition and surmount their troubles to become the stars they were born to be.

Babes in Arms. Metro-Goldwyn-Mayer. Produced by Arthur Freed. Directed by Busby Berkeley. Screenplay by Jack McGowan and Kay Van Riper, from the musical by Richard Rodgers and Lorenz Hart. Photography by Ray June. Music by Richard Rodgers, Lorenz Hart, Arthur Freed, Nacio Herb Brown, and others. Art direction by Cedric Gibbons. Costumes by Dolly Tree. Edited by Frank Sullivan. Cast: Mickey Rooney, Judy Garland, Charles Winninger, Guy Kibbee, June Preisser, Grace Hayes, Betty Jaynes, Douglas McPhail, and Margaret Hamilton.

In the Lincoln Memorial, Jeff Smith (James Stewart) watches a boy reading the inscription to his grandfather. Capra claimed that the scene was inspired by his visit to the Memorial, where he actually saw an eight-year-old boy reading the words in a clear and innocent voice to an elderly man whose sight was failing.

Lamb Among the Wolves:
Mr. Smith Goes to Washington

"I'm not licked, and I'm gonna stay right here and
fight for this lost cause!"
—James Stewart in *Mr. Smith Goes to Washington*

Americans who have weathered presidential campaigns, at least those in recent years, can surely be forgiven for taking a jaundiced view toward politics and politicans. After a steady barrage of outrageous distortions and deceitful allegations, after hour upon hour of television time glutted with simplistic slogans and empty rhetoric, small wonder that thinking citizens frequently look upon office-seekers with enough grains of salt to fill a few miles of the Dead Sea. Even (or maybe especially) on the municipal level, graft and corruption sometimes seem to run rampant through the body politic. Despite all the honorable, responsible men and women who seek roles in the government, we sometimes suspect that the politician's outstretched hand is reaching for shekels rather than support.

Transposed to film over the years, the image of the politician has been anything but favorable. More often than not, the cinematic road to holding office has been paved with bad intentions, and movie annals are filled with either ruthless, conniving despots or laughable buffoons who have cheated or bulldozed their way to the top. Some are part of film legend: "Boss" Gettys (Ray Collins) in *Citizen Kane* (1941), shamelessly blackmailing a not-so-spotless Charles Foster Kane into withdrawing from the race for governor; Willie Stark (Broderick Crawford) in *All the King's Men* (1949), storming his way to political power; and Frank Skeffington (Spencer Tracy) in *The Last Hurrah* (1958), neither despot nor buffoon but the perfect political animal who knows how to serve his constituents while remaining firmly in control. Even more prevalent are the political clowns: either comically inept bumblers (the senators in *Louisiana Purchase*, 1941, and *The Senator Was Indiscreet*, 1948) or harebrained puppets whose strings are pulled by the all-powerful "boss" (*The Dark Horse*, 1932; *The Great McGinty*, 1940).

On the other side of the ledger have been the political novices, men and women who have somehow retained their ideals and their illusions and have ventured into politics to serve with honesty and integrity. In the movie-eye view, these are the naïve dreamers who enter the mainstream and come perilously close to being devoured by the sharks. Their fates vary: Sometimes their virtue acts as a shield, and they not only survive but also win the day over the sharks (Loretta Young as a simple but cagey farm girl who becomes a senator in *The Farmer's Daughter*, 1947). Other times, they withdraw from the race, bruised but enlightened (Spencer Tracy, playing the presidential game in *State of the Union*, 1948), or they learn the advantages of compromise while holding fast to their ideals (Henry Fonda as a presidential contender in *The Best Man*, 1964). Occasionally, these men are destroyed, as in *Advise and Consent* (1962), in which a senator (Don Murray) commits suicide when a rival senator threatens to expose a sordid incident in his past. In recent years, as the world has turned more cynical, filmmakers have shown young and idealistic politicians learning to understand, and to live with, the moral laxity that surrounds them. In *The Candidate* (1972), a liberal senatorial candidate (Robert Redford) wins the election but becomes neutralized in the process. (In his moment of triumph, he asks querulously, "What do we do now?") *The Seduction of Joe Tynan* (1979) has Alan Alda experiencing a double "seduction," first by an attractive worker in his campaign (Meryl Streep), and then by the exigencies of getting elected. In our time, it is no longer possible to believe in the shining knight who will right wrongs with his slashing sword of truth.

Once upon a better time, it was not only possible for moviegoers to believe in this knight but also likely that they would applaud his efforts all the way to his final triumphant moment. And no figure ever wore armor that shone as brightly, or even provoked lustier cheers from audiences, than young Jefferson Smith, the junior senator who chose to do battle against the formidable forces of corruption even as they reached into the sacred chamber of the U.S. Senate. As embodied for all time by James Stewart, Jeff Smith was the resolute hero of Frank Capra's comedy-drama *Mr. Smith Goes to Washington*.

For Frank Capra, Senator Smith represented the embodiment of an ideal he had been constructing in his life and work since coming to the United States as a Sicilian boy of six in the early years of the century. Intensely, fervently patriotic, Capra believed that ordinary Americans, even the most naïve and gullible, had within their power the ability to rout the forces of evil and venality that threatened to destroy them. Through what he called their "courage, wit, and love," they could triumph over their environment. Capra's belief could not have come at a better time. After working in the twenties as a gag writer for Mack Sennett, where he helped to develop the childlike personality of comedian Harry Langdon, Capra went to the "Poverty Row" of Columbia, where he began

Director Frank Capra and James Stewart stand before the intricately detailed set of the Senate Chamber. Fiercely patriotic, Capra wrote in his autobiography about "the bad case of goose pimples" he got when he saw the chamber spread out before him, "as awe-inspiring as an empty cathedral."

directing films. His early films were mostly perfunctory, but in the midst of the bleak Depression, with despair and hopelessness ravaging the country, his natural optimism soon found a voice.

As he developed his craft, learning to shoot sequences in the lively, accelerated pace that kept viewers watching, Capra was drawn increasingly to material that revolved around the everyday lives of people who had reserves of strength and resilience, the very people who were struggling to survive the Depression. Embedded in the heavy sentimentality of Capra's *Lady for a Day* (1933) was a genuine affection for the Runyonesque derelicts who banded together to help one of their own. More importantly, Capra's landmark comedy *It Happened One Night* (1934) folded into its breezy cross-country romance a genuine concern for worn-at-the-heels Americans who rode the buses and lived in the motor courts. Capra struck such a deep chord of recognition that to everyone's surprise, including Capra's, the movie won five Oscars and drew large, enthusiastic audiences. The movie also displayed Capra's ability to obtain unaffected performances from his actors.

With *Mr. Deeds Goes to Town* (1936), another major success, Capra discovered that moviegoers shared his affinity for the naïve, idealistic "Everyman" hero. As Longfellow Deeds, the eccentric small-town greeting-card poet who inherits a fortune, Gary Cooper took on the greedy financiers, the pretentious "culture vultures," and the crass opportunists who were wresting the country away from

Fumbling Jeff Smith is introduced to Susan Paine (Astrid Allwyn) by her father, Senator Joe Paine (Claude Rains). Capra felt that Rains ''had the artistry, power, and depth to play the soul-tortured idealist whose feet had turned to clay.''

Returning from his first excursion in Washington, Jeff expresses his elation at viewing the Capitol Building and the Lincoln Memorial to a dubious Saunders (Jean Arthur) and reporter Diz Moore (Thomas Mitchell). ''I don't think I've ever been so thrilled in my whole life!'' he tells them.

the little people. Audiences who needed a rationale for their plight flocked to see the "pixilated" Deeds rout the villains, with the help of his once-dubious, now-adoring girlfriend (Jean Arthur). Wisely, Capra mixed large dollops of rowdy humor into the proceedings, diluting with laughter any note of sanctimonious preaching. The combination of "chin-up" sentiment and comedy, handled sure-footedly by Capra, proved to be irresistible.

When Capra came to *Mr. Smith Goes to Washington*, he knew at once that he could repeat this successful formula in a new setting. The idea had come to his desk by a circuitous route. Director Rouben Mamoulian had purchased the rights to an out-of-print novel by Lewis R. Foster called *The Gentleman from Montana* for $1,500. Harry Cohn, the rough-hewn head of Columbia Pictures, wanted to buy it from Mamoulian for $75,000, but mysteriously (as the story goes) Mamoulian agreed to sell it to him for the same sum he had paid, provided Cohn would let him direct the film version of Clifford Odets's play *Golden Boy*. Unable to pass up such a bargain, Cohn agreed to the terms and showed the Foster story to Frank Capra. Capra read the first page of a two-page synopsis and leaped at the idea of filming it. He saw it immediately as a vehicle for Jimmy Stewart and Jean Arthur, whom he had teamed felicitously the year before in *You Can't Take It With You*. After Sidney Buchman had written a flavorsome and richly detailed screenplay,* *Mr. Smith Goes to Washington* went into production with Stewart and Arthur in the leading roles.

Casting most of the other principal roles proved to be a relatively easy task. Edward Arnold, a stout character actor with a booming laugh, was the inevitable choice to play ruthless political boss Jim Taylor, and the part of Senator Joseph Paine, the white-haired "Silver Knight" whose corruption was concealed beneath a dignified bearing, went to the distinguished British actor Claude Rains, who was gifted with one of the most mellifluous voices in films. The reliable Thomas Mitchell was chosen to play the pixieish, tippling reporter Diz Moore, and other roles went to Guy Kibbee as the inept Governor Hubert Hopper and Eugene Pallette, bulky and frog-voiced, as Taylor's aide Chick McCann.

The part of the Vice-President, who must oversee and control the upheavals that rattle the walls of the film's Senate chamber, was originally offered to Edward Ellis, a longtime character actor whose dignified mien seemed appropriate. Angrily, Ellis turned down the role, citing that the Vice-President was given only a few lines to say and spent most of his time on-camera hammering his gavel. Capra then offered the role to Harry Carey, the veteran cowboy actor, who was eager to do it. Working his way into the role with some difficulty— after so many Westerns, he was apparently intimidated by playing the nation's

---

*Robert Rifkin, Capra's favorite scenarist, had gone to Goldwyn as an associate producer but returned later to write other Capra films, notably *Meet John Doe* (1941).

Pointing to the lighted dome of the Capitol Building, Jeff voices his deep feelings about liberty. Although Stewart's brilliant performance won him an Oscar nomination, he received the award the following year for an engaging but lesser performance in *The Philadelphia Story*.

Vice-President—Carey finally evolved a performance that won him an Academy Award nomination as Best Supporting Actor. With only a handful of lines and a series of sly half-smiles, he managed to create a memorable character.

Since the film called for the reproduction or background use of many prominent Washington locales, a considerable amount of work had to be done before shooting began. While Capra and Sidney Buchman explored the area, steeping themselves in its flavor and traditions, cameraman Joseph Walker and assistant director Art Black photographed the sites so that they could be rear-projected on the screen or re-created authentically on the Columbia lot. All the intricate details of the Senate chamber—its seats, doorknobs, chandeliers, walls—were photographed, with each shot carefully scaled for the studio's set builders. To ensure accuracy in showing Senate procedures, Capra hired Jim Preston, superintendent of the Senate press gallery, whose substantial knowledge proved indispensable to the production. According to Capra, Preston could describe the composite model of a U.S. senator, easing the way for him to cast ninety-

Knowing that Jeff is a victim of political chicanery, Saunders urges him to leave Washington: "Why don't you go home? . . . This is no place for you. You're halfway decent!" One of the deftest actresses of the thirties and forties, Arthur had a distinctive crackling voice that remains one of the most pleasing memories of that era.

six actors who would resemble real senators at their desks.* Perhaps the most difficult task went to art director Lionel Banks and his team. They were asked to reproduce, in one hundred days, exact and workable replicas of the sites it had taken over one hundred years to build. Poring over dust-laden blueprints gleaned from the depths of the Capitol, plus thousands of old photographs, they worked long hours to duplicate the committee rooms, cloak rooms, hotel suites, monuments, and the Press Club of Washington.

As in all of his films, Capra assumed total control over every aspect of the production. To write the musical score, he signed Dimitri Tiomkin, the Russian-born composer who had worked in Hollywood since the early thirties. The heavily accented Tiomkin, who admitted frankly to borrowing his musical themes from the work of both European and American composers, was asked by Capra to avoid drawing from the masters of his native land and to use native American themes instead. Capra suggested Stephen Foster, John Philip Sousa, or W. C. Handy. According to the director, Tiomkin replied, "Fronk, vat you theenk, I'm

---

*In his autobiography, Capra relates that during the filming, an agitated Preston stopped the shooting of a scene on the Vice-President's rostrum, noting that there was no lock on the big clock over the rostrum. It seems that a lock had been placed on the clock to keep the senators from advancing the time so that they could adjourn and go to a ball game. Preston insisted that the absence of the lock would cause laughter in the Washington Press Club. The lock was added.

like children? Papichka, in my head is notes like apple pie so American." Capra also worked closely with the Yugoslavian-born Slavko Vorkapich, the acknowledged master of the montage.

The filming of *Mr. Smith* proceeded with very few hitches, with Capra setting a brisk pace for his seasoned cast members. By late summer, he had assembled a rough print of the film, and its prospects for rousing success seemed very good indeed. In July, the National Press Club had asked him whether they could sponsor the world premiere of the film in Washington, and in mid-September, a press preview had drawn enthusiastic notices. (Hedda Hopper, self-appointed watchdog and weather vane for the film industry, compared the movie to Lincoln's Gettysburg Address.) Capra and Columbia happily prepared for a massive publicity coup, in which Washington leaders would proclaim and celebrate the virtues of *Mr. Smith Goes to Washington*.

At first, "Mr. Smith" day (October 16, 1939) went very well. At a dinner given by the Press Club in honor of Jim Preston, there was an overflowing of camaraderie and good cheer. Cocktails were raised in flowery toasts; patriotic marches were followed by extravagant speeches in which pillars of the Press Club praised Jim Preston while Capra conceded that "without Mr. Preston, there could have been no *Mr. Smith*." The director was convinced that the first showing of the film that night at Constitution Hall would be the culmination of a dream that his immigrant father would have been thrilled to share.

It was not to be. At the premiere that evening, with the cream of Washington society in attendance, disaster was in the air. Scattered whispers and fidgeting accelerated into walkouts. Members of the audience, muttering imprecations under their breath, hurried out of the theater. Soon enough, Capra could hear such words as "Outrage!" and "Insult!" hurled at his bewildered head. As *Mr. Smith* sputtered to its end, most of the attendees had vanished into the night, leaving behind the bloodied bodies of the participants. There was even worse to come. Later, at the Press Club, Capra cowered as Washington's press correspondents vilified him for having made such a scurrilous film. His sins were double: He had shown that corruption could appear in the noble Senate chamber, and he had drawn one of their own members as a souse. To Capra, the reasons for their vilification were evident: "Clearly, the National Press Club envied and feared film as a rival opinion maker. Clearly, they detested *Mr. Smith Goes to Washington* because it was the first important film to muscle in on their private Washington preserve."*

The situation grew worse. At the same time that the film was winning enthusiastic advance reviews from nationwide critics, government leaders and film industry executives, believing that releasing *Mr. Smith* would not be "in

*Frank Capra, *The Name Above the Title* (New York: Macmillan Company, 1971), p. 283.

Jeff meets the enemy in the burly person of political boss Jim Taylor (Edward Arnold). A sturdy character actor since the early thirties, Arnold usually played villainous or overbearing characters. The year before, he had appeared as James Stewart's father in *You Can't Take It With You*.

the best interests" of the country, were aiming their weapons at Columbia. Claiming to speak for his colleagues, Senator Alben Barkley of Kentucky condemned the movie as "a grotesque distortion" of the way the Senate was run, while Senator James F. Byrnes of South Carolina called it "exactly the kind of picture that dictators of totalitarian governments would like to have their subjects believe exists in a democracy." It was reported that the major studios would offer Columbia a large reimbursement if they withdrew the movie from circulation. The most damaging blow occurred when Joseph P. Kennedy, America's ambassador in London, called Harry Cohn, asserting that the film would do untold harm to America's prestige in Europe, and urging him to withdraw it immediately from European distribution and exhibition.

Deeply troubled, Harry Cohn looked for a solution to the problem raised by Kennedy and all the others who wanted *Mr. Smith* executed for treason. Capra defended the film vehemently, claiming that his movie could not have come at a more appropriate time. With war newly raging in Europe, with Hitler at the throat of every country in Europe, it was time for the "Mr. Smiths" of the world to stand up for freedom, to show dictators that America was the envy and the hope of all "kicked-around" people. He assembled hundreds of opinions, editorials, and comments on the film and sent them to Ambassador Ken-

In an effort to vindicate himself, Jeff begins his filibuster in the Senate. Stewart's heartfelt performance in this long and difficult sequence helped to turn him from an amiable, lightweight leading man into an important screen actor.

nedy in London. Somewhat mollified, Kennedy still concluded that the film would do "inestimable harm" to America, and he continued to urge its withdrawal. To his credit, Cohn refused to concede, and the film went into general release. Three years later, Frank Capra was moved when he learned that *Mr. Smith* was the last film to be shown in the theaters of Nazi-occupied France before American and British films were banned by the Germans. *Mr. Smith* played continuously during the final thirty days before the ban.

Viewing *Mr. Smith Goes to Washington* from the vantage point of our more cynical age, it is not difficult to equate Jefferson Smith's wide-eyed naïveté with the film's ingenuous point of view. Like Mr. Smith, the movie harbors the innocent notions that America's government officials are primarily responsible to the people rather than to their own greedy ambitions, that the freedoms we once fought to win are worth any sacrifice to preserve, and that one stalwart individual can make a profound difference in the quality of our lives. In a time when corruption seems to flow through our system like raw sewage, such ideas seem not only naïve but positively subversive. And yet, from first frame to last, *Mr. Smith Goes to Washington* overrides our cynicism, confounds our sophistication, and sends us whirling with Jeff Smith into an exhilarating vortex of conflicting emotions. Somehow, despite our better judgment, it all works beautifully, and Frank Capra is the man who makes it so through sheer cinematic skill.

The movie begins in high gear as an old senator dies suddenly, and someone is needed to replace him in a state under the powerful thumb of political boss Jim Taylor (Arnold). The bumbling governor (Kibbee) is asked to find a patsy as the replacement, a dumb party man who will play along with Taylor and the state's revered but corrupt other senator, Joseph Paine (Rains). At the urging of his many children (all brash and irreverent in the style of thirties movie brats), the governor appoints young Jefferson Smith (Stewart), the popular head of a chain of boys' clubs, and an all-round nice fellow. Taylor is assured they can handle this "simpleton of all time, this big-eyed patriot." Senator Paine scoffs at the very notion of this "young patriot, turned loose in our nation's capital."

Capra clearly savors our first view of Jeff Smith: At the send-off banquet in his honor, the camera moves to his lanky frame as, with genuine awe at his new responsibility, he addresses the assembled well-wishers. His first words are: "I can't help feeling that there's been a big mistake." Senator Paine, beaming at his protégé, is startled to learn that Jeff's father, a newspaper editor murdered because of his outspoken ways, was an old friend who championed "lost causes," as Paine himself once did. Jeff's arrival in Washington is a model of artfully handled exposition: Through a series of deft comic touches and montages arranged by the masterly Slavko Vorkapich, we see Smith both as a tangle-footed hayseed out of place in the Washington jungle and as a tourist genuinely awed by the symbols of the nation's capital. At one moment, he is shy at meeting Senator Paine's pretty young daughter Susan (Astrid Allwyn)—the camera photographs his hat continually falling out of his nervous hands—and at another, he is gazing in wonder at the Lincoln Memorial, while a young boy reads the inscription to his grandfather. (Capra never counted subtlety among his virtues—he also has an old black man, hat in hand, looking up reverently at Lincoln's solemn visage.)

All this patriotic fervor calls for a dose of down-to-earth practicality, and the film provides it in the attractive person of Jean Arthur as Saunders, Jeff's Washington-wise secretary. Cynical about Jeff's appointment, and fully aware of the machinations practiced by Taylor and Paine, she carelessly throws Jeff to the snapping wolves of the fourth estate, who gleefully mock and humiliate him in print. Diz Moore (Mitchell), Saunders's hard-drinking friend and would-be husband, is among the reporters.* Jeff's shaky first day in the Senate is marred by all this bad publicity, and in a rage, he seeks out the offending reporters and knocks them down, only to be verbally attacked by them as an "incompetent clown" and "honorary stooge." To placate Jeff, Paine urges him to prepare his first bill calling for the construction of a boys' camp in the state. Paine, however, is unaware that Jeff's bill would conflict dangerously with a piece of legislation for a new dam that he is currently rushing through the Senate with Taylor's backing. It happens that the site for the projected boys' camp and that for the dam are identical, and that the land surrounding the dam site has been bought up by Taylor and his cronies under assumed names, with the intention of selling it back to the government at a huge profit.

Jeff's enthusiasm for his bill, and for the principles that inspired it, is contagious; even Saunders's attitude is softened by the quiet eloquence with which he talks about liberty: "Liberty is too precious a thing to be buried in books, Miss Saunders. Men should hold it up in front of them every single day of their lives and say, 'I'm free—to think and to speak. My ancestors couldn't. I can. And my children will.' " Stewart reads these lines with such conviction and intensity that he succeeds in making the character seem less like the vacuous bumpkin of the first reel and more like the persuasive champion of justice and right he will later become. So impressed is Saunders by his credibility that she helps him prepare the bill for the boys' camp, only to learn to her dismay that the bill will directly oppose Paine's grafting legislation. When Taylor's forces conspire to keep Jeff out of the Senate so that the bill for the dam can be passed,

---

*Those who believe that today's hard-driving, insensitive paparazzi are a phenomenon of recent times have never viewed thirties movies in which newspaper people were depicted as vultures who would do anything to get a good "story." Mervyn LeRoy's *Five Star Final* (1931) comes to mind as a powerful early example.

Saunders urges him to go home before it is too late: "You don't belong here. You're halfway decent."

Of course, Jeff's integrity cannot be compromised (certainly not in a Frank Capra film), and a worried Paine has him finally meet Taylor. In a classic confrontation—Jeff wary and concerned, Taylor trying his best to appear avuncular—Jeff learns the painful truth about his idol's long record of expedient corruption. ("Joe Paine has been taking my advice for twenty years.") Paine tries to explain the reality of the situation ("You've been living in a boy's world"), but a heartsick Jeff can see only the clay feet of the man he worshiped. He has no choice but to introduce his bill into the Senate. Taylor's forces, however, are prepared—Paine interrupts Jeff to accuse him of owning the land on which his boys' camp would be built. In ringing terms, he denounces Jeff as unfit to sit in the Senate. To his bewilderment, Jeff is being ground up in the wheels of Jim Taylor's machine.

Perhaps only Frank Capra could carry off the scene at the Lincoln Memorial in which Saunders finds Jeff, weeping in despair and ready to return home a broken man. He finds no solace in the "words and the monuments" and wants only to get away from "the whole rotten show." Her voice charged with emotion, Saunders urges him to stay and fight. "You can't quit now," she tells him. Her cynicism replaced by love, she has come to believe in his "plain, decent, everyday common rightness," and we sense that scenarist Buchman and director Capra believe in it, too. Perhaps one of the reasons that *Mr. Smith Goes to Washington* has survived the years is the utter conviction with which its ideas are presented; it earns rather than manipulates our feelings for Jeff's plight.

At any rate, Saunders convinces Jeff to stand fast with the truth, leading to the film's stirring climax. When the move is made to expel him from the Senate, he rises to begin a filibuster that will keep him standing until his cause and his position have been fully set forth. With Saunders as his guide and support in the visitors' gallery, he launches his counterattack on Taylor and Paine. Sensing danger, Taylor musters his machine to stop Jeff, organizing rallies against him and urging his ouster in banner headlines splashed across the newspapers he controls. When Jeff's supporters try to print their own paper, Taylor's men even hurt the loyal boys who try to distribute them. As Jeff hangs on in the Senate and Taylor's opposition grows, the scenes keep up an unflagging pace that sweeps up the viewer with a rare urgency and excitement.

His body sagging with weariness, his voice a hoarse whisper, Jeff continues to state his principles: "There's no place out there for graft or greed or lies. . . . This country is bigger than the Taylors or you and me." Stewart's performance reaches a peak of eloquence as he aims his words at Senator Paine: "You know that you fight for the lost causes harder than for any others. Yes, you even die for them. . . . I'm not licked and I'm gonna stay right here and fight for this

In a scene that was deleted from the final print, Jeff and Saunders celebrate his victory in the Senate. Joining them in the car are his mother (Beulah Bondi), Senator Paine, and Jeff's adoring Boy Rangers.

lost cause!'' When thousands of letters denouncing him are wheeled onto the Senate floor, his cause seems hopelessly lost, and he finally collapses. At this moment, Senator Paine, unable to live with his conscience any longer, tries to shoot himself, shouting, ''Every word that boy said is true!'' Jeff has been vindicated, as cheers resound throughout the Senate. If this is the sort of political miracle that could occur only in a Frank Capra movie, there is no denying its effectiveness, or the eminently satisfactory way in which it brings the film to its conclusion.

Although Capra remains the dominant force behind the film's durability, many elements contributed to its success. Joseph Walker's photography (bolstered by Slavko Vorkapich's montages) propels the viewer into the Washington hullabaloo, crowding frame after frame with vivid, precisely selected images. Dimitri Tiomkin's ''apple pie-American'' score artfully blends a number of classic American songs, including ''Red River Valley,'' ''Bury Me Not on the Lone Prairie,'' ''The Battle Hymn of the Republic,'' and ''Jeannie with the Light Brown Hair.'' Lionel Banks's reconstruction of Washington sites, especially the Senate chamber, gives us added reason to admire the special skills of the art director.

Yet Frank Capra remains the film's principal architect, building its exhilarating mood and leading his cast to exemplary performances. James Stewart's Jeff Smith is indisputably one of his finest acting jobs, earning him an Academy Award nomination as Best Actor and winning him the New York Film Critics Award for Best Male Performance. Jean Arthur's piquant style was never more appealing, and Claude Rains brings depth and conviction to the role of Senator Paine. In his usual fashion, Capra also gives some of his supporting players their own moments to shine; we remember Eugene Pallette's oversized political sharpshooter trying to extract himself from a telephone booth; Thomas Mitchell's bemused reporter, proposing marriage once again to Saunders with the remark, "I'll cherish you"; or, most memorably, Harry Carey's Vice-President, smiling benignly behind his hand at Jeff Smith's youthful naïveté.

Viewed against the background of cynicism and double-dealing in the political arena of recent decades, *Mr. Smith Goes to Washington* seems the very soul of innocence. Today, a new young senator is more likely to consult immediately with his media people and poll-takers than to visit the Lincoln Memorial, though no doubt there are legislators who share Jeff Smith's (and Capra's) conviction that one righteous man can make a difference in the government. Today, Jefferson Smith has become something of an anachronism, an idealist in a world where ideals seem to have little consequence.

Still, we can watch *Mr. Smith Goes to Washington* and cheer whenever the neophyte senator triumphs over the villainous powers-that-be. Once again, we can be grateful for the magic—and the myth—of the movies.

Mr. Smith Goes to Washington. Columbia. Produced and directed by Frank Capra. Screenplay by Sidney Buchman, from a novel by Lewis R. Foster. Photography by Joseph Walker. Montage effects by Slavko Vorkapich. Art direction by Lionel Banks. Costumes by Robert Kalloch. Edited by Gene Havlick and Al Clark. Cast: Jean Arthur, James Stewart, Claude Rains, Edward Arnold, Thomas Mitchell, Guy Kibbee, Eugene Pallette, Beulah Bondi, Harry Carey, H. B. Warner, and Ruth Donnelly. Remade in 1977 as *Billy Jack Goes to Washington.*

Rockefeller Center opens for business in New York City . . . Listeners for radio's soap operas are at an all-time high . . . The New York World's Fair closes after 26 million paid admissions . . . The National Women's Party urges immediate congressional action on E.R.A . . . The Nobel Committee offers no peace prize for 1939 . . . The Russians invade Finland, leaving wide areas of Helsinki in flames . . . The Irish Republican Army explodes three bombs in Piccadilly Circus . . . The Nazis destroy a statue of Woodrow Wilson in Posen, Poland, calling it an eyesore . . . Hitler escapes an attempt on his life . . .

. . . and the amazing movie year ends with Garbo's laughter in *Ninotchka*, Marlene Dietrich's comeback in *Destry Rides Again*, and the arrival of the most eagerly awaited film in screen history, *Gone With the Wind* . . .

Greta Garbo as the transformed Ninotchka.

The Thawing of a Comrade: Ninotchka

> "I always felt a little hurt when our swallows
> deserted us in winter for capitalistic countries. Now
> I know why. We have the high ideals. They have
> the climate."
> —Greta Garbo in *Ninotchka*

There have always been two schools of opinion about Greta Garbo. The more prominent one maintains that after more than four decades since her last film, she remains the screen's most consummate actress and most beautiful woman. They rhapsodize, often in hyperbolic terms, about the extraordinary face that radiates a luminous glow in the camera's eye, and about an acting gift that can bring depths of meaning to a glance or a phrase. In Europe, Garbo is still known as "La Divina," and in America, reams of prose are still written about the inimitably throaty voice that can express infinite variations of sorrow and longing, and the enigmatic tragic mask, the tabula rasa that kept viewers enthralled in films both terrible and sublime. Indeed, it is not difficult to subscribe to this point of view when watching her Anna Karenina, all hope lost, racing to meet her tragic destiny, or her Camille, expiring in the arms of her beloved Armand.

A minority opinion, however, holds that Garbo is a limited actress who was able to transmute an eminently photogenic face and chilly Swedish personality into a mystique beyond mere words. Those who refuse to participate in the panegyrics for Garbo point out that while Garbo was often able to rise above the romantic twaddle she was saddled with at MGM in the silent and early sound years, she also resorted to occasionally posturing and "attitudinizing" instead of acting. When the material defeated her, some critics insist, she could be as bad as any actress who never received the benefit of an extensive publicity campaign.

By the end of the thirties, enough evidence had accumulated to give some weight to both schools of opinion. On the one hand, she had not only demonstrated the full breadth of her art in *Queen Christina*, *Anna Karenina*, and *Camille* but she had also brought vitality to some of the hard-breathing moral melodramas that the studio kept tossing her way; there are moments in such overwrought movies as *Wild Orchids* (1929) in which the power of her acting makes one care about the fate of her character. On the other hand, there are scenes that even her most ardent supporter would find it difficult to accept or admire. Grappling with English for the first time, she is perilously close to absurd in parts of *Anna Christie* (1930), especially in her climactic love scene with Charles Bickford. In *Mata Hari* (1932), her seductive spy edges toward parody more than once. And (is it sacrilegious to say this?) as the world-weary ballerina Grusinskaya in *Grand Hotel* (1932), she never seems fully convincing in John Barrymore's arms. Flinging her head back to suggest passionate abandon, murmuring "Flix! Flix!" she seems to be assuming a pose rather than becoming the character she had chosen to portray.

By the time she came gloriously to *Ninotchka*, Garbo had retained her popularity, at least with women who admired her style, her air of mystery, and her all-for-love attitude. Yet signs and portents told the actress that it was time for a professional change. Although she had survived her last movie, *Conquest* (1937), sailing sadly away from her lover, Napoleon, the poor reviews and box-office reception had convinced her that she had perhaps suffered enough in her films. To date, she had drowned, crashed to her death, perished before a firing squad, thrown herself under a train, and expired of tuberculosis. She decided that lighter, less doom-laden roles were in order, and she began her campaign for a comedy, threatening, as usual, to return to Sweden if she was denied. Reluctantly, the studio began to look for a suitable vehicle. According to one report, Garbo, by way of her good friend Salka Viertel, learned of a story by Hungarian writer Melchior Lengyel concerning a grim Communist girl who finds romance in Paris. She liked the idea and insisted that MGM buy it for her. Lengyel was paid fifteen thousand dollars for his three-page outline.

At first, Louis B. Mayer was not at all happy with the idea, nor with the screenplay that Billy Wilder, Charles Brackett, and Walter Reisch finally fashioned from it.* He not only thought that Garbo was ill-advised to venture into the untried genre of comedy but also maintained that the subject of Communism was repugnant to him and every American moviegoer, even when Communists were the targets of the humor. In spite of his militant anti-Communism, he was also aware that many people, including influential intellectuals of the day, ad-

---

*Others who tried—and failed—to write a usable screenplay included Jacques Deval, the author of *Tovarich*, and S. N. Behrman, the stylish playwright who had written dialogue for several of Garbo's films. (In Behrman's version, Ninotchka went to Paris to make a deal for the ore in a Siberian silver mine.) Brackett and Wilder were then signed to work with Walter Reisch, a friend of Lubitsch's and an MGM studio writer.

Greta Garbo on the set of *Ninotchka* with director Ernst Lubitsch. Witty and erudite, the Berlin-born Lubitsch brought a wry, sardonic flavor and a visual elegance to such previous films as *Trouble in Paradise* (1932) and *The Merry Widow* (1934).

mired Russia and would object to any criticism of that country. Garbo, however, remained adamant, recognizing that her career was on the line—one wrong move could send her tumbling into obscurity. Mayer finally consented, and after a game of musical chairs (a popular Hollywood pastime), Ernst Lubitsch was chosen to direct her. It happened this way: After George Cukor was fired from *Gone With the Wind* following a dispute with David Selznick, he was assigned by MGM to direct the film version of Clare Luce's vitriolic play *The Women*. Lubitsch, who was originally scheduled to direct *The Women*, was transferred to *Ninotchka*, with happy results.

Apparently Lubitsch, a director with an elegant visual style and a brilliant, sardonic wit, had been interested for a number of years in making a film with Garbo. According to an autobiography by Mercedes de Acosta, the director had met Garbo after she completed *As You Desire Me* in 1932. Struck by her extraordinary beauty and talent, he had said, "*Gott*, how I would love to direct a picture with you!" Smiling, Garbo had answered, "You tell them, Ernst. I'm far too tired to talk to studio executives." "Vat fools they are," Lubitsch exclaimed.

The Grand Duchess Swana of Russia (Ina Claire) discusses ways of recovering her jewels with her suave lover Count Leon d'Algout (Melvyn Douglas). One of the stage's most elegant comediennes, Claire appeared in only a handful of films over the years.

"How vonderful Greta and I would be together. What a vonderful picture we could make together.' " The years passed, as Lubitsch went on to direct such high-style films as *Trouble in Paradise* (1932), *Design for Living* (1933), and *The Merry Widow* (1934). In 1937, he received a special Academy Award for his twenty-five year contribution to motion pictures, but, like Garbo, he needed a film that would bring him fully back on course as a master director. Finally, he had the chance to make that "vonderful picture" with the actress he so admired, and the production got under way.

To play opposite Garbo, Lubitsch—or the studio—made the wisest choice possible. A popular and reliable actor since his debut in 1931 in *Tonight or Never*, Melvyn Douglas had excelled at playing dapper men-about-town opposite many of the screen's leading ladies, including Irene Dunne, Marlene Dietrich, and Joan Crawford. (He had previously appeared with Garbo in *As You Desire Me*.) He seemed, and proved to be, ideal for playing the role of Leon, the suave Parisian playboy who romances Ninotchka. Another superb choice was Ina Claire, one of the stage's most adroit comediennes, who would appear as the

Nina Ivanovna Yakushova (Greta Garbo), otherwise known as Ninotchka, arrives at her lavish hotel suite in Paris. "Which part of the room is mine?" she askes the flustered Soviet emissaries.

Grand Duchess Swana, Leon's Russian mistress and the original owner of the jewels that trigger the plot of the film. Although she had been a Broadway favorite for many years, she had made only a few films, but in *Ninotchka*, her brittle sophistication ("My face doesn't compose well. It's all highlights.") contrasted brilliantly with Garbo's languorous soul-searching, and their climactic scene together is a highlight of the film. To play the Russian emissaries who succumb to French hedonism, MGM signed the always sturdy, always excitable Sig Rumann; Felix Bressart, the German character actor who invariably brought an underlying note of melancholy to his comic roles; and Polish stage actor Alexander Granach. In one of his rare nonhorror roles, Bela Lugosi was signed to play Soviet Commissar Razinin.

The production of *Ninotchka* began in May 1939 and ended only fifty-eight days later.* As usual, Lubitsch had worked closely with the writers, helping to fine-tune the elegant, expert dialogue. In his customary fashion, he had also created a detailed blueprint of every scene so that he knew exactly what he wanted well before the cameras began turning. From all reports, his directorial style was firm without being autocratic or overbearing. And with Garbo, he was the soul of gallantry and thoughtfulness, knowing (as all directors did) that she required special handling. This was especially necessary with *Ninotchka*, since she was venturing forth for the first time into the maze of comedy.

According to John Bainbridge's book on Garbo, Lubitsch would arrive on the set in the morning and formally pay his respects to Garbo in her dressing room. He would then remove his coat and work in his shirt-sleeves for the rest of the day. At the end of the work period, he would again put on his coat and call at the actress's dressing room to bid her a good evening. Lubitsch continued this unprecedented behavior throughout the shooting of the film. On occasion, he would stage little tricks to keep the reticent Garbo in a light frame of mind. Bainbridge reports that one day Garbo noticed Lubitsch reading a book entitled *Parisian Nights*. Lubitsch pretended not to notice her curiosity as they began talking about a scene in the movie. Garbo kept stealing glances at the book until her curiosity could no longer be restrained. When she opened the book, it went off with a bang, and everyone laughed, including Garbo. Lubitsch later said, "She is probably the most inhibited person I ever worked with. When you finally break through the inhibitions, and she really feels a scene, she's wonderful. But if you don't succeed in making her feel it, she can't do it cold-bloodedly on technique."

---

*MGM executives made many title changes; some of them wildly improbable, before settling on *Ninotchka*. Among them were: *We Want to Be Alone, A Kiss from Moscow, This Time for Keeps, Time Out for Love*, and *A Kiss for the Commissar*. For those who might be put off by the title finally chosen, the ads proclaimed: "Don't pronounce it—see it!"

In a Paris restaurant, Leon topples from his chair after a futile attempt to make Ninotchka laugh. For the moment, Ninotchka retains her stony countenance, then (inset) explodes with laughter. The ads proclaimed: "Garbo Laughs!"

Many years later, in his autobiography,* Melvyn Douglas commented on Garbo's acting technique: "Garbo has an extraordinary face, plastic and luminous, the kind of subject sculptors adore. . . . Her best work was done in love scenes. . . . Her technical abilities for other kinds of scenes were not as fully developed, however. Perhaps because English was not her first language, she did not 'underline,' she did not pick out the most important phrases in a speech or color individual words for subtle shades of meaning. In spite of *Ninotchka*'s billing as the film in which 'Garbo laughs,' she was unable to articulate so much as a titter during the shooting of the restaurant scene. I never learned whether the laughter, which must have been added in the dubbing room, was Garbo or not."

Lubitsch also recalled Garbo's extreme difficulty with certain scenes. According to the director, she was highly apprehensive about the crucial sequence

*Melvyn Douglas and Tom Arthur, *See You at the Movies: The Autobiography of Melvyn Douglas* (New York and London: University Press of America, 1986), p. 89.

in which Ninotchka becomes tipsy in a restaurant as she savors the capitalistic way of life. Extremely nervous about playing in front of many extras, she told Lubitsch, "I don't think I can play it." Lubitsch insisted that she had no choice, telling her, "I'll do anything you want. I'll change the script, the dialogue, anything, but this can't be changed. Too much depends on it. You must make up your mind that you'll have to play it." He later noted, "I waited two weeks before starting that particular scene. When we did get to it, she was very—afraid is too strong a word—timid. But I finally got her to relax completely by talking to her and being patient. . . . I gave her confidence, gradually, so that when she came to the drinking scene she was completely at ease. And she played it beautifully."* Garbo was able to look at the film only after it had been cut and edited. Accompanied by Lubitsch, she attended a private showing of the film at the studio. "Do you like yourself in it?" Lubitsch asked her as the lights went up. "Even then," he remembered, "she didn't seem to know if she was bad or good."

She need not have worried. From her first entrance into the film, a dour and gloomy Russian envoy in a plain dress, to her transformed Ninotchka, rapturously kissing the man she loves, Garbo plays with a glowing enchantment that lights the entire film and makes one regret that she came so late to comedy. True, she has the support of a first-rate cast and a screenplay that bubbles like vintage champagne. (Why has wit vanished in screenwriting? Or is it merely hiding?) Even the opening legend tells us that we will spend the next 110 minutes in a departed but fondly remembered world: "This picture takes place in Paris in those wonderful days when a siren was a brunette and not an alarm . . . and if a Frenchman turned out the light it was not on account of an air raid!"

The opening sequences, before Ninotchka enters the scene, introduce us to Iranoff (Sig Rumann), Buljanoff (Felix Bressart), and Kopalski (Alexander Granach), the three Russian emissaries who have been sent to Paris to sell the imperial jewels for a starving Russia. Awed at first by the splendor of the hotel, they waste little time in taking advantage of all the "amenities." (Kopalski says, "Comrades, why should we lie to each other? It's wonderful.") The satire in these early scenes and, for that matter, in all the scenes that follow is actually so good-humored and toothless that it should be considered more of an affectionate spoof than true satire. At any rate, a Czarist spy at the hotel rushes to tell the Grand Duchess Swana (Ina Claire) that her jewels are being sold in Paris by three Communist emissaries.

The Grand Duchess and her dapper lover, Count Leon D'Algout (Melvyn Douglas), are clearly characters out of a world that was disappearing even in

---

*Bainbridge, John, *Garbo*. New York: Holt, Rinehart & Winston, 1971, p. 245.

Tipsy and deliriously happy in her love for Leon, Ninotchka demands to be "shot" as a traitor for betraying "the Russian ideal." Blindfolded, she awaits the gunshot (actually the pop of a champagne cork), but Leon has romance in mind.

1939; she is brittle, vain, and self-absorbed, and he is a well-heeled gigolo, living resourcefully by his wits, which are considerable. Swana wants her jewels back, and Leon is just the man to get them. He approaches the harried Russians, knowing full well that the Soviet government will never return the jewels. He must adopt a different plan, and with the practiced hand and eye of a true Parisian, he sets about seducing the vulnerable Russians with the pleasures of Paris. He also sends the movie spinning merrily into orbit as the Russians succumb. In a quintessentially Lubitschian sequence, we remain outside their hotel room as waiters first enter with platters of food to the sound of a satisfied "Ahh!" followed by a cigarette girl who provokes a joyful "Ah-ah!" from the men. The slightly flustered girl soon exits, only to return a moment later with two more cigarette girls. This time we hear an explosive "AH-AHH!" Economically, teasingly, and with cinematic flair, Lubitsch has told us everything we need to know about the human frailty behind the impassive Soviet mien.

Enter Nina Ivanovna Yakushova (a.k.a. Ninotchka), Envoy Extraordinary from Moscow and the very model of an unemotional, serious-minded Communist woman. She has been dispatched by the concerned Commissar to learn the reason for the delay in selling the jewels. From her first appearance, Garbo manages to be enchanting, absurd, and funny as she insists on carrying her own bags,* marvels at a chic Parisian hat ("How can such a civilization survive which permits their women to put things like that on their heads?"), and criticizes the bewildered emissaries for their extravagant hotel suite ("If I stay here a week, I will cost the Russian people seven cows."). On her way to tour the public utilities of Paris, she meets Leon, who is amused and entranced by this astonishing woman. His airy boulevardier patter collides with her no-nonsense practicality (*Ninotchka:* "Must you flirt?" *Leon:* "Well, I don't have to but I find it natural." *Ninotchka:* "Suppress it." *Leon:* "I'll try."). As they view the glories of Paris from the top of the Eiffel Tower, Ninotchka can see only a city about to become extinct, while Leon can see only a woman ripe for seduction.

In his apartment, in a scene of incomparable romantic charm, Leon works his practiced wiles on the cool and languorous Ninotchka. At first his words are hollow and insincere, the standard patter of a man-about-Paris, but soon, her extraordinary beauty and her ineffable air of mystery turn him into the victim instead of the prey. Although Ninotchka is determined to keep their relationship on a purely scientific level, a chemical meeting of male and female, Leon's feelings cannot be contained ("Oh, my barbaric Ninotchka! My divine, statistical Ninotchka!") as he tries to explain the complex emotion of love. She simply responds, "You are very talkative." Finally, he kisses her ("Was that

---

*When she tells the porter that his working for others is "social injustice," he replies with one of the best lines in the screenplay: "That depends on the tip."

Back in Moscow, Ninotchka enjoys a reunion with her friends (left to right) Kopalski (Alexander Granach), Iranoff (Sig Rumann), and Buljanoff (Felix Bressart). The three "Westernized" emissaries contributed delightful performances—Rumann and Bressart, in particular, were skilled actors who brightened many movies in the thirties and forties.

talkative?" "No, that was restful."), but all too soon, reality intrudes and he learns her identity. It appears that they are adversaries who cannot be lovers, yet a captivated Leon is not so sure.

This being romantic comedy, Ninotchka and Leon are destined to meet again soon, and they do, in a little working-class restaurant, where she orders raw beets and carrots. ("Madame," the owner tells her, "this is a restaurant, not a meadow.") Leon shows up, all affable charm as he tries to assure her that he is at home among working men. He tries to coax her into laughter with a few jokes but she remains stony-faced, until he tumbles from his chair. As Ninotchka explodes with laughter, we witness the first crack in her wall of Russian reserve and determination. Ninotchka begins to respond to the lure of Paris and as we see a new woman, we also see a new Garbo, relaxed, cheerful, and altogether winning. The actress moves radiantly through Ninotchka's scenes of discovery, shyly showing off her new hat for Leon, responding with ardor to his kisses, and even becoming jealous of his photograph of Swana.

At a restaurant, Ninotchka and Leon are spotted by the Grand Duchess, but Ninotchka is too blissfully in love to notice her rival. The two women finally meet and exchange sharp-edged banter, which leads Ninotchka, sad about her future with Leon, to her first unaccustomed bout with champagne. If Garbo was ill at ease about this scene, it certainly does not show on the screen. In thirties romantic comedy, it was customary for the leading lady to lose some of her inhibitions through alcohol, and the actress often seemed uncomfortable, a goddess pretending to be "one of the guys." Garbo makes no such mistake here—her tipsiness seems to be a natural manifestation of her newly released spirit. In the scene that follows in Leon's apartment, Garbo was perhaps never more rapturously beautiful. In her happy state of inebriation, she insists on being "shot" as a traitor for betraying the Russian ideal. Leon blindfolds her and stands her against the wall, and as the cork pops from the champagne, she sinks to the floor. ("I've paid the penalty. Now let's have some music.") After they look at the jewels together ("the tears of old Russia"), Leon places the sleepy Ninotchka in her bed and tiptoes out of the room, leaving audiences to savor an irresistibly funny and tender scene.

All too soon, Ninotchka has her happiness shattered by a visit from the Grand Duchess Swana. Eager to have Ninotchka leave Leon and Paris forever, Swana has a proposition. She also has the jewels, stolen from Ninotchka's safe by the loyal Czarist waiter. Swana promises to hand over the jewels only if Ninotchka will take the plane to Moscow. The scene offers a classic confrontation between two actresses whose acting styles could not be more different, with Garbo trained to keep part of herself elusive from the all-seeing eye of the camera, and Claire trained by the stage to project a character to the upper balcony. In this instance, the contrasting styles serve the characters well, creating a memorable sequence in which Lubitsch keeps them together in the frame to heighten the contrast. On the telephone with Leon, knowing that she must leave him, Garbo suggests something of her usual tragic roles. When he sends her a bottle of goat milk as a gift, she responds with a subtle mixture of sadness and delight.

Ninotchka returns to Russia, while Leon tries in vain to get a visa to follow her. In an amusing scene with the Russian visa official (George Tobias), he reacts angrily to the official's suspicions about his reason for visiting Russia ("I'll boycott you, that's what I'll do! No more vodka, no more caviar! No more Tchaikovsky! [the worst threat] No more borscht!"). Ninotchka leads her usual life in Russia, softened somewhat by her memories and by a happy reunion with those three "scoundrels," Iranoff, Buljanoff, and Kopalski. She also receives a letter from Leon, so heavily censored that all that remains is the salutation ("Ninotchka, my darling") and the closing ("Yours, Leon").

Later, Commissar Razinin (Bela Lugosi) summons Ninotchka to tell her that her help is needed again. Her three old friends are now in Constantinople (on her recommendation) but they have been unable to sell any fur to the government. Instead, they have been "dragging the good name of the country through every café and nightclub." Ninotchka goes on her mission reluctantly, but in Constantinople, she is greeted warmly by her three friends, all dressed in the height of capitalistic splendor and all proud owners of a new restaurant. She also discovers Leon, who has arranged for all this to happen. "They wouldn't let me in. So I had to get you out." As they kiss joyfully, the scene fades to a last shot of Kopalski, picketing his restaurant, where his is the only name not brightly lit in the sign. He is carrying a placard reading: BULJANOFF AND IRANOFF UNFAIR TO KOPALSKI.

In spite of enthusiastic reviews and three Oscar nominations (Best Picture, Best Actress, Best Original Story), *Ninotchka* proved to be a disappointment at the box office. Louis Mayer, who had opposed the film from the beginning, used it as an example of "classy" versus commercial entertainment. He would later say: "*Ninotchka* got everything but money. A Hardy picture cost twenty-five thousand less than Lubitsch was paid alone. But any good Hardy picture made five hundred thousand dollars more than *Ninotchka* made." Garbo would make only one more film, a rather dreary and tasteless comedy called *Two-Faced Woman*, this time under the direction of George Cukor.

Although *Ninotchka* may have ended on the wrong side of the business ledger at the time, a half-century later it has certainly earned its keep as well as a permanent place among the screen's great romantic comedies. Its gentle thrusts of satire may no longer apply, and its air of chic elegance may have grown a bit dusty. Yet in addition to having an historical role as the last great film of two masters—Greta Garbo and Ernst Lubitsch—it continues to delight us with its charm and wit. We never seem to tire of watching dour Ninotchka as she blossoms amidst the heart-lifting pleasures of the city of lights.*

Ninotchka. Metro-Goldwyn-Mayer. Produced and directed by Ernst Lubitsch. Screenplay by Charles Brackett, Billy Wilder, and Walter Reisch, from a story by Melchior Lengyel. Photography by William Daniels. Art direction by Cedric Gibbons. Costumes by Adrian. Edited by Gene Ruggiero. Cast: Greta Garbo, Melvyn Douglas, Ina Claire, Sig Rumann, Felix Bressart, Alexander Granach, and Bela Lugosi.

---

*Over the years, *Ninotchka* has had several remakes and spin-offs. The year after its release, MGM tried another romantic comedy that spoofed the strictness of the Soviet regime, but *Comrade X* (1940), with Clark Gable and beautiful Austrian actress Hedy Lamarr, was feeble at best. In 1955, *Ninotchka* was turned into a Cole Porter stage musical called *Silk Stockings*, which was filmed by Rouben Mamoulian in 1957, with Fred Astaire and Cyd Charisse. Ralph Thomas's 1956 movie *The Iron Petticoat*, starring the unlikely team of Bob Hope and Katharine Hepburn, lifted the *Ninotchka* theme in its story of a Russian lady aviator and an American Air Force officer.

Marlene Dietrich as Frenchy, the role that revitalized her career.

Showdown in Bottleneck: Destry Rides Again

"I'm gonna stay here and do this job I come for.
My pa did it the old way, and I'm gonna do it
the new way."
—James Stewart in *Destry Rides Again*

By the late thirties, some of the movie icons of earlier years were slipping into limbo. Greta Garbo, whose classic beauty and tragic demeanor had never been seen to better advantage than in *Camille* (1937), had followed that film with *Conquest* (1937), a turgid costume drama concerning the romance between Napoleon (Charles Boyer) and Polish countess Marie Walewska (Garbo). Shirley Temple's curls and dimples were not enchanting audiences as they had earlier in the decade, and after the poorly received *Blue Bird* in 1940, she would leave Fox studios forever. Although some stars, such as Bette Davis, Clark Gable, and James Cagney, were at the peak of their popularity, others were required to move in a new direction to reassert their status. In 1939, Fred Astaire made *The Story of Vernon and Irene Castle*, the last (and one of the least) of his RKO musical films with Ginger Rogers, then floundered for several years until regaining momentum in the early forties.

Another movie goddess was in severe decline in the late thirties. After some years as a mysteriously glamorous if rather remote figure in her mentor Josef von Sternberg's elegant melodramas and costume films, Marlene Dietrich had fallen on hard times. After leaving Sternberg in 1935, she made three films in which her masklike countenance and enigmatic personality no longer seemed quite as alluring. (Audiences preferred the no-nonsense directness of such home-grown actresses as Ginger Rogers.) Frank Borzage's *Desire* (1936), a romantic bauble concerning a beautiful jewel thief who falls in love with an American engineer (Gary Cooper), at least had a measure of wit in the screenplay and in Borzage's assured direction. Borzage also displayed more than a touch of the style of Ernst Lubitsch, Paramount's head of production at the time. Richard

Boleslawski's *The Garden of Allah* (1936) and Jacques Feyder's *Knight Without Armor* (1937), however, proved to be florid and heavy-handed romantic dramas that offered little more than a stunningly photographed Dietrich. *Angel* (1937), Ernst Lubitsch's return to direction after two years of producing, had some of his elegant style, but Samson Raphaelson's screenplay involving a triangular romance (Dietrich, with husband Herbert Marshall and lover Melvyn Douglas) was pallid and uninteresting, and the movie was not a success. When Paramount dropped her contract, Dietrich moved to Paris, convinced that her American career was ended.

Preparing to film a movie with French director Julien Duvivier, Dietrich received a surprising telegram from an old friend, producer Joe Pasternak, asking whether she would be interested in appearing in a new movie for Universal. She was astonished to learn that it would be a Western, a long distance from the exotic romances she had adorned for years. At first, she was both amused and dubious. "You must be crazy," she told Pasternak. "Haven't you heard? I'm box-office poison." Gallantly, Pasternak assured her that she would never be box-office poison, and after further cajoling, she accepted the role, none too enthusiastically. Even after she returned to Hollywood, she was convinced that she was making a serious mistake. The movie was *Destry Rides Again*, a loose version of a Max Brand novel that Universal had filmed in 1932 as cowboy star Tom Mix's first venture into sound.

Under the direction of George Marshall, a veteran of film comedy since the silent era, Dietrich would play the role of Frenchy, the rowdy saloon queen and singer on the wrong side of the law, who changes sides when she falls for the gentle but persuasive Destry. Pasternak surrounded Dietrich with a solidly professional cast: gawky, extremely likable Jimmy Stewart, who had just scored as a naïve senator in *Mr. Smith Goes to Washington*, as the deputy who refuses to carry a gun; Charles Winninger as the hard-drinking sheriff Wash Dimsdale; Mischa Auer as the comic gambler improbably named Boris Callahan, whose domineering wife Lily Belle (Una Merkel) insists on his using the name of her late first husband; and Brian Donlevy as Kent, the wicked town boss who owns and runs the saloon. Although she would no longer have the flattering, luminous photography that Lee Garmes brought to many of her Sternberg films, Dietrich could rely on the seasoned expertise of cameraman Hal Mohr to give her new image at least a suggestion of the old glamour. She met the challenge with a boisterous, all-stops-out performance that gave her a second career.

Dietrich's entry into the film is delayed so that the audience can get to know the Wild West town of Bottleneck. Even before the credits, we see the sign WELCOME TO BOTTLENECK and hear the raucous sounds of a town where gunfights are as common as poker games. In the aptly named Last Chance Saloon, bartender Loupgerou (Billy Gilbert) serves drinks to the rowdy clientele while Kent

Frenchy sings "You've Got That Look," backed by the dancing girls at the Last Chance Saloon. In the film, Dietrich sang three tunes by Frank Loesser and Frederick Hollander.

keeps a steely eye on the proceedings. Then we hear that inimitable voice, smoky, monotoned, and insinuating, and the camera moves through the crowd to stop at Frenchy, who is singing. She turns to face the camera, winks mischievously, and rolls a cigarette, all the while intoning the lyrics of "Little Joe the Wrangler."* With Frenchy, Dietrich has returned to the coarse, frank sensuality of her Lola-Lola in *The Blue Angel*, but this is Lola-Lola with a heart of gold concealed beneath her spangled costume. Frenchy answers to no man but Kent, yet she is domestic enough to offer sandwiches to the cardplayers in the back room. And although she participates in Kent's crooked scheme to cheat a farmer out of his property, we sense from the start that the right person could tap a deep well of decency that she has never acknowledged, even to herself.

Events are triggered when Kent's men kill the town's conscientious sheriff, and Wash Dimsdale, the local drunkard and universal object of derision, is mockingly appointed the new "sheriff" by Kent. Ostensibly, nothing will change in Bottleneck: Law and order will remain a joke; Kent will stay in control; and Frenchy will continue to entertain the men at the Last Chance Saloon. As Frenchy sings "You've Got That Look," the camera moves in for a close-up of Dietrich's

---

*All of Dietrich's songs in *Destry Rides Again* were written by Frank Loesser and Frederick Hollander. Earlier, Hollander had composed "Falling in Love Again," the song that the actress had immortalized in *The Blue Angel* (1930).

Amiable, drawling, and unarmed, Tom Destry (James Stewart) is welcomed to Bottleneck by an incredulous Wash (Charles Winninger) and Lily Belle Callahan (Una Merkel). Other new arrivals are brother and sister Janice and Jack Tyndall (Irene Hervey and Jack Carson).

Frenchy wins the pants of Boris Callahan (Mischa Auer, seated at her left) in a card game. A fixture in films of the thirties and forties, Auer frequently played eccentric, madcap Russians. (He was born in St. Petersburg.) Auer is perhaps best remembered for his lunatic gigolo who impersonated a gorilla for Alice Brady's amusement in *My Man Godfrey* (1936).

face, and an expression of brazen amusement passes across that famous enigmatic mask. But suddenly, everything is not the same: Taking his new job seriously, Wash sobers up long enough to send for Tom Destry, Jr., the son of the tough, legendary sheriff and town-tamer, whom Wash once served as deputy. "Destry will ride again!" he proclaims.

To Wash's amazement and chagrin, young Tom Destry (Stewart) turns out to be a sober, thoughtful, quiet-speaking man who refuses to carry a gun. (Asked by a baffled, amused Kent, why he will not use a gun, Tom drawls, "If I hadda gun, why, one of us might have got hurt, and it might have been me. I wouldn't have liked that, would I?") Tom also has the disconcerting habit of making his point by relating a story about a "friend" of his, who was in a similar predicament. Although his gentle ways meet with scorn from the townspeople, Tom manages to get results. His first chance is when he becomes involved in a wild brawl between Frenchy and Lily Belle Callahan over Boris's gambling debt. (Boris lost his pants to Frenchy in a card game.) When Tom stops the fight by pouring water over the scuffling ladies, a furious Frenchy threatens him with a gun and wrecks everything in sight.

One of the best-remembered cat fights in movie history, rivaled only by the Rosalind Russell–Paulette Goddard brawl in *The Women,* or possibly the Shirley MacLaine–Anne Bancroft imbroglio in *The Turning Point* (1977), the Frenchy–Lily Belle encounter left both actresses badly bruised. Dietrich refused to have a stand-in; she pulled hair, wrestled, punched, kicked, threw a succession of beer steins, buckets, and bottles, and was doused with cold water three times. The entire scene required five days of shooting, but at the end of it, the cool European seductress had become a hot-tempered, embattled saloon queen.

Tom's pacifism amuses everyone until they begin to realize the resolve behind it. "I'm gonna stay here and do this job I come for," he tells Wash. "My pa did it the old way, and I'm gonna do it the new way." Quietly, he begins to investigate the mysterious disappearance of the late sheriff, and he visits Frenchy to hint at her involvement in Kent's crooked dealings. Their scene together has a surprising depth of feeling: At first angry at his insinuation, Frenchy is startled when he suggests that another woman lurks behind all the makeup. "I'll bet you have a lovely face behind all that paint," he tells her. "Why don't you wipe it off someday and have a good look—and figure out how you can live up to it?" When he leaves, she gazes into the mirror and touches her face as if seeing it for the first time. Expertly played, the scene has a touching quality that deepens the story, at least for a moment.

While the women of the town, under Lily Belle's leadership, are organizing to oppose Kent, Tom goes about his plan of trapping Kent and his men into revealing the whereabouts of the body of the murdered sheriff. He persists, despite Frenchy's urgent warning—she has come to like and admire him, and her feelings may be even stronger. At the same time, she continues to entertain at the saloon, rendering the song "The Boys in the Back Room," which became one of the actress's trademark numbers. Transported from a Berlin cabaret to the Last Chance Saloon, Dietrich gives the song a brash, uninhibited directness that no other performer could hope to match. (Nearly a decade later, in Billy Wilder's *A Foreign Affair* (1948), Dietrich would indeed return to a Berlin cabaret, adding world-weary cynicism to the mix with new songs by Frederick Hollander, such as "Black Market" and "Illusions.")

When Tom finally arrests Gyp Watson (Warren Hymer), one of Kent's henchmen, for the sheriff's murder, the situation becomes tense and dangerous. Knowing that there can be no fair trial in Bottleneck with the corrupt judge (Samuel S. Hinds) presiding—he is also the mayor—Tom arranges for a federal judge to be sent to the town. To thwart a trial, Kent plans to break Gyp out of the jailhouse. Frenchy deliberately keeps Tom away to prevent him from being killed in the breakout, and so Wash alone is fatally shot. Tom's face expresses both rage and quiet sorrow as he cradles his dying old friend in his arms. Strapping on his guns, he expresses the common credo of the day: A man must take a stand against violent assault, even, if necessary, by taking up arms against the enemy. Tom Destry's earlier defense of the moral power of law and order vanishes before the brutal onslaught of Kent, and now armed, he ventures into the saloon for a showdown with Kent.*

He has help: The women of the town, fired into taking action by Frenchy, join together to march down its center, wielding clubs and determined to oust Kent and his men. A wild melee ensues as they storm into the saloon and take up battle with the enemy. In the midst of the fracas, Frenchy sees Kent stalking Tom, and she hurls herself in front of him, taking the bullet instead. Kent is shot dead, but now Frenchy has been fatally wounded. As Tom holds her, she gasps, saying, "Won't you kiss me goodbye?" wipes her hand across her mouth to remove her lipstick as a final gesture, and dies. (Originally, her line was: "Kiss me, good fella.") Afterward, we see the new Bottleneck, now peaceful and governed by law and order. But as a group of children sing about "Little Joe," a slight smile passes across Tom's face as he remembers Frenchy and her ultimate sacrifice.

George Marshall's direction is brisk but commonplace, yet *Destry Rides Again* never fails to divert with its combination of raucous farce and standard Western action, and its robust performances, especially by Stewart and the new unre-

---

*Thirteen years later, in an entirely different era, Sheriff Will Kane (Gary Cooper), in Fred Zinneman's *High Noon* (1952), also takes a stand against evil forces, but this time instead of urging him on, the townspeople retreat into cowardice and desert him entirely. One might deduce that the aggressive prewar spirit of 1939 had been replaced by the uneasy McCarthyism of 1952.

One of the great movie catfights: Frenchy vs. Lily Belle. "Ya gilded lily!" Lily Belle shrieks, and the melee begins. The sequence removed forever the image of Dietrich as the icy, exotic glamour queen.

strained Dietrich. Much of the screenplay, credited to Felix Jackson, Gertrude Purcell, and Henry Myers, includes sly send-ups of Western conventions. The town's mayor (also judge) is not the usual bumbling, ineffectual fool but a happily self-serving, cardplaying crook who wears a stovepipe hat. Frenchy's black maid is not a devoted, adoring mammy but a sassy minx who welcomes Frenchy's cast-off clothing. The Last Chance's bartender is no surly stoic who dispenses drinks but a harassed, complaining oaf. The film's climactic brawl involves not only a bevy of cowboys and gunslingers but also a contingent of club-wielding, *Lysistrata*-like women, out to settle accounts with the town's wild, corrupt element. With great humor, *Destry Rides Again* turns the clichés of the genre on their ear, applying a comic context that would later broaden into Mel Brooks's Western burlesque *Blazing Saddles* (1974).

Frenchy sings "(See What) The Boys in the Back Room (Will Have)" to a highly receptive audience. Dietrich's Frenchy had some of the coarseness of Lola-Lola, the tawdry nightclub singer she had made famous in *The Blue Angel* (1930). The important difference was that Frenchy, unlike Lola-Lola, had a proverbial heart of gold beneath her brassy exterior.

Fatally shot, Frenchy dies in Tom's arms, but not before wiping her hand across her mouth to remove her lipstick as a final gesture to the man she clearly loves. Dietrich received glowing notices for her lusty performance.

The film won high praise from the critics, who found it a refreshing approach to a perennial genre, but not unexpectedly, much of the enthusiasm was reserved for the "new" Dietrich. From *Destry Rides Again*, she went on to play other flamboyant women of questionable reputation, most notably in her next two films, Tay Garnett's *Seven Sinners* (1940) and René Clair's *The Flame of New Orleans* (1941), where her aggressive sexuality dominated the action in amusing style. Later, she would be ill-served when her character would be shunted into the background so that the two male leads could battle for her favors—Edward G. Robinson and George Raft fought over her in *Manpower* (1941), and John Wayne and Randolph Scott clashed twice, in *The Spoilers* and *Pittsburgh*, both released in 1942. Jimmy Stewart would forgo Westerns until the fifties, when he started to appear in a series of superior Western films directed by Anthony Mann, where layers of ambiguity and subtle new coloration were added to his easygoing personality. *Destry Rides Again* would be remade twice, first as *Frenchie* (1951), in which Shelley Winters tried gamely to suggest the bold manner of a saloon queen, and *Destry* (1954), which had Audie Murphy as the laid-back hero who tames Bottleneck. George Marshall repeated as director, without matching or even approaching his earlier success.

Destry Rides Again was one of the year's successes, earning no Academy Award nominations but attracting large audiences who enjoyed its raucous humor or were curious to see the "transformation" of Marlene Dietrich. Many years later, in her one-woman show, the actress would receive enthusiastic applause whenever she began singing about "The Boys in the Back Room." ("Just see what the boys in the back room will have. And tell them I died of the same.") It signaled that, although decades had passed since Frenchy had given up her life for Tom Destry, the character—and the actress who played her—had left an indelible impression on our collective memory.

Destry Rides Again. Universal. Produced by Joseph Pasternak. Directed by George Marshall. Screenplay by Felix Jackson, Gertrude Purcell, and Henry Myers, from a novel by Max Brand. Photography by Hal Mohr. Songs by Frank Loesser and Frederick Hollander. Art direction by Jack Otterson. Costumes by Vera West. Edited by Milton Carruth. Cast: Marlene Dietrich, James Stewart, Charles Winninger, Mischa Auer, Brian Donlevy, Una Merkel, Samuel S. Hinds, Irene Hervey, Billy Gilbert, Warren Hymer, and Jack Carson. Previously filmed in 1932, and remade as *Frenchie* in 1951 and as *Destry* in 1954.

In one of the film's first scenes, Scarlett O'Hara (Vivien Leigh) revels in the attention of her adoring suitors. From the beginning, Leigh succeeds in capturing Scarlett's Southern-belle flirtatiousness and mercurial temperament.

A Dream Remembered:
Gone With the Wind

"We're alike—bad lots, both of us. Selfish and
shrewd, but able to look things in the eyes and call
them by their right name."
—Clark Gable to Vivien Leigh in *Gone With the Wind*

GWTW. Then and now, the letters are
sufficient to evoke the movie: David O. Selznick's massive production of Margaret Mitchell's novel of the Old South, *Gone With the Wind*. In a decade of filmmaking that had closed with an extraordinary number of memorable movies, *GWTW* marked a summit, a splendid and matchless amalgam of talent, skill, and ballyhoo. When the film had its premiere in Atlanta, Los Angeles, and New York City, in December of 1939, Selznick and the American public held their collective breath. For Selznick, it was the culmination of years of agonizing, exhilarating—and extremely costly—effort. For the public, the movie was the visualization of a novel that had enthralled them with its romantic story. It was a triumph all around: Selznick saw his vision justified; the public saw the characters and events of a favorite book spring to life on the screen. Amazingly, a half-century later, the same film, in a restored version, was shown to audiences in three special, reserved-seat performances at New York City's showplace— Radio City Music Hall. The same letters were all that were needed: *GWTW*.

It all began with a teletype message on May 20, 1936, from Katharine (Kay) Brown, Selznick International's Eastern Story Editor, to her boss, producer David O. Selznick. The message read: WE HAVE JUST AIRMAILED DETAILED SYNOPSIS OF GONE WITH THE WIND BY MARGARET MITCHELL. ALSO COPY OF BOOK. I BEG, URGE, COAX AND PLEAD WITH YOU TO READ IT AT ONCE. I KNOW THAT AFTER YOU DO YOU WILL DROP EVERYTHING AND BUY IT. Kay Brown was wrong. Five days later, Selznick wrote her a long memo turning down the book. ". . . I do not feel we can take such a gamble," he said, concluding that he was "most sorry to have to say no in face of your enthusiasm for this story."

Kay Brown's "enthusiasm" was entirely understandable, considering the unprecedented nationwide acclaim and excitement that were being generated by Margaret Mitchell's panoramic novel revolving around a willful Southern vixen named Scarlett O'Hara. Even before its official publication date of June 30, the word of mouth was astonishing. Over sixty thousand copies had already been shipped to retailers, which, together with the forty thousand ordered by the Book-of-the-Month Club, brought a total of one hundred thousand copies into print. Nobody was more amazed than the author herself, a thirty-five-year-old Atlanta woman married (for the second time) to an advertising executive named John Marsh. As "Peggy Mitchell," she had been a popular columnist with the *Atlanta Journal* from 1923 to 1926, and after leaving the newspaper, incapacitated by arthritis and a badly sprained ankle, she had started to write a novel about the Civil War, filling ream after ream of paper with material typed on her Remington portable. By 1930, when she was about two-thirds of the way into the book, many stacks of manila envelopes filled her closet. By the time the book was largely completed, early in 1935, the size of the manuscript was staggering.

When the book came to the attention of a traveling Macmillan editor named Harold Latham, Peggy Marsh was extremely reluctant to show it to him. (At first, she even denied that she had written a novel!) She felt that she could not be taken seriously as a writer and, in fact, asked Latham to return the manuscript to her, after she had submitted it at a friend's suggestion. Latham, however, was impressed and recommended publication. By late July, she had received a contract offering her an advance payment of five hundred dollars and a royalty of ten percent for the first ten thousand copies, with an escalation to fifteen percent after that point. For the next few months, she worked on making substantial revisions, incidentally changing her heroine's name from Pansy to Scarlett and finding her title in a line from a famous poem by Ernest Dowson: "I have forgot much, Cynara! Gone with the wind." She believed the line suggested something of the destruction of the Old South's gentle and refined ways by the ravages of the Civil War.

The book's publication in mid-1936 brought an unprecedented response from the public. Within weeks, all copies were disappearing from the stores, and a startled Macmillan found itself unable to keep pace with the demand. By mid-July, the publisher was promising a sixth printing and stating gleefully that an amazing total of 140,000 copies was already in print. The raging enthusiasm continued to spread throughout the summer months—after all, could there be any better vacation reading?—and by September, with 370,000 copies in print, *Gone With the Wind* (or *GWTW* as it was called in the press) had become the

Mammy (Hattie McDaniel) expresses her usual disapproval of Scarlett's behavior. Forty-nine when she appeared in the film, McDaniel had toured the black theatrical belt for many years, playing in tent shows, vaudeville, cabarets, and on the legitimate stage. Her well-deserved Oscar for this performance was the first awarded to a black actress.

fastest-selling book of all time. The reviews, on the whole, were extremely favorable, although no critic felt that it belonged in the realm of durable literature. *The New York Times* reviewer J. Donald Adams, while conceding that it was not a great novel, found it "a book of uncommon quality, a superb piece of story-telling which nobody who finds pleasure in the art of fiction can afford to neglect." Even *The New Yorker* praised Margaret Mitchell as "a staggeringly gifted storyteller," calling the book "more than a novel, perhaps a whole library in itself." The trade magazine *Publishers Weekly* went so far as to call *Gone With the Wind* "very possibly the greatest American novel."

If Kay Brown had caught "Scarlett fever," other movie people were as immune as David Selznick to the book's potential as a film. At Metro-Goldwyn-Mayer, production head Irving Thalberg told Louis B. Mayer, "Forget it. No Civil War picture ever made a nickel." Jack Warner turned down the book for his studio, buttressed by director Mervyn LeRoy's claim that Civil War films never succeeded at the box office. RKO head Pandro Berman rejected the book because he could only see Katharine Hepburn as Scarlett and the actress was currently "box-office poison." Selznick only reconsidered when wealthy John Hay ("Jock") Whitney, his company's chairman of the board and principal backer, enthusiastic about the novel, wired Selznick that he would consider buying the property himself if the producer didn't buy it for their company. By July 1936,

Selznick had wired Kay Brown: IF YOU CAN CLOSE "GONE WITH THE WIND" FOR 50,000, DO SO. . . . I CANNOT SEE MY WAY CLEAR TO PAYING ANY MORE THAN 50,000. The offer was accepted, a contract was signed on July 30, and Selznick began the monumental task of turning a widely beloved book into an epic motion picture.

Any discussion of *Gone With the Wind* must begin and end with Selznick, who was undeniably the single driving force behind its creation. A dynamic, intensely ambitious man with a quicksilver mind and an all-consuming passion for moviemaking, Selznick had already made an impressive mark in the film industry by 1939. The son of Lewis J. Selznick, a once-prominent film magnate whose various business ventures had ultimately toppled, he shared his younger brother Myron's belief that other film tycoons were responsible for his father's downfall. Myron became one of Hollywood's most powerful agents, delighting in drawing blood from studio moguls. David, however, had other ideas. Determined to restore the family name, he joined a floundering RKO Pictures in October 1931, where, as Vice President in Charge of Production, he helped to reverse the studio's fortunes with such profitable movies as *A Bill of Divorcement* (1932), *What Price Hollywood* (1932), and that classic tale of monster love, *King Kong* (1933). Going to Metro-Goldwyn-Mayer in February 1933 at the behest of his father-in-law, Louis B. Mayer, Selznick produced some of the studio's most glittering triumphs of the period, including *Dinner at Eight* (1933), *David Copperfield* (1934), and *A Tale of Two Cities* (1935). Still, he was anxious to head his own company, and despite the huge risks, he left MGM in June 1935 to form Selznick International. Assuming full control of every production, overseeing every detail through an extraordinary stream of memoranda that were known to anger or intimidate many of his directors, he turned out a number of polished entertainments such as *A Star Is Born, The Prisoner of Zenda,* and *Nothing Sacred,* all released in 1937. By the time he was ready to produce *Gone With the Wind,* he had established a firm reputation, but his company was far from solvent.

By the fall of 1936, Selznick had set in motion the extraordinarily complex project that would take him through three years of decision making, infighting, and reversals, followed by acclaim in the waning months of 1939. Although most of the country's—and the world's—attention focused on the casting, especially the role of Scarlett O'Hara, there was no aspect of the production that escaped the scrutiny of the trade papers, which dutifully recorded every portentous announcement of every clash of wills and temperaments between Selznick and many of the participants. At first, his decisions came easily. To write the screenplay, he chose Sidney Howard, the brilliant, reclusive dramatist who had already adapted several of his own plays to the screen (*The Silver Cord,* 1933; *Dodsworth,* 1936, among others). To direct the film, he selected George Cukor, an erudite, fastidious man whose long association with the producer extended

Rhett Butler (Clark Gable), "that most daring of all blockade-runners," shocks Atlanta society by insisting on young widow Scarlett as his partner for the Virginia reel. He tells Scarlett, "I expect a very fancy profit out of it."

back to RKO and MGM, where he directed a number of Selznick's most successful films. Within months of signing Cukor for the formidable job, Selznick had him hunting locations in the South and starting a preliminary search for Scarlett. Almost before the ink was dry on the contract purchasing the book, Selznick's memoranda began to spill over with suggestions for the principal roles. Yet before the film was completed, a large number of writers would have grappled with the screenplay, several other directors would have worked on the film, and during the first year, the brouhaha over casting would assume gargantuan proportions.

If *Gone With the Wind* can be called the ultimate Hollywood movie, the principal steps that went into its production can be called the ultimate Hollywood story: a tangled web of outsize egos, ambitions, and talents in furious contention. As always, David Selznick stood at the spinning center, determined to have his way with every aspect of his most important film. The record of his relationships with the numerous writers shows a man with firm ideas about how to compress Margaret Mitchell's massive tale of the Old South into a screenplay that would not be impossibly long or cluttered. He also fancied himself as a writer as well, and much of the finished script contains his handiwork. When Sidney Howard completed his adaptation in January 1937, Selznick worked diligently with him on revisions, and even after the "official" screenplay was completed in November of that year, many other writers worked on it, under Selznick's close supervision, even after shooting began early in 1939. Some of the writers, such as F. Scott Fitzgerald and John Van Druten, had achieved fame in fiction and the theater, while others, such as Oliver H. P. Garrett, Jo Swerling, and John Lee Mahin, had labored long and hard in the Hollywood mills.

One of the most colorful writers who contributed to the screenplay was Ben Hecht, the cantankerous, eccentric novelist and journalist who loathed Hollywood but found it a convenient source of sizable income. (He wrote, doctored, or collaborated on a great many scripts.) Only weeks into the filming of *Gone With the Wind*, Hecht was summoned by Selznick to revise the screenplay, which by now was a patchwork of changes by various hands. Working feverishly for five days, with Selznick very close at hand, Hecht reshaped and tightened Sidney Howard's original screenplay—which he admired—cutting away the excess material that had grown around the many rewrites. Accounts vary as to what actually happened—Hecht's own version may have been distorted or exaggerated—but apparently on the fourth or fifth day of work, Selznick collapsed while eating a banana and had to be revived by a doctor. His exhaustion may have been due in part to his lack of sleep—Selznick would sometimes stay awake for seventy-two hours, working or gambling compulsively. Hecht seems to have survived the ordeal, considerably richer for having principally contributed the rather flowery series of titles that connect the main sections of the film.*

No aspect of the production created as much of a nationwide uproar as the casting. From the time the film was announced, countless people seemed to feel that the book was *their* personal property and that the screen incarnations of

---

*Other writers who worked, or were reputed to have worked, on the screenplay include: John Balderston, Michael Foster, Barbara Keon, Wilbur G. Kurtz, Val Lewton, Charles MacArthur, Edwin Justus Mayer, Winston Miller, and Donald Ogden Stewart. Doubtlessly, many of the writers could relate stories as odd as Hecht's. Jo Swerling, for example, traveled to Bermuda with Selznick and four cases packed with drafts of the screenplay. Two months later, the script was not much improved. Final credit for the screenplay went solely to Sidney Howard.

the characters, especially that of Scarlett O'Hara, had to meet *their* specifications. There were threats of retaliation if a Southern girl was not cast as Margaret Mitchell's tempestuous heroine. Readers who had devoured the book felt that it was their sworn duty to make known to the producer their choices for the role. When Selznick launched a nationwide search for the actress who would play Scarlett, the reverberations could be heard from Maine to California. In Hollywood, virtually every young actress who could draw breath, with the possible exception of Shirley Temple, began to see herself in crinoline, exclaiming "Fiddle-dee-dee!"

The other central roles presented problems, but there was much less hoopla surrounding them, and the process of selection remained a largely private affair. It was clear from the start that virtually everyone saw only Clark Gable in the part of the dashing, roguish Rhett Butler. MGM's leading box-office attraction for years, Gable projected a virility and a bemused "take them or leave them" attitude toward women that his legion of fans found singularly attractive. He seemed the embodiment of Rhett Butler, and although other actors (Gary Cooper, Ronald Colman) were considered fleetingly, Selznick knew early on that he had to have Gable. He began negotiations with his father-in-law, Louis B. Mayer, who would have preferred to see Selznick back at MGM rather than heading a rival company. After considerable haggling, Selznick and Mayer came to terms: MGM would lend Gable at a figure considerably larger than his usual salary and provide half of the film's financing in return for the world distribution rights and half of the total profits.* It was a fine arrangement for MGM, but Gable himself was not overjoyed. Cautious and insecure despite his rugged public persona, he was extremely nervous about tackling a role that embodied countless fantasies. (He was quoted as saying, "I don't want the part for money, marbles, or chalk.") The money was excellent, however, and facing the cost of a dissolving marriage—he was in love with actress Carole Lombard and would marry her during the filming of the movie—he agreed to take on the role of Rhett Butler.

Gable was not the only actor who resisted appearing in a major role in *Gone With the Wind*. Although he figures importantly in the story, the character of Ashley Wilkes, Melanie's ineffectual husband and the object of Scarlett's over-the-years adoration, was not exactly an actor's dream. While many actors coveted the part, and Melvyn Douglas and Jeffrey Lynn were among those tested, Selznick's only real choice for Ashley was British actor Leslie Howard. Blondly handsome and refined, Howard seemed at least physically appropriate for the role, despite his British accent and his age. (He was forty-six at the time and

---

*Another offer had come earlier from Warners. They would lend Bette Davis as Scarlett, Errol Flynn as Rhett, and Olivia de Havilland as Melanie in exchange for only twenty-five percent of the profit. Selznick gave the offer only momentary consideration, since he was unenthusiastic about Davis as Scarlett.

Melanie (Olivia de Havilland) gratefully accepts a donation of money from Belle Watling (Ona Munson), a notorious Atlanta madam and Rhett Butler's good friend. Scarlett and Mrs. Meade (Leona Roberts) show their disapproval. De Havilland's sensitive performance managed to bring some dimension to a one-note character.

actually some years too old for Ashley.) Like Gable, Howard was extremely reluctant to accept the part, feeling that he had played perhaps one too many pallid and genteel young men. When Selznick promised to make him the associate producer of his next film, *Intermezzo* (1939), in which he would costar with Swedish actress Ingrid Bergman, Howard agreed to play the role.

No actress demonstrated an equal reluctance to appear in *Gone With the Wind.* The role of Melanie, forever sweet-natured, steadfast, and loyal, required an actress who could suggest the strength and courage behind all the stifling virtue. As usual, many actresses were tested, including Andrea Leeds, Anne Shirley, and a starlet at RKO named Lucille Ball, but the leading contender was Warners' contract player Olivia de Havilland, who had been recommended to Selznick by her sister Joan Fontaine, a candidate for Scarlett. When Jack Warner refused to lend her, claiming that she was being groomed for major stardom, the firm-minded de Havilland campaigned actively to be released for the part, and she finally succeeded. Her radiant beauty, and her intelligent approach to a fairly one-dimensional role, helped to give the film an emotional resonance, especially in the second half.

Other women's roles were well cast, none more so than the central role of Mammy, the tenacious and sassy black housekeeper who weathers the storms that destroy Tara and the Old South. To play Mammy, Selznick chose Hattie McDaniel, an actress who, by way of her color and bulk, had been relegated for years to the traditional servant roles in such films as *The Little Colonel* (1935) and *Show Boat* (1936). In *Gone With the Wind*, she was once again the loyal servant, but McDaniel endowed the role with such vigor and conviction that she made it her own: a figure of dignity who was able to see clearly through all the sham and hypocrisy that surrounded her. Another black actress in the cast was less fortunate—as the simpleminded Prissy ("Ah don' know nothin' 'bout birthin' babies"), Butterfly McQueen was required to play the epitome of "darkie" dumbness; for many years afterward, into the present day, she regretted playing the role.* Other important parts went to Ona Munson as the good-hearted madam Belle Watling (reputedly, Tallulah Bankhead rejected the role with a barrage of insults); to Laura Hope Crews as the fluttery Aunt Pittypat; and to Barbara O'Neil, a character actress who often brought a touch of nervous fragility to her roles, as the ill-fated Mrs. O'Hara.

As other roles were filled (Thomas Mitchell as Gerald O'Hara; Evelyn Keyes as Suellen O'Hara; Harry Davenport as Dr. Meade), the central question remained: Who would play Scarlett O'Hara, that light-headed Southern belle who becomes a hardheaded and tenacious Southern woman? The selection of the actress for the all-important role soon turned into much more than a simple process of testing and elimination; under the direction of Selznick's publicity director Russell Birdwell, it became a worldwide guessing game, a topic of national interest that loomed even larger than any rumblings of war across the ocean, and a bonanza for newspapers and magazines. The roll call of actresses who would have probably lied, cheated, or even killed for the role reads like a veritable "Who's Who" of the silver screen of the time, although some of the candidates provoke a startled "Who?"

From the vantage point of half a century, it is difficult to imagine how Selznick could have taken some of the contenders seriously. Although Alabama born and bred, Tallulah Bankhead, the first of the thirty-two actresses tested for the role, would have turned Scarlett into a basso-profundo blunderbuss. Katharine Hepburn was strongly considered, but she was just coming out of a long period as "box-office poison," and it would have been hard to transform her Bryn Mawr twang into a Southern drawl. Norma Shearer, a popular favorite in the running, claimed that she rejected the role because it went against her

---

*Shortly after the movie's release, there was strong adverse reaction by the black press, which denounced it as crude, subversive propaganda. The protest was short-lived, especially after Hattie McDaniel won the Oscar.

fans' perception of her as ladylike and invariably soignée; more likely, she recognized her unsuitability for the fiery young Scarlett of the early reels. Bette Davis seemed a reasonable choice, and when she was out of the running, she retaliated by starring at Warners as another willful Southern belle in William Wyler's *Jezebel* (1938). Her Oscar-winning performance must have compensated in part for losing *Gone With the Wind*.*

The months passed, and potential Scarletts came and went. Surviving screen tests reveal a number of woefully inexperienced young actresses with only the vaguest grasp of the role. Among them were a pouting, teenaged Lana Turner, a coy Susan Hayward (then known as Edythe Marrener), and such pretty but vapid ingenues as Frances Dee and Anita Louise. One actress emerged as a leading candidate. Paulette Goddard, who had appeared opposite Charlie Chaplin in *Modern Times* (1936), impressed Selznick with her spirited and credible reading of the part (existing scenes from her test reveal that she was surprisingly good), and for a while she was the front-runner. When rumors about her "questionable" relationship with Chaplin began to surface, Selznick pushed the panic button and changed his mind, especially after Goddard refused to produce a marriage license.

By November 1938, only months away from the start of filming, Selznick still had no Scarlett O'Hara. Many months earlier, in February of 1937, he had heard of a young British actress named Vivien Leigh, but he had not seen even a photograph of her or screened one of her films. He remained unimpressed after seeing her in *Fire Over England* (1937), where she appeared opposite Laurence Olivier and Flora Robson. By the time that Selznick had started to exhaust his supply of potential Scarletts, Leigh had arrived in Hollywood to visit Olivier, with whom she was very much in love. (He was filming *Wuthering Heights*, and she was harboring a secret thought that she might replace Merle Oberon in the leading role.) She also coveted the role of Scarlett O'Hara; since the book's publication, she had pored over its pages, imagining herself in the role and convinced that she would someday get the chance to play it.

By now, the fateful meeting of David Selznick and Vivien Leigh has acquired legendary status, and even if one questions some of the details or wonders whether it was actually a pre-arranged publicity stunt, it remains a fascinating tale of Hollywood. Before the filming began in January 1939, Selznick had been convinced that he could get a sizable head start by shooting the crucial sequence of the burning of Atlanta. Old sets, strewn over forty acres, including the imposing Great Gate that was meant to keep King Kong out of the native village,

---

*After *Jezebel* was released, Selznick sent an angry letter to Jack Warner about its similarities to *Gone With the Wind*. ("The picture throughout is permeated with characterizations, attitudes, and scenes which unfortunately resemble *Gone With the Wind*. . . .")

With Melanie in labor, Scarlett sends Prissy (Butterfly McQueen) to find Dr. Meade. One of today's few survivors of the filming, McQueen often expressed her disapproval of the stereotyped character she played, but most viewers fondly remember her dim-witted, shrieking Prissy.

would be set afire and doubles of the cast would ride through the conflagration consuming the city. On Saturday evening, December 10, with the complex logistics nervously in place, the fire was started while Selznick, his workers, and virtually every firefighter in Culver City watched with awe and trepidation. Legend enters at this point. According to most reliable reports, Myron Selznick arrived on the set with his dinner guests Vivien Leigh and Laurence Olivier. When his brother was within earshot, Myron invited him to meet the actress who would play Scarlett O'Hara.* Selznick turned to see Vivien Leigh's lovely face illuminated by the light of the blaze. Years afterward, he maintained, "I took one look and knew that she was right—at least right as far as her appearance went . . . at least right as far as my conception of how Scarlett O'Hara looked. . . .

---

*Accounts vary as to what Myron Selznick actually said to his brother. Alexander Walker's account in his book *Vivien* (New York: Weidenfeld and Nicolson, 1987) sounds most persuasive. According to Walker, Myron, three sheets to the wind as usual, and often sarcastic with David, said, "Hey, genius, meet your Scarlett O'Hara!" The documentary on the making of the film confirms this account.

I'll never recover from that first look." In mid-January of 1939, after a search that had taken two years and had cost $92,000, he announced his signing of Vivien Leigh to play Scarlett.

The course of the director's lot on *Gone With the Wind* proved to have its own share of pitfalls and problems. Although George Cukor had been part of the production virtually from its inception, his relationship with David Selznick was becoming increasingly tense as filming got under way on January 26, 1939. Three weeks into the filming, Selznick was complaining vociferously about Cukor's slow pace, his muted use of color,* and his continual refusal to agree with his (Selznick's) judgment. For his part, Cukor felt that he was failing but that the fault lay with an inferior screenplay, not with him. He wanted the Sidney Howard version restored. There was also the question of Cukor's seeming preference for working with his female stars Vivien Leigh and Olivia de Havilland, and his coolness toward his male star Clark Gable, which may not have had any basis in truth. At any rate, a joint announcement by Selznick and Cukor on February 13 stated that "As a result of a series of disagreements . . . we have mutually decided that the only solution is for a new director to be selected at as early a date as is practicable." Despite ardent protests by Leigh and de Havilland, Selznick was adamant about firing Cukor, who went on to direct *The Women*. However, most of his work remains in the film, especially in the early part of the story during which characters are strongly established.

After the production closed down briefly, Cukor was replaced by Victor Fleming, an MGM director who was finishing *The Wizard of Oz* for the studio. A vigorous "man's man," and a close friend of Gable's, Fleming was extremely reluctant to take on the massive problems of *Gone With the Wind*, but he was finally persuaded. The filming resumed with a more relaxed Gable and a much uneasier Leigh and de Havilland, who were extremely distressed by Cukor's firing, and who were, unknown to each other, receiving private coaching from Cukor in the evenings. Under the stress of the long hours, the amazingly complex and outsize physical production, and the friction between the participants, Victor Fleming's health deteriorated. (Selznick himself was surviving on thyroid extract and Benzedrine.) Shortly after filming Melanie's death scene, Fleming became embroiled in yet another argument with Vivien Leigh and stormed off the set in a state of nervous collapse. (He later admitted that he considered driving his car off a cliff.) Director Sam Wood was quickly summoned from MGM and after two weeks of rest, Fleming was cajoled by Selznick into returning to complete the film. His first job was to film the famous climactic sequence in

---

*Cinematographer Lee Garmes was later replaced by Ernest Haller, who gave Selznick what he wanted. Much later, however, Selznick admitted that he had acted unfairly in dismissing Garmes.

In the war-ravaged Tara, Scarlett comes upon a Union deserter (Paul Hurst), who is desperately looking for food. A moment later, she will shoot him in the face, and Melanie, drawing on her waning energy, will help her dispose of the body.

which Scarlett, unbroken by her tribulations, vows at dawn to "never go hungry again."*

No account, however brief, of the making of *Gone With the Wind* can fail to mention the principal behind-the-camera figures who managed to weather the turbulence of an epic production and survive with their skill and artistry intact. Perhaps the most important of these figures was William Cameron Menzies, the veteran art director who coordinated the composition and color design of the entire film, giving it a richness and glow that survive to the present day. (Menzies

*In a long, impassioned letter to Frank Capra on January 22, 1940, Selznick defended his treatment of the directors, apparently after having been accused by the Directors Guild of being unfair and high-handed in his treatment of them on *Gone With the Wind*.

made more than twenty-five hundred sketches to guide the director and cinematographers in reconstructing the look of the Old South from the pre-to-post-Civil War days. He even suggested lighting and camera angles.) Other significant contributions were made by Walter Plunkett's sumptuous costumes, Lyle Wheeler's impeccable art direction, Jack Cosgrove's special effects, Hal Kern and James E. Newcom's editing, and the dazzling camera work of Ernest Haller and Ray Rennahan. (Rennahan was assigned as special adviser from the Technicolor company.) Also worth noting is Wilbur G. Kurtz, a Georgia historian who was hired by Selznick to oversee the film's historical accuracy.

Max Steiner's lush musical score for *Gone With the Wind* almost never made it into the film. Borrowed from Warners to write the score, Steiner worked on an almost impossible deadline, trying to compose the music for both *Gone With the Wind* and the Warners drama *Four Daughters* (1938). When he told Selznick that he was unable to finish the score, Selznick let it be known that he intended to replace Steiner with Herbert Stothart, head of MGM's music department. According to a Selznick memo, Stothart was "simply frantic with eagerness and enthusiasm to do it." A furious Steiner redoubled his efforts, composing almost all of the more than three hours of music that the film required. His original melodies, including the soaring "Tara" theme, were blended with Civil War songs and American folk tunes. (In his authoritative book on Selznick,* Ronald Haver notes that fragments of scores from other films can be found at several points in *Gone With the Wind*.)

As the filming continued throughout the spring, nerves became increasingly frayed and tensions mounted steadily as the race to complete the project accelerated. By June, the company confronted the last major production problem, that of filming the scene of Scarlett searching for Dr. Meade among the wounded and dying soldiers sprawled at the Atlanta railroad station. To achieve the memorably panoramic effect, the studio had to locate the largest construction crane in Southern California, one that had an extension range of 125 feet. A crane was found that required special handling, but another dilemma loomed in trying to assemble the nearly two thousand extras required for the scene. When Central Casting could provide only eight hundred extras, it was decided to use hundred of dummies, interspersed among the extras. An elaborate rigging was set up allowing many of the dummies to "move" as if real.

On June 27, the final scene was shot under Victor Fleming's direction.† Surprisingly, considering the fragmented nature of the production, it was close to the very end of the film, when Rhett leaves Scarlett, ostensibly forever. Aware

---

* *David O. Selznick's Hollywood* (New York: Bonanza Books, 1980).

† Selznick wired John Hay Whitney: SOUND THE SIREN. SCARLETT OHARA COMPLETED HER PERFORMANCE AT NOON TODAY.

that the existing motion-picture code prohibited the use of the word *damn*, Selznick filmed the scene in two versions, with Rhett saying "Frankly, my dear, I don't give a damn" ("frankly" was added at the last minute) and also "I just don't care." But now, as the massive job of editing got under way, and preparations began for the first previews, Selznick also knew that faithful readers of the book would never accept the substitution. In a letter to Will Hays, who administered the code for the Motion Picture Producers and Distributors of America, he pleaded to be allowed to use the word "damn." (". . . this word as used in the picture is not an oath or a curse. The worst that could be said against it is that it is a vulgarism. . . .") The word remained, but Selznick was required to pay a five-thousand-dollar fee before the code seal could be granted.

Working intensely with editor Hal Kern, Selznick began the enormous task of reducing thirty hours of printed film to roughly four, and within a few months, exhausted but exhilarated, they had assembled a first cut. As late as October, some scenes were being reshot by Victor Fleming, including the opening scene at Tara, which had been filmed a number of times before. Others worked assiduously as well—driven by Selznick and his barrage of memoranda to complete their jobs in record time. The first secret preview, held at the Arlington Theatre in Santa Barbara, drew a wildly enthusiastic response, and yet Selznick continued to make changes and additions, smoothing out what he regarded as rough or incomplete portions of the narrative. By the time of the first official screening in Hollywood on December 12 for members of the world press corps and their guests, anticipation was at fever pitch. After nearly two years, and an unprecedented cost of $4,085,070, *Gone With the Wind* was ready to be seen.

The film's gala premiere in Atlanta on December 15 marked a peak in the long and colorful history of movie ballyhoo: an event in which Hollywood glitter and Georgia pride converged in unabashed splendor. Preceded by three days of festive parades and celebrations, the premiere took place at the Grand Theatre in downtown Atlanta, where over two thousand seats, at ten dollars per seat, had long been sold out. (Georgia's governor declared the day of the opening a state holiday.) In the audience were David O. Selznick, Margaret Mitchell, Clark Gable, Vivien Leigh, Olivia de Havilland, and other members of the film's cast, all cheered by the enormous crowd waiting outside the theater.* The next day, *The Atlanta Constitution* devoted much of its issue to the premiere (GONE WITH THE WIND ENTHRALLS AUDIENCE WITH MAGNIFICENCE), eager to point out its "eye-arresting, pulse-quickening, heart-warming details" that would be remembered forever. The premieres that followed in New York and Hollywood were equally

---

*Victor Fleming was conspicuous by his absence from the premiere. He had been insulted by Selznick's query about giving credit to the other directors who had worked on the film, and he was enraged by Selznick's statement in the program that the film's directors had all been "supervised personally by David Selznick." The two men never reconciled.

One of the film's most memorable sequences: Scarlett walks among the war's wounded and dying at Atlanta's railroad station. Many of the "soldiers" were actually dummies interspersed among the extras.

extravagant. To Selznick's gratification, business boomed and reviews, on the whole, were hugely favorable.

David Selznick had gambled and won. For several years, he had poured his energy and his talent into a massive venture that would not only be the longest, most expensive film ever made but that also brought Hollywood's rich and varied technical skills to the pinnacle of achievement, especially in Technicolor photography. He had made it clear from the start that it was *his* film, and as he argued with directors, cajoled actors, and deluged personnel with on-the-set comments and memoranda, he knew that it was *his* reputation that was at stake. In a letter written but never mailed to Al Lichtman, vice-president at MGM, he wrote, "This picture represents the greatest work of my life, in the past and very likely in the future."

Unfortunately, he was right. Selznick was never able to surpass or even duplicate his achievement with *Gone With the Wind*, no matter how desperately or conscientiously he strived. Although he went on to produce other notable films, he could never match the romantic splendor or the special immutable charisma of *GWTW*. Revival after revival proved that the light of its beacon was too strong ever to be dimmed.

From its opening credits, as each letter of the title sweeps across the screen from right to left, we sense that a screen "event" is about to take place, and despite the flowery introductory title ("a land of cavaliers and cotton fields"), the first sequence at Tara does not disappoint. (It was shot perhaps more times than any other.) Scarlett, twittering amidst her many beaux, is a perfect embodiment of Margaret Mitchell's heroine. We learn immediately about her infatuation with Ashley Wilkes, and her dismay over his engagement to his demure cousin, Melanie Hamilton. More important, a petulant Scarlett is instructed by her father (Thomas Mitchell) in the value and permanence of "the land"—a lesson that only the ravages of war can make real to her. His words are reinforced by the soaring Tara theme, but Scarlett is too upset by the news about Ashley to hear them.

The barbecue and ball at Twelve Oaks is the film's first lavish scene, beautifully costumed and photographed and marred only slightly by some obvious rear projection. Superficially, the sequence is intended to show us the serenity and splendor of the Old South at its peak just before the war begins. More relevantly, since *Gone With the Wind* concerns character even more than action, the sequence offers a strong and immediate contrast between Rhett Butler and Ashley Wilkes, the two important men in Scarlett's life. Rhett's entrance into the film is brilliantly managed; the camera catches him smiling roguishly up at Scarlett from the bottom of a staircase, then moves down to emphasize his devilish presence amid all the blond and red-haired young Southerners. (Scarlett refs to him as "the nasty dark one," and responds instantly to his sexual attraction: "He looks like he knows what I look like without my shimmy.") Ashley Wilkes, on the other hand, is a pale and inadequate ghost of a man, reacting to Scarlett's ardor with the undeniable comment, "You have all the passion for life that I lack!" Having overheard Scarlett's importunate pleas to Ashley in the library, Rhett looks at her with detached amusement, mixed with an unmistakable sexual interest. In a way that is rather bold and surprising for a film of this period, it is the sexual bond between Scarlett and Rhett that influences much of what happens to their lives during the film.

The war comes swiftly, and just as swiftly, Scarlett, oblivious to the tumult and aware that Ashley loves only Melanie, agrees to marry Melanie's brother Charles (Rand Brooks). A letter informing her of Charles's death from pneumonia turns her into an attractive but reluctant widow, not averse to attending a Monster Bazaar in Atlanta to raise money for the "glorious cause." There she meets Rhett Butler again, now acclaimed as a war hero because of his blockade running, but sardonic about the war and his role in the fighting. It is clear from their dialogue in this scene that he is no callow swain but a worldly, self-involved man attracted to a woman whose affected "Southern belle" whims and fancies amuse him. For her part, she is intimidated yet challenged by his boldness, so challenged, in fact, that she is willing to shock Atlanta society by accepting Rhett's bid for her to dance the Virginia reel with him. In one of the movie's indelible moments, Rhett holds her in his arms and exclaims, "Someday I want you to say to me the words I heard you say to Ashley Wilkes: 'I love you!' " Despite her pretense of rejecting him, Scarlett is willing to accept his attentions, sensing that he will play an important role in turning her from a flighty young girl into a passionate woman whose innocence can never be reclaimed.

As the war continues, the beleaguered South begins to crumble under the weight of defeat. Surprisingly, for a film in which the war is a central event, the battle scenes are confined to a few quick montages. However, the impact of the fighting on the life of Atlanta is dramatized eloquently in the scene in which the casualty lists appear before its weary and frightened populace. (A woman nods sadly to her bandmaster husband, who turns to lead his musicians in a rendition of "Dixie.") It falls to Rhett to state the obvious: "The cause of living in the past is dying right in front of us." The impact of this defeat has yet to register with Scarlett; throughout Ashley's Christmas leave, she pines for him and openly declares her continued love for him. Leslie Howard's stiff portrayal of the vapid Ashley makes this devotion somewhat less than convincing.

Although historically inaccurate (the city actually survived somewhat longer than indicated), the siege of Atlanta constitutes the film's most spectacular section. This long sequence, dominated by Scarlett and Rhett's flight to Tara with Melanie, her baby, and Prissy, has a sweep and a scope unmatched by any other. Memorable moments abound: a priest continuing to pray as the church window shatters from a shell blast; the rows of dying and wounded soldiers in the hospital, the camera catching their agony in a slow pan; Scarlett, weary and repelled by the horror at the hospital, fleeing with others through the besieged city. The appearance of Rhett, coolly cynical and realistic as always, offers the only reassurance. Through the chaos that surrounds them, Rhett can still take full measure of Scarlett: "We belong together, being the same sort." For a time, however, Scarlett must face a crucial test of her courage and endurance. Searching for Dr. Meade to deliver Melanie's baby, she wanders into the railroad depot, where several thousand soldiers lay wounded and dying. In perhaps the film's single most famous shot, the camera moves back to take in a panoramic view of this scene of human desolation and carnage with a tattered Confederate flag in the foreground. Revealingly, Scarlett seems almost indifferent to the suffering around her, and when she wants to leave Atlanta, only her promise to Ashley to take care of Melanie keeps her from running away.

The escape from a burning Atlanta, highlighted by a series of dazzling effects (the collapse of a blazing building, an exploding boxcar), takes Scarlett and Rhett to the edge of the city, where a shaken Scarlett seems to have finally absorbed the desperate futility of the war. Yet vestiges of the self-centeredness remain— she refuses to understand why Rhett would desert her to return to the fighting. The ordeal that follows—the dangerous journey back to Tara, the discovery of her mother's death and her father's mindless state—finally gives her the maturity that erases all memory of the simpering Southern belle. This section contains its share of unforgettable images: Tara suddenly emerging from behind a cloud, or Scarlett coming upon the body of her mother, laid out on a table in a room. Characteristically, Scarlett doesn't gain compassion or nobility through her suffering; she becomes hard, resilient, and defiant. Wandering through the barren fields, she plucks a radish from the fields and retches when she tries to eat it. As the Tara theme soars on the sound track, she raises her fist to the skies and cries, "As God is my witness, they're not going to lick me. . . . I'm going to live through this and when it's over I'll never be hungry again. No, nor any of my folks! If I have to lie—steal—cheat—kill—as God is my witness, I'll never be hungry again!" The film's first part closes on this indelible moment in film history.

Part Two of *Gone With the Wind*, much grimmer, darker, and ultimately less satisfying than the first, reveals a South—and Tara—in ruins, broken by poverty and despair. Scarlett has taken over her helpless father's role as head of the family and also echoes his old reverence for the land. She shows her newfound strength when she shoots the Union deserter who has come into the house, bent on robbery and rape. (A startling moment shows the surprised face of the

Surrounded by desolation after the war, Scarlett contemplates a bleak future with her now-mindless father (Thomas Mitchell). Her reverence for Tara and the land, taught by her father in happier times, sustains her through the ordeal.

soldier [Paul Hurst], bloodied by the gun blast.) Amusingly, Melanie displays an unexpected coolness by taking the killing in stride. With Ashley's return from the war, the newly business-minded Scarlett feels that she can restore Tara's cotton fields with his help, while the romantic-minded Scarlett still harbors the hope that she can win his love. She turns out to be wrong on both counts. In a scene with Ashley, marred by Leslie Howard's inability to breathe life into an ineffectual character, she flings herself at him, only to be confronted by his old prattle about "honor." "I love your courage and your stubbornness," Ashley tells her, which is not exactly what she wants to hear. Realizing that she has lost him forever, Scarlett turns (as she always does) back to the soil of Tara.

The next section of the film is perhaps the weakest, somewhat cluttered with incidents not always clearly motivated or worked out in the screenplay. After the death of her father in a fall from a horse, Scarlett's obsession with becoming solvent again fills her every waking moment. Dressed in a gown made from draperies, she tries to charm an imprisoned Rhett for the tax money she owes on Tara, and when this fails, she tricks her sister's beau, Frank Kennedy (Carroll Nye), into marrying her, then builds up his lumber business by exploiting cheap labor. The narrative becomes curiously tentative at this point, when Scarlett, obstinate as always, insists on riding through Shantytown and is assaulted there. In a retaliatory raid on Shantytown, Frank is killed and Ashley, who joins him in the raid, is wounded. Once again, Rhett comes to the rescue, extricating Ashley from a dangerous situation. These scenes generate a certain amount of tension (the waiting women, trying to stay calm; the suspicious Yankee captain), but they seem perfunctory and unformed, partly because we are never given any reason for gentle Ashley's involvement in violence.

With Rhett's proposal to Scarlett, the film returns to what is, after all, its central concern: their complex relationship over the years, made up of a combination of antagonism, sexual attraction, and a mutual understanding that they are "a bad lot." His proposal sets the tone for their marriage—knowing that she conceals her steely nature behind a mask of Southern refinement, he asks for her hand mockingly, in the style of an Atlanta gentlemen ("A feeling more beautiful, more pure, more sacred . . . Dare I name it? Can it be—love?"). As they enter into marriage at last, they are each under the assumption (wrongly, as it turns out) that the other will fulfill his or her needs. For Rhett, Scarlett will be that desirable woman he has wanted to possess since he first gazed up at her from the bottom of the Twelve Oaks staircase. For Scarlett, Rhett will be the security she has longed to recover, the man who can keep her safe from the nightmare of poverty and hunger. But after an idyllic period, Rhett finds her sexually cold, still dreaming of Ashley, while Scarlett becomes bored and restless with her recovered wealth. Their only link—and it is a link infinitely stronger for Rhett than for Scarlett—is their little daughter, Bonnie Blue (Cammie King).

Never on too secure a footing, their marriage begins to disintegrate, especially after Scarlett scandalizes Atlanta society by being seen embracing Ashley. When Scarlett and Rhett are invited to Melanie's party for Ashley, Rhett insists angrily on her facing the guests alone. True to her generous nature, Melanie welcomes Scarlett, but everyone else is cold and stiffly formal toward her. In the sequence that follows—one of the most famous and most pivotal in the film—Scarlett and Rhett have their inevitable confrontation. Drunk, desperate, and aware (as always) of how much they are alike, Rhett would like to crush the image of Ashley from her head (we have never seen him so physically aggressive). When she rejects him, he kisses her fiercely, exclaiming, "This is one night you're not turning me out!" and carries her up the long staircase, two steps at a time. Today, this scene would be infinitely franker but no more powerful. As beautifully directed by Victor Fleming, it is as bold as a 1939 film could get in depicting the sexual wars between men and women. Scarlett's

Scarlett with Ashley Wilkes (Leslie Howard), the one true love of her life. Howard tried to breathe life into the weak-willed and gentlemanly Ashley, but in the end, the role defeated him.

pleased purring the next morning tells us that Rhett may have won the battle, but their bitter encounter afterward lets us know that neither has won the war.

The remainder of the film crowds one calamitous event after another in a way that smacks inevitably of soap opera. Still, there are highlights. Scarlett's miscarriage from a fall down the stairs gives Gable the chance to act in a scene he was extremely reluctant to undertake, but he manages it capably. Bonnie's death in a riding accident leads to Hattie McDaniel's finest moment as Mammy; distraught by Rhett's refusal to relinquish the child's body for burial, she has lost all the strength and resilience that made her the family's mainstay. Sobbing as the camera tracks alongside her when they mount the stairs, she tells Melanie about Rhett's overpowering grief ("I never seen no man, black or white, set such store on any child."), and about his bitter exchanges with Scarlett ("It's like to turn my blood cold—the things they say to one another!") No doubt her affecting performance in this scene earned her the Oscar as Best Supporting Actress.

Melanie's death soon afterward finally frees Scarlett from her obsession with Ashley. When she sees that he is completely broken, unable to live without Melanie, her lifelong fantasy comes to an end. Yet there is nothing left to replace it. When she returns home, she discovers that Rhett is leaving her forever. The one strong link between them has been severed, and he can no longer tolerate her selfishness, her coldness, or her endless manipulations. Ironically, the man who once looked disdainfully on the decline of the Old South wants "to see if there isn't something left of charm and grace." Bewildered, Scarlett tries to claim that she loves him, but now he has lost his desire for her. When she protests that she has no place to go, he replies with the line that has echoed down the years: "Frankly, my dear, I don't give a damn," and he vanishes into the fog. Summoning up all her old strength, Scarlett is reminded of its source in Tara: "I'll go home—and I'll think of some way to get him back. After all, tomorrow is another day!"

How can we account for the never-ending popularity of *Gone With the Wind*? Those who have seen it many times, who are perennially fascinated by the body of fact and fancy that has developed about this single film, are hardly concerned with the innovative quality of its color, or with its status as the longest, most expensive, most widely publicized movie to that date. Only film historians really care that *Gone With the Wind* represents the peak of Hollywood filmmaking in the thirties: a glorious culmination of the screen's resources and techniques. Even those who admire the film greatly acknowledge its weaknesses. Then why the cachet bestowed on this film?

Once again, we return to the characters of Scarlett O'Hara and Rhett Butler. Against a backdrop of war and its desolate aftermath, these two people are locked in a fierce conflict between their opposing wills and their irresistible attraction to each other. Once we strip away the clutter of the narrative, we come down to the bare bones of a love-hate relationship that may be timeless in any decade. Ask first-time or many-time viewers what they recall best from *Gone With the Wind* and chances are that, apart from the siege of Atlanta or the view of a resilient Scarlett, vowing that she'll "never be hungry again," they will remember Rhett clutching Scarlett against a flaming red sky on the road to Tara, or Rhett carrying Scarlett in his arms up that long flight of stairs. At the film's end, they are standing at opposite poles from where they began. Scarlett has moved from frivolous Southern belle to shrewd businesswoman, while Rhett has gone from cynic to idealist, pursuing a lost dream of "charm and grace."

There are, of course, other reasons for the film's durability: the mythic central performances of Vivien Leigh, Clark Gable, and Olivia de Havilland (de Havilland has never been credited enough with making Melanie touchingly real despite her one-note goodness); the matchless scope of a physical production that suggests size without the necessity of spectacle; and especially the film's message of survival in the face of defeat. It was reported that when the movie, previously banned, was released in liberated cities at the end of World War II, the reception was frequently emotional from people who understood what it meant to be crushed and humiliated.

Whatever the reasons it has endured, *Gone With the Wind* remains one of the screen's great romantic sagas, and one of the last, most memorable vestiges of an innocent era.* When Margaret Mitchell, in 1926, typed her first sentence on that portable Remington, she could hardly have envisioned that her story would come to life in a film that has stirred our imagination for fifty years. David O. Selznick realized his dream, and we have made it our recurring dream ever since.

Gone With the Wind. Metro-Goldwyn-Mayer. Produced by David O. Selznick. Directed by Victor Fleming. Screenplay by Sidney Howard, from the novel by Margaret Mitchell. Photography by Ernest Haller. Art direction by Lyle Wheeler. Costumes by Walter Plunkett. Edited by Hal C. Kern and James E. Newcom. Production designed by William Cameron Menzies. Cast: Clark Gable, Vivien Leigh, Olivia de Havilland, Leslie Howard, Hattie McDaniel, Thomas Mitchell, Barbara O'Neil, Butterfly McQueen, Evelyn Keyes, Ann Rutherford, Victor Jory, Laura Hope Crews, Carroll Nye, Oscar Polk, and Eddie Anderson.

---

*It also received a total of ten Academy Awards, more than any previous film to date, including: Best Picture, Best Actress (Leigh), Best Director (Fleming), Best Supporting Actress (McDaniel), Best Screenplay (Howard), Best Cinematography—Color (Ernest Haller and Ray Rennahan), Best Art Direction (Lyle Wheeler), Best Film Editing (Hal Kern and James E. Newcom), a special award to William Cameron Menzies for his use of color, and a special technical award to Don Musgrave for pioneering in the use of coordinated equipment in the production of *Gone With the Wind.*

The following productions also warrant attention as 1939 films of considerable merit and interest.

BACHELOR MOTHER

Eager to establish her reputation as an actress and not only as Fred Astaire's dancing partner, Ginger Rogers had started to appear in straight dramatic roles that took advantage of her piquant, down-to-earth personality. She was particularly effective in Gregory La Cava's *Stage Door* (1937) and George Stevens's *Vivacious Lady* (1938), where she dispensed wisecracks with the aplomb of an assured "screwball" comedienne. After making *The Story of Vernon and Irene Castle* (1939) with Astaire, she discarded her dancing shoes for a decade.

Bachelor Mother represents a peak in her nondancing career in the late thirties. A charming, even rather racy comedy, it cast Rogers as a department store salesgirl who finds an abandoned baby. When she tries to return it, everyone assumes that she is an unwed mother. Rogers becomes romantically involved with the playboy son (David Niven) of the department store owner (Charles Coburn), who makes the same assumption. At the film's end, everything is resolved, and Rogers and Niven will be married.

Playing against the commonly held belief that unwed motherhood was only a fit subject for tragedy, Norman Krasna's script treats Rogers's dilemma with lighthearted, offhand humor, while Garson Kanin's direction handles the material with easy assurance. Many of the laughs in the film's early portions stem from Niven's growing anger about Rogers's seemingly cold-blooded desire to get rid of her baby, and his efforts to change her mind lead to some funny

Bachelor Mother. Salesgirl Polly Parrish (Ginger Rogers) confronts playboy David Merlin (David Niven) and his fiancée (Jane Wilkins).

scenes in which Niven displays a surprising skill for playing farce. Rogers brings a pleasingly wry touch to her role, moving smoothly from incredulity through dismay to resignation at her predicament. The stars get strong help from the unfailing Charles Coburn as the crusty old man who is delighted to assume that the abandoned baby is his grandson. He draws the film's biggest laugh when, during one especially chaotic moment, he shouts, "I don't care who the father is. *I'm* the grandfather!"

Having just directed two well-regarded "sleepers" (*A Man to Remember,* 1938; *The Great Man Votes,* 1939), Garson Kanin was riding high at RKO, and *Bachelor Mother* marked his first attempt at handling a major production. He came through with one of the year's brighter comedies. The film was poorly remade in 1956 as a musical entitled *Bundle of Joy,* with Debbie Reynolds in the Rogers role and then-husband Eddie Fisher (in his movie debut) as her leading man.

Bachelor Mother. Produced by B.G. De Sylva and Pandro S. Berman. Directed by Garson Kanin. Screenplay by Norman Krasna, from a story by Felix Jackson. Cast: Ginger Rogers, David Niven, Charles Coburn, Frank Albertson, Ernest Truex, and Ferike Boros. Remade in 1956 as *Bundle of Joy.*

CONFESSIONS OF A NAZI SPY

Throughout the thirties, Warners had established a reputation for combining topical, socially conscious themes with hard-hitting action. As the rumblings of war grew louder in Europe, the studio decided to widen its scope by taking aim against the growing inroads of fascism in this country. It produced the bluntly titled *Confessions of a Nazi Spy*, a film designed to point up the threat represented by the infiltration of Nazi agents into America's way of life.

Edward G. Robinson, who was gradually divesting himself of the gangster persona that brought him to stardom in *Little Caesar*, appeared as an FBI man assigned to rout the Nazi underground. His investigation leads him to a reluctant spy (Francis Lederer), and then to two Nazi "bigwigs" played by George Sanders and Paul Lukas. Lukas, whose job is to recruit young people for the Nazi Bund, wants to inform on Sanders, but he is kidnapped and beaten senseless. Robinson perseveres until he can destroy the Nazi network.

Although the film was conventional at heart, the semi-documentary approach gave it a dramatic urgency that had audiences, already fearful of sinister spies in their midst, sit up and take notice. Newsreel footage, including clips from the 1937 trial in which four Nazis were convicted of espionage, was mixed into the fictional story. Robinson played his role quietly and persuasively, in contrast with the actors whose vicious, sneering villains foreshadowed the many propagandistic war films (often produced by Warners) that emerged during World War II.

Inevitably, the movie provoked cries of outrage from Nazi Bundists, and from Germany, which banned it immediately. Eighteen other countries followed suit, afraid of offending Hitler. Distributors were warned about the possibility of riots provoked by Nazi agitators, but there seems to have been little clamor in the theaters. Warners continued its assault on fascism, seldom forgetting to stir in some stardust and a healthy portion of fast-paced entertainment.

Confessions of a Nazi Spy. Warner Bros. Produced by Robert Lord. Directed by Anatole Litvak. Screenplay by Milton Krims and John Wexley, from a story by Krims and Wexley and materials gathered by former FBI agent Leon G. Turrou. Cast: Edward G. Robinson, George Sanders, Francis Lederer, Paul Lukas, Henry O'Neill, Lya Lys, James Stephenson, and Sig Rumann.

DRUMS ALONG THE MOHAWK

John Ford's first color film, made after *Young Mr. Lincoln*, this Technicolor saga dealt with rugged pioneer life in the early years of the American Revolution, a subject not often covered in films. Joining again with Ford, Henry Fonda played Gil Martin, a young farmer trying to build a life for himself and his wife Lana (Claudette Colbert) on the frontier of the Mohawk Valley in upstate New York. In addition to the rigors of the wilderness, the couple and other homesteaders

Drums Along the Mohawk. The pioneers, including Ward Bond, Henry Fonda, and Claudette Colbert, are poised for an Indian attack.

must contend with attacks by marauding Indians, spurred on by ruthless Tories. Against overwhelming odds, Gil and Lana survive to face the future.

Filmed on location in the lush valleys and forests of northern Utah, *Drums Along the Mohawk* contains familiar Fordian themes: the enduring strength of America's pioneers, the strong bonds of community life, and the daily rituals of life and death. As usual, Ford never allows his themes to get in the way of a crackling-good adventure story, and this one is first-rate, moving from one exciting sequence to another. Despite its rather simplistic views of pioneers as models of courage and fortitude and Indians as "filthy, painted heathens,"* the screenplay, based on Walter D. Edmonds's popular 1936 novel, is rich in authentic period detail, and the photography by Bert Glennon and Ray Rennahan bathes every scene in the most vivid Technicolor hues.

Ford brings an expert touch to many key sequences, most notably one in which Gil Martin eludes the Indians as he races through the night across plains, forests, and streams in search of help for the beleaguered pioneers. The final scene, in which the settlers gaze at the thirteen-starred Continental flag as it is raised to the top of a church tower, closes the film on a stirring note.

Henry Fonda is singularly fine as the determined farmer, especially in the scene where he returns exhausted from battle to describe the horrors of what he has seen and his pride in the men who fought: "We proved we can lick them. We showed them they couldn't take the valley." Claudette Colbert never seems quite at home in her role; although we are supposed to believe that she has made the transition from refined Easterner to brave frontier wife, the artifice shows through. As the feisty Widow McKlennar, who refuses to surrender her

---

*Interestingly, the Indians in *Drums Along the Mohawk* have a terrifying immediacy they lack to some extent in Ford's *Stagecoach,* where they seem more like forces of nature than painted savages.

In Name Only. The eternal triangle: Alec Walker (Cary Grant), Julie Eden (Carole Lombard), the girl he loves, and Maida (Kay Francis), his scheming wife.

bed to the Indians, Edna May Oliver, mistress of the tart remark and the sour grimace, nearly walks away with the film. (She was nominated for an Oscar.)

Although it may not rank among John Ford's classic films, *Drums Along the Mohawk* demonstrates his storytelling ability and his undisputed mastery of American themes.

Drums Along the Mohawk. Twentieth Century-Fox. Produced by Raymond Griffith. Directed by John Ford. Screenplay by Lamar Trotti and Sonya Levien, from the novel by Walter D. Edmonds. Cast: Claudette Colbert, Henry Fonda, Edna May Oliver, Eddie Collins, Ward Bond, John Carradine, Arthur Shields, and Jessie Ralph.

IN NAME ONLY

Pleased with her dramatic role in *Made for Each Other* opposite James Stewart, Carole Lombard agreed to make another serious film, under the same director (John Cromwell) and with a new leading man (Cary Grant). A high-gloss soap opera, replete with marital strife and anguished separated lovers, *In Name Only* boasts one advantage that lifts it above the suds: a well-crafted, intelligent screenplay by Richard Sherman (based on a novel by Bessie Breuer). Although the sides of the romantic triangle are clearly delineated (young widow vs. grasping wife fight for the husband), the characters are never simplistic cardboard, cut from a too-familiar pattern.

Lombard plays Julie Eden, a commercial artist with a home in Connecticut, who meets Alec Walker (Grant) and falls in love with him. He reciprocates, but the fly in the ointment is his wife Maida (Kay Francis), a cold, scheming woman who wants the money and social position that come with being Mrs. Walker and refuses to divorce him. The situation appears hopeless for Julie and Alec, until a despairing Alec becomes critically ill with pneumonia. Julie helps him to rally by lying to him about their status, but then Maida inadvertently reveals her true nasty self to Alec's gullible parents. The future now seems bright for the lovers.

The story is undoubtedly pulpish and the characters are trite. (They include Maida's malicious, flirtatious best friend—a nice turn by Helen Vinson—and the usual omniscient doctor, played by Maurice Moscovich.) Yet *In Name Only* somehow transcends its "ladies magazine" story to become a highly watchable domestic drama. Surprisingly, the reason for the extra interest it evokes rests with the character of Maida Walker. As written by Richard Sherman and played by Kay Francis, Maida has an icy assurance that cannot be broken until the end. She covers her lies and deceptions with honey, evoking sympathy from everyone but Alec. Her scenes with Alec crackle with tension and hostility—they no longer have illusions about each other and can only speak the stinging truth. Secretly, however, Maida has no intention of releasing him. When a friend wonders whether she will really give him up to Julie, Maida replies, "What do *you* think?" Her poised, masklike face is in sharp focus.

The climax involving Alec's near-fatal illness has its share of absurdities (doctor to Julie: "His chances of recovery depend on your seeing him. You must tell him that there is hope—in fact that there is certainty"), but as in *Made for Each Other*, Lombard has the ability to make them believable. Grant is less successful—his jaunty persona was so established by this time that his sickbed scenes are somewhat less than convincing. The other actors (Charles Coburn, Nella Walker, little Peggy Ann Garner) are up to their supporting roles, but Katherine Alexander excels as one of the screenplay's most interesting characters, Lombard's bitter, neurotic sister Ellen.

In Name Only is hardly burnished gold—it is not easy to make gold out of soap. Yet it merits our respectful attention as the sort of polished triangular drama that was once a staple in Hollywood's golden era.

In Name Only. RKO. Produced by Pandro S. Berman. Directed by John Cromwell. Screenplay by Richard Sherman, from the novel by Bessie Breuer. Cast: Carole Lombard, Cary Grant, Kay Francis, Charles Coburn, Helen Vinson, Nella Walker, Peggy Ann Garner, Katherine Alexander, and Maurice Moscovich.

INTERMEZZO: A LOVE STORY

A popular Swedish actress by 1938, Ingrid Bergman was seen by producer David O. Selznick in a Swedish-language version of the romantic drama *Intermezzo*. Stunned by what he called "the combination of exciting beauty and fresh purity," he signed her at once to repeat the leading role opposite Leslie Howard in an English-language version. Bergman became an immediate star and reigned as one of the screen's leading actresses until her death in 1982.

A relatively short (70 minutes) but quietly touching film, *Intermezzo* cast Howard as a celebrated violinist, married and with a young son and daughter, who falls deeply in love with Bergman, a music student. Their romance flourishes as she becomes his accompanist, but Bergman comes to recognize how much Howard misses his children, and how much their own happiness is built on the unhappiness of another. She leaves him, and he returns to his family. After a family crisis—his daughter is struck by a car and seriously hurt—Howard seeks to leave again, feeling he has failed his family, but his wife (Edna Best) asks him to return.

The year being 1939, the film was obliged to make it abundantly clear that Howard and Bergman, no matter how deeply in love, were committing adultery and had to pay for their sin. Howard must confront the misery of his devoted wife and loving children, while Bergman receives a verbal lashing from Howard's friend and confidant (John Halliday), who warns her that her recklessness in falling in love with a married man will cost her dearly. The wife's willingness to take her straying husband back into the family fold is viewed as an act of surpassing nobility.

Intermezzo: A Love Story (billed in this way to avoid any uncertainty about the title) is actually a rather slight film, placidly directed by Gregory Ratoff (who replaced William Wyler). Yet Bergman's star quality is immediately evident. Gregg Toland's luminous photography captures her extraordinarily beautiful face, and the ethereal quality that audiences found so appealing throughout her career seems genuine and spontaneous here. Critical and audience response was enthusiastic, yet Selznick was unable to find another suitable role for her, and her next two films, made on loan to Columbia and MGM, were disappointing. It was not until *Casablanca* (1942) that she became a "bankable" star, capable of drawing moviegoers into the theater.

A side note: The film's score by Lou Forbes was nominated for an Oscar, and its haunting theme, written by Heinz Provost, became internationally popular. (It was also used in the Swedish version.)

Intermezzo: A Love Story. Produced by David O. Selznick. Directed by Gregory Ratoff. Screenplay by George O'Neil, from the story by Gosta Stevens and Gustav Molander. Cast: Leslie Howard, Ingrid Bergman, Edna Best, John Halliday, Cecil Kellaway, Ann Todd, and Douglas Scott. Remade in 1957 as *Interlude*.

Jesse James. Jesse (Tyrone Power) bids farewell to wife Zee (Nancy Kelly), while brother Frank (Henry Fonda) looks on.

JESSE JAMES

From all historical accounts, the legendary outlaw Jesse James was actually a ruthless gunman who left a trail of human desolation as he robbed banks and trains with his brother Frank. Casting truth to the winds, Fox fashioned this lively Technicolor Western, which portrayed Jesse (Tyrone Power) and Frank (Henry Fonda) as honorable young men who turn outlaw to wreak vengeance on the nasty representatives of the St. Louis Midland Railroad, whom they blame for the murder of their mother (Jane Darwell). Jesse and Frank become national legends (which was actually the case), but Jesse is shot down by "that dirty little coward" Bob Ford (John Carradine).

Despite its falsification of most of the facts, *Jesse James* has the pace and vigor of a first-rate Western film. Written by Nunnally Johnson and photographed in the vivid color Fox used for some of its major productions at this time, the film moves along at a fast clip under Henry King's direction. Many of the action scenes are well handled. An ill-fated bank robbery in which the James boys and their gang ride into an ambush could stand as a model for this sort of sequence. The movie works less well in suggesting Jesse's brooding, fatalistic state of mind. At this relatively early period in his career, Tyrone Power lacked the skill to suggest the depths of feeling in this man.

At the film's end, the crusading newspaper editor (Henry Hull), who has consistently defended Jesse's actions, delivers a graveside speech that summarizes America's fondness for glorifying its less respectable figures: "Jesse was a bandit, an outlaw, a criminal. But we ain't ashamed of him, maybe because he was bold, lawless. Like we all like to be sometimes. . . . Or maybe because he was so good at what he was doin'."

Although Tyrone Power acts competently as Jesse, he is edged out by Henry Fonda's laconic, quiet-spoken Frank. (Fonda repeated the role in a 1940 sequel, *The Return of Frank James.*) Nancy Kelly is appealing as Jesse's loyal, worried wife Zee, and Randolph Scott remains discreetly in the background as a decent marshal who would rather not hunt down Jesse. Brian Donlevy, Donald Meek, and John Carradine provide the proper amount of bombast as villainous types.

Jesse James fits handily into the late-thirties theme that a corrupt society precipitates criminal behavior. Nevertheless, it gets by more on its hard-riding action than on any sociological point. As such, it is a superior Western that has held up well over the years.

Jesse James. Twentieth Century-Fox. Produced by Nunnally Johnson. Directed by Henry King. Screenplay by Nunnally Johnson. Cast: Tyrone Power, Henry Fonda, Randolph Scott, Nancy Kelly, Brian Donlevy, Slim Summerville, J. Edward Bromberg, John Carradine, Donald Meek, and Jane Darwell.

JUAREZ

As virtually the only Hollywood studio to directly acknowledge the very real threat of totalitarianism in that troubled year of 1939, Warners was seldom circumspect about its militant stance. Even in an elaborate historical drama such as *Juarez*, it was abundantly clear that the story of Mexico's Benito Juarez and his clash with the imperialist forces of Louis Napoleon was actually a cautionary tale warning America about the need to defend democracy against tyranny. Under William Dieterle's direction, *Juarez* sounded an urgent plea for "truth, liberty, and justice."

Paul Muni stars as Juarez, the tiny, stoic man who rallies his forces against the greedy designs of Napoleon. Claiming his conquest of Mexico as a "holy mission," Napoleon creates a puppet regime by arranging to have the Archduke Maximilian of Austria (Brian Aherne) declared Emperor of Mexico. A gentle, well-meaning, but ineffectual man, Maximilian is duped into believing that the people want him. His unstable wife Carlotta (Bette Davis) is enraged when she learns the truth, but Maximilian, out of a sense of moral duty, refuses to abdicate even after Juarez's forces are triumphant. Maximilian is executed, and Carlotta goes mad.

Although handsomely produced and meticulously detailed, *Juarez* seldom rises to the intended heights. The principal fault lies with the splintered screenplay, which divides the audience's attention between Juarez, who is depicted as something of a cipher, a symbol rather than a human being, and Maximilian, who is by far the more interesting and complex character. Although Juarez is given the requisite didactic lines ("The defense of democracy is an imperative duty," for example) we are never stirred by him, whereas foolish, compassionate Maximilian, despite his royalist views, earns our sympathy. The screenplay would like us to equate Juarez with Abraham Lincoln (Juarez admires Lincoln and grieves at his assassination), but our feelings go out to Maximilian as he stands before the firing squad. Inevitably, the film's lack of clear focus induces confusion and weariness.

Wearing nut-brown makeup and a stovepipe hat (no doubt in tribute to Juarez's American idol), Paul Muni tries to breathe some life into his character, without much success,* nor is he helped by John Garfield, who, as Juarez's chief aide Porfirio Diaz, seems to have just arrived in Mexico from New York City. As the hapless Empress Carlotta, Bette Davis gets to perform several pyrotechnic displays of acting (blistering rage, intense despair, staring madness), but hers is actually a large supporting role. The film's acting honors really belong to Brian Aherne as Maximilian, his well-trimmed beard fairly bristling with rectitude as he calmly resists abdication. (He received a nomination as Best Supporting Actor.)

More effective as a clarion call against fascism than as drama, *Juarez* won the respect and even admiration of critics who were impressed by its theme, but it failed to catch fire at the box office. Warners' two leading stars, who never meet in the film, were never paired again.

Juarez. Warner Bros. Produced by Henry Blanke. Directed by William Dieterle. Screenplay by John Huston, Wolfgang Reinhardt, and Aeneas MacKenzie, from a play by Franz Werfel and a novel by Bertita Harding. Cast: Paul Muni, Bette Davis, Brian Aherne, Claude Rains, John Garfield, Donald Crisp, Gale Sondergaard, Joseph Calleia, and Gilbert Roland.

THE LITTLE PRINCESS

By 1939, Shirley Temple's phenomenal popularity was starting to wane. At the ripe old age of eleven, on the brink of adolescence, she was still an extraordinarily talented child, but her last two films (*Little Miss Broadway* and *Just Around the Corner*, both 1938) had received fairly scant production values from the studio and less than enthusiastic reviews from the critics. Hoping for a last burst of glory, Fox decided to star her in her first color film, a lavish remake of *The Little Princess*, the Frances Hodgson Burnett novel previously filmed in 1917, with Mary Pickford. It turned out to be what many regard as her best film.

In this charming Victorian fable, set in 1899, Shirley plays Sara Crewe, a spunky little girl who is sent to Miss Minchin's Boarding School when her father (Ian Hunter) goes off to fight in the Boer War.† When he is presumed killed in

---

*A notoriously difficult actor, Muni insisted on adding more scenes for himself, even after shooting was completed, so that some footage with Davis and Aherne had to be cut.

†In some of her films, Shirley portrayed a motherless child whose attachment to her father was slightly alarming. In *The Poor Little Rich Girl* (1936), she sings to daddy (Michael Whalen), "Marry me and let me be your wife."

The Little Princess. Sara Crewe (Shirley Temple) and her friend Bertie (Arthur Treacher).

action, Sara is forced to become a much put-upon slavey at the school. Unwilling to believe that her beloved daddy is dead, Sara continues to search for him, making sympathetic friends along the way. Ultimately, with the intervention of Queen Victoria herself (Beryl Mercer), she is reunited with her shell-shocked father.

As usual, Shirley plays a resilient and resourceful little girl who steals everyone's heart, everyone, that is, except the mean Miss Minchin (Mary Nash). (Sara is never snobbish—even as a pampered "princess," her best friend is Becky [Sybil Jason], the cockney servant girl.) Shirley plays Sarah with spirit and vivacity, even getting to sing and dance delightfully to "The Old Kent Road" with Arthur Treacher as Miss Minchin's sympathetic brother Bertie. To take advantage of the film's lavish Technicolor trappings, the studio included an elaborate fantasy sequence in which Shirley performs in tutu and ballet slippers. Her support in the film included Richard Greene, Anita Louise, Cesar Romero, and young Marcia Mae Jones as the requisite "meanie" who torments Shirley during her slavey period.

After *The Little Princess,* Shirley made three more films for Fox, but they proved to be unsuccessful, and one, *The Blue Bird,* was an expensive disaster, a rather heavy-handed fantasy that compared unfavorably with the previous year's *The Wizard of Oz.* She departed the studio in 1940 to face an uncertain screen career as an adolescent. However, she left behind the durable memory of a gifted tyke who brightened America's bleak Depression years. Although it came late in her career as a child star, *The Little Princess* gives us a permanent record of her special appeal.

The Little Princess. Twentieth Century-Fox. Produced by Gene Markey. Directed by Walter Lang. Screenplay by Ethel Hill and Walter Ferris, from the novel by Frances Hodgson Burnett. Cast: Shirley Temple, Richard Greene, Anita Louise, Ian Hunter, Cesar Romero, Arthur Treacher, Mary Nash, Sybil Jason, Beryl Mercer, and Marcia Mae Jones. Previously filmed in 1917.

MADE FOR EACH OTHER

After establishing her reputation as an attractive and skilled comedienne in such films as *My Man Godfrey* (1936) and *Nothing Sacred* (1937), Carole Lombard longed to play a dramatic role that would demonstrate her versatility as an actress. She chose to appear opposite James Stewart in David O. Selznick's domestic drama *Made for Each Other*. It turned out to be a suitable choice.

Lombard and Stewart play Jane and John Mason, a newly married couple giddily in love until problems intrude. A struggling young attorney, John is burdened with a gruff, insensitive boss (Charles Coburn) who thinks nothing of interrupting their honeymoon. An even more grievous problem is presented by John's mother (Lucile Watson), an overbearing tyrant who keeps John under her thumb. Defeated at every turn, the Masons face a bleak future until, joyously, their baby arrives. The baby becomes critically ill, and only a special serum, flown through a snowstorm against almost insurmountable odds, can save his life. The serum arrives in time, and everything ends happily for the Masons.

Jo Swerling's screenplay unveils the moss-covered clichés as if they were being freshly discovered, and director John Cromwell works strenuously to smooth over the many worn patches. Yet what the film lacks is the artistry and skill that King Vidor brought to a very similar film, *The Crowd*, in 1928. Fortunately, the stars bring such warmth and conviction to their roles that the movie becomes pleasing and even, on occasion, genuinely touching. As the wife who tries to build the esteem of her weak, unachieving, and mother-dominated husband, Lombard proves that she could handle dramatic as well as comic scenes convincingly. Stewart is on thinner ice but manages capably. Playing something of a bumbling fool who is passed over for a junior partnership, Stewart must keep the character sympathetic, a difficult task considering his mealymouthed behavior throughout most of the film. Yet the actor's charm and appeal shine through the role in the way that it would later in the year when he played another naïve young man in *Mr. Smith Goes to Washington*. Their best support comes from veteran actress Lucile Watson, who has a moving speech as they keep vigil for the sick child. ("I wasn't always a bitter old woman. I wasn't always a pest and a nuisance.")

The cliffhanger climax, which induces winces with its calculated melodramatics (ice-covered plane flying through a blizzard; waiting anguished parents), was added to the film by Selznick after the first previews were disappointing. He remembered using a similar plot device in his 1933 MGM production of *Night Flight,* which, in turn, had been based on a true incident. His brother Myron (Lombard's agent) had fallen ill in California and required a serum found only in New York City. The chartered plane completed the flight in record time, and Myron's life was saved. With the crisis over, David declared, "This is too good to waste on Myron. Let's put it in the picture." Revived for *Made for Each Other,* the device gave the movie a dramatic if cornball finish.

Made for Each Other has the glossy professional sheen of a Selznick film. If the story has more suds than substance, it still affords the opportunity to watch Carole Lombard at peak form, bringing luster to a lusterless role.

Made for Each Other. Selznick-United Artists. Produced by David O. Selznick. Directed by John Cromwell. Screenplay by Jo Swerling. Cast: Carole Lombard, James Stewart, Charles Coburn, Lucile Watson, Eddie Quillan, Alma Kruger, Harry Davenport, Louise Beavers, and Ward Bond.

THE ROARING TWENTIES

At the start of the thirties, James Cagney had exploded on the screen in *The Public Enemy* (1931). It was his sixth film, but the first in which his raw urban energy and jaunty Irish charm collided head-on with his role as a ruthless gangster to produce a fusion that stunned audiences. Along with *Little Caesar,* *The Public Enemy* launched a cycle of gangster films that pleased Depression audiences. By the middle of the decade, however, protest against the violence of these films was vocal and organized, and Hollywood sensed that a change was in order. Cagney joined the side of law and order in *G-Men* (1935), and even as an unregenerate killer in *Angels with Dirty Faces* (1938), he pretended to go to the electric chair as a shrieking coward in order to set his teenage admirers on the straight road to a decent life.

In *The Roaring Twenties,* Cagney plays his most sympathetic gangster role. As Eddie Bartlett, he resorts to crime only in desperation after World War I, when society turns its back on him. A sentimentalist behind his gruff, violent exterior, he falls in love with a demure nightclub singer (Priscilla Lane), who turns him down for a young attorney (Jeffrey Lynn), who is sworn to battle the mob. In a gallant gesture, Eddie sacrifices his own life to save the attorney— now his beloved girl's husband—from assassination. Tom Powers of *The Public Enemy* would have scorned Eddie Bartlett and probably riddled him with bullets. Lying dead on the steps of a church, Eddie gets a kind of epitaph from Panama

Smith (Gladys George), the blowsy chanteuse who knew and loved him. "He used to be a big shot," she tells the police.

Under Raoul Walsh's direction, *The Roaring Twenties* has the sort of driving pace one associates immediately with Warner Brothers. There are few surprises, but characteristically, Walsh stages the action scenes in bravura style. The gang's robbery of a shipment of liquor confiscated by the government during Prohibition is a model of efficient filmmaking and a blazing shootout sparked by Eddie after his best friend (Frank McHugh) has been murdered by the mob fairly blisters the screen. Eddie's descent into near oblivion after the stock market crash lowers the film's temperature for a while, but his final fatal encounter with George Hally (Humphrey Bogart), the vicious kingpin hood who betrayed him, rekindles the excitement.

Inevitably, it is Cagney who keeps *The Roaring Twenties* roaring; his Eddie Bartlett has a dancer's grace and the coiled tension of a predatory animal on the prowl, but he also has an underlying generosity and honesty that keep him appealing and make his fate poignant. All the other actors, including Bogart as one of the snarling villains he played before stardom, move to Cagney's beat, but Gladys George excels as the Texas Guinan-like Panama Smith, croaking her sad songs in low dives and eyeing Eddie with love and understanding.

A decade later, in Raoul Walsh's *White Heat* (1949), Cagney would revive his cold-blooded *Public Enemy* gangster and add a few touches of pathological behavior. Standing midway between the twin poles of gangsterism, *The Roaring Twenties* stands as a transition point in Cagney's career, taking him from his cocky hoods of the early thirties to the cocky song-and-dance man of *Yankee Doodle Dandy* in 1942.

The Roaring Twenties. Warner Bros. Produced by Hal B. Wallis. Directed by Raoul Walsh. Screenplay by Jerry Wald, Richard Macaulay, and Robert Rossen, from a story by Mark Hellinger. Cast: James Cagney, Priscilla Lane, Humphrey Bogart, Jeffrey Lynn, Frank McHugh, Gladys George, and Paul Kelly.

UNION PACIFIC

A long, large-scale Western directed by master showman Cecil B. De Mille, *Union Pacific* purported to be the story of the building of the Union Pacific Railroad in the late 1860s. Joel McCrea starred as the overseer of the construction of the railroad, who must battle the opposition backing the Union Pacific's rival, the Central Pacific. Among his nemeses are a crooked gambler (Brian Donlevy) hired to cause havoc at the Union Pacific, and a gunslinger (Robert Preston), who was once a good friend and war buddy of McCrea's. Barbara Stanwyck costarred as the spirited Union Pacific postmistress who is romantically involved with both McCrea and Preston.

As usual, De Mille churns up a goodly amount of action, paying scant attention to such niceties as credible dialogue. Highlights include a spectacular train crash, several Indian attacks, a breathtaking last-minute rescue, and a final ceremony at which the last rail is laid for the Union Pacific ("This great nation is united with a wedding ring of iron."). Subtlety may be lacking, but De Mille knows his business, and he manages a number of exciting brawls, scrapes, and chases in the film's over two-hour running time. His skill at handling hordes of extras is evident in the scenes depicting the building of the railroad.

Dwarfed by the continual action, the cast performs competently, although Barbara Stanwyck, in the role originally offered to Vivien Leigh, has obvious difficulty with the Irish brogue she is called upon to effect as a hot-tempered colleen. Curiously, she has a climactic scene that directly parallels a scene in John Ford's *Stagecoach:* During a ferocious Indian attack, when all seems lost, Joel McCrea prepares to shoot her as she prays, but a last-minute rescue by soldiers saves their lives. (Both *Stagecoach* and *Union Pacific* were adapted from stories by Ernest Haycox.)

In the fashion of the day, *Union Pacific* portrays Indians as shrieking, infantile savages. In one especially disgraceful scene, the screenplay has "tamed," child-like Indians playing with pieces of cloth and firing in fright at a player piano when it suddenly begins to play.

Over the years, De Mille refused to veer from the simple, direct, flamboyant style he had adopted in the silent era, and he paid for his recalcitrance with dismissal by most serious critics. Yet *Union Pacific,* for all its lumbering ways, demonstrates De Mille's talent as a consummate storyteller who served his audiences well.

Union Pacific. Paramount. Produced and directed by Cecil B. De Mille. Screenplay by Walter DeLeon, C. Gardner Sullivan, Jesse Lasky, Jr., and Jack Cunningham, from the novel *Trouble Shooter* by Ernest Haycox. Cast: Barbara Stanwyck, Joel McCrea, Robert Preston, Brian Donlevy, Akim Tamiroff, Lynne Overman, Robert Barrat, and Anthony Quinn.

Innocent victims of a hostile society, Leni (Jane Bryan) and Dr. David Newcome (Paul Muni) are sentenced to death.

WE ARE NOT ALONE

One of Warners' most prestigious actors (often billed with an intimidating "Mr." before his name), Paul Muni won acclaim and honors for his performances in *I Am a Fugitive from a Chain Gang* (Oscar nomination, 1932), *The Story of Louis Pasteur* (Academy Award, 1936), and *The Life of Emile Zola* (Oscar nomination, 1937). Today, his acting seems mannered and overly busy, drenched more in greasepaint than in genuine feeling.

His last performance for Warners, in Edmund Goulding's adaptation of James Hilton's novel *We Are Not Alone*, is one of his best, restrained and often affecting, with few actor's tricks. He plays David Newcome, a gentle, absentminded English doctor living in a small town in 1914 with his repressed, severe wife Jessica (Flora Robson) and young son Gerald (Raymond Severn). In all innocence, he befriends Leni (Jane Bryan), an unhappy young Austrian girl, and brings her to his house as governess to Gerald. When Jessica is poisoned accidentally, David and Leni are accused of murdering her out of illicit passion for each other, and they are brought to trial. Circumstantial evidence, vicious gossip, and growing war fever (Leni is suspected of being a German spy) conspire to render a guilty verdict, and they are hanged.

Edmund Goulding stages this mournful tale (based on a true incident) at a steady, unhurried pace, savoring the details of small-town life and allowing the characterizations in James Hilton and Milton Krims's screenplay to take precedence over the melodrama. He gets help from the actors. As the cold, tightly wound Jessica, who terrifies her overly sensitive son,* Flora Robson gives a splendid performance, taut with a lifetime of stifled emotions, and Jane Bryan, an enormously appealing young actress who retired early in her career, turns Leni into a heartbreaking figure, frightened and bewildered. Given a character whose fumbling naïveté threatens to exasperate rather than move the viewer, Paul Muni plays in a low-keyed, soft-spoken style that makes his plight all the more poignant. His most effective moment comes on the witness stand when he suddenly realizes that he does love Leni after all ("I hadn't thought of it. But of course I do! Yes, I do!"). Together for the first and last time after their sentencing, David and Leni make a pitiable couple, affirming their innocence but reconciled to their fate.

Curiously, *We Are Not Alone* ends with a coda that tries to lift the story out of its domestic boundaries and turn it into one with worldwide implications. In an impassioned—and unexpected—speech, David tries to equate their fate with the victims of the approaching First World War. Obviously, his words are meant to refer to 1939 as well as 1914: "We are not alone," he tells Leni. "Every minute, every second, out there . . . thousands are dying, or sent to die, who have done no wrong." Inexplicably, considering his perilous dilemma, his thoughts move to the world outside as he addresses the sword-rattling leaders: "Why have you let things come to this? We simple people only ask to live in peace and do our work. Haven't you learned anything in two thousand years?" For a few awkward moments, the voices of the screenwriters can be clearly heard over the voice of the character.

Apart from this false and arbitrary ending, *We Are Not Alone* is a superior drama that deserved wider popularity. Its tragic story could hardly be expected to appeal to general audiences (as *Wuthering Heights* attested, many viewers were not partial to unhappy endings), but within its modest aims, this film has more resonance and power than many "larger" films.

We Are Not Alone. Warner Bros. Produced by Henry Blanke. Directed by Edmund Goulding. Screenplay by James Hilton and Milton Krims, from the novel by James Hilton. Cast: Paul Muni, Jane Bryan, Flora Robson, Raymond Severn, Una O'Connor, Henry Daniell, and James Stephenson.

---

*A memorable moment occurs as Jessica bathes her son, who has lost his fears under Leni's warm tutelage. "What are you not afraid of anymore?" Jessica asks him. His eyes gaze at her directly as he says, "Of you, Mother."

Still Other Notable Films
Released in 1939

The name of the director appears in italics following the studio.

The Adventures of Sherlock Holmes. Twentieth Century-Fox. *Alfred Werker.* Screenplay by Edwin Blum and William Drake, from a play by William Gillette. Cast: Basil Rathbone, Nigel Bruce, Ida Lupino, Alan Marshal, George Zucco, and Terry Kilburn. Fox's *The Hound of the Baskervilles* was so successful that the studio quickly made another Sherlock Holmes feature to cash in on its popularity. Modestly but neatly made, this film is based on William Gillette's long-running play, *Sherlock Holmes,* in which the devilishly clever detective outwits the nefarious Professor Moriarty (Zucco) in his attempt to steal the Crown jewels. Universal picked up the series, and with Rathbone and Bruce repeating as Holmes and Watson, ran it into the ground by the mid-forties.

Beau Geste. Paramount. *William Wellman.* Screenplay by Robert Carson, from the novel by Percival C. Wren. Cast: Gary Cooper, Ray Milland, Robert Preston, Susan Hayward, Brian Donlevy, Albert Dekker, Broderick Crawford, J. Carrol Naish, and Donald O'Connor. The best-remembered version of the novel about honor, treachery, and brotherly devotion in the French Foreign Legion. There are some rousing action scenes, and everyone recalls the fort "defended" by dead soldiers, but the acting and dialogue are faintly absurd. Brian Donlevy stands out as a sadistic officer. Previously filmed in 1926 and remade in 1966. Comedian Marty Feldman also directed and starred in a 1977 parody entitled *The Last Remake of Beau Geste.*

The Cat and the Canary. Paramount. *Elliott Nugent.* Screenplay by Walter DeLeon and Lynn Starling, from the play by John Willard. Cast: Bob Hope, Paulette

Goddard, John Beal, Douglass Montgomery, Gale Sondergaard, Elizabeth Patterson, and George Zucco. The popular 1922 stage mystery, filmed in 1927 and 1930 (as *The Cat Creeps*), was retooled to accommodate the brash personality and quick-fire gags of Bob Hope. The movie includes—and takes seriously—all the familiar trappings of the "haunted house" thriller—mysterious sliding doors, clutching hands, etc.—but Nugent tempers the terror with Hope's barrage of jokes. The result is both frightening and surprisingly funny.

Each Dawn I Die. Warner Bros. *William Keighley*. Screenplay by Norman Reilly Raine and Warren Duff, from a novel by Jerome Odlum. Cast: James Cagney, George Raft, Jane Bryan, George Bancroft, Maxie Rosenbloom, Stanley Ridges, and Alan Baxter. Prison films had been a staple subgenre of the thirties, many of them coming from the melodrama mill at Warners. *Each Dawn I Die* was yet another entry: a tough, intermittently effective tale of a crusading reporter (Cagney) who is framed by gangsters and sent to prison. He becomes involved in a breakout headed by big-shot gangster Raft. The story becomes implausible, but Cagney gives it his dynamic, swaggering best. Best scene: A "stoolie" is stabbed in the prison theater.

Golden Boy. Columbia. *Rouben Mamoulian*. Screenplay by Lewis Meltzer, Daniel Taradash, Sara Y. Mason, and Victor Heerman, from the play by Clifford Odets. Cast: Barbara Stanwyck, Adolphe Menjou, William Holden, Lee J. Cobb, Joseph Calleia, Sam Levene, and Edward Brophy. This adaptation of Odets's play keeps the basic, much-parodied premise (young fighter must choose between his fists and his violin playing), but removes most of the social intent (selling one's artistic soul in a corrupt society). Twenty-one-year-old Holden made his film debut as the fighter, ably supported by Stanwyck as the tough girl who comes to love him. Cobb repeated his stage role as Holden's Italian papa, giving what must be termed an excruciating performance. Excellent fight sequences are the film's highlights.

The Great Man Votes. RKO. *Garson Kanin*. Screenplay by John Twist, from a story by Gordon Malherbe Hillman. Cast: John Barrymore, Virginia Weidler, Peter Holden, Katherine Alexander, and Donald MacBride. Well-handled by writer-director Garson Kanin (his third film as director), this slight but engaging film marks one of Barrymore's best screen performances. He plays an ex-college professor who sinks into an alcoholic haze after his wife's death. Through the efforts of his two young children, he gains back his self-respect.

The Hound of the Baskervilles. Twentieth Century-Fox. *Sidney Lanfield*. Screenplay by Ernest Pascal, from the novel by Sir Arthur Conan Doyle. Cast: Basil

Rathbone, Richard Greene, Nigel Bruce, Wendy Barrie, Lionel Atwill, and John Carradine. The first entry in the long-running Sherlock Holmes series starring Rathbone and Bruce. Obviously made on a small budget, the movie still manages to generate a chilling atmosphere. The casting of Rathbone and Bruce was so felicitous that moviegoers wanted more of the same. *The Adventures of Sherlock Holmes* followed in a few months. Both Fox films were superior to most of the later films made at Universal.

The Hunchback of Notre Dame. RKO. *William Dieterle.* Screenplay by Sonya Levien and Bruno Frank, from the novel by Victor Hugo. Cast: Charles Laughton, Maureen O'Hara, Thomas Mitchell, Edmond O'Brien, Sir Cedric Hardwicke, Alan Marshal, and Walter Hampden. An elaborate, rather cumbersome adaptation of the Hugo novel, filmed before in a famous 1923 version with Lon Chaney. Wearing horrific makeup, Charles Laughton gives a bravura performance as the deformed, pathetic bellringer Quasimodo, who protects the beautiful Esmeralda (O'Hara) amid the terror and corruption of the Middle Ages. The film's best feature: a rousing score by Alfred Newman.

Let Us Live. Columbia. *John Brahm.* Screenplay by Anthony Veiller and Allen Rivkin, from a story by Joseph F. Dineen. Cast: Henry Fonda, Maureen O'Sullivan, Ralph Bellamy, Alan Baxter, Stanley Ridges, Henry Kolker. Very similar to Fritz Lang's *You Only Live Once* (1937), this expressionistic melodrama again cast Fonda as a desperate man pursued by the law. Here, he is mistakenly accused and convicted on a murder charge, finally—with the efforts of his girlfriend (O'Sullivan) and a detective (Bellamy)—winning his freedom just before his execution. Earnest and glum, but also effectively acted.

The Light That Failed. Paramount. *William Wellman.* Screenplay by Robert Carson, from the novel by Rudyard Kipling. Cast: Ronald Colman, Walter Huston, Ida Lupino, Muriel Angelus, Dudley Digges, Ernest Cossart, and Ferike Boros. Adapted from Kipling's first novel, this drama starred Colman as a soldier turned painter, whose masterwork is destroyed, out of frustration and rage, by the streetwise prostitute (Lupino) who posed for it. Ultimately, Colman goes blind and dies heroically in battle. Although Colman acquits himself creditably, as always, the film belongs to Lupino, whose performance as the vengeful prostitute revealed her star potential for the first time. Previously filmed in three silent versions.

Nurse Edith Cavell. RKO. *Herbert Wilcox.* Screenplay by Michael Hogan, from a novel by Captain Reginald Berkeley. Cast: Anna Neagle, Edna May Oliver, George Sanders, May Robson, ZaSu Pitts, and H. B. Warner. British actress

Anna Neagle starred as the heroic nurse who worked with the Belgian underground to help wounded soldiers in World War I. The film has somewhat less of the overwrought propaganda that was customary at the time, and it also features some fine acting turns by an estimable supporting cast. Interestingly, a 1928 silent version (*Dawn*) with Dame Sybil Thorndike provoked outrage from leading Englishmen who saw it as an effort to undermine efforts toward peace and goodwill with Germany.

On Borrowed Time. MGM. *Harold S. Bucquet.* Screenplay by Alice Duer Miller, Frank O'Neil, and Claudine West, from the play by Paul Osborn and the novel by Lawrence Edward Watkin. Cast: Lionel Barrymore, Sir Cedric Hardwicke, Beulah Bondi, Bobs Watson, Una Merkel, and Eily Malyon. A modest, gentle, somewhat watered-down version of the Osborn play about an old man (Barrymore) who chases Death—here in the form of Mr. Brink (Hardwicke)—up a tree to keep from dying before he can take his young grandson (Watson) out of the clutches of a mercenary aunt (Malyon). Barrymore is characteristically hammy, but the movie, even with its conventional Hollywood heaven, has undeniable charm.

The Private Lives of Elizabeth and Essex. Warner Bros. *Michael Curtiz.* Screenplay by Norman Reilly Raine and Aeneas MacKenzie, from a play by Maxwell Anderson. Cast: Bette Davis, Errol Flynn, Olivia de Havilland, Donald Crisp, Alan Hale, Vincent Price, Henry Stephenson, Henry Daniell, and Nanette Fabares. A lavish, none-too-compelling historical drama (actually more fiction than history) concerning the ill-starred romance between—and battle for power of—Queen Elizabeth (Davis) and the Earl of Essex (Flynn). Reputedly, Davis loathed Flynn—she wanted Laurence Olivier in his role—and their scenes together are patently unconvincing. The sets and costumes, filmed in vivid Technicolor, are a feast for the eyes, however, and Davis, wearing what seem to be pounds of makeup, appears to be enjoying the tirades she must deliver as the embattled queen. (At one point, she smashes virtually all the mirrors in the palace in a pyrotechnic display of fury.)

The Rains Came. Twentieth Century-Fox. *Clarence Brown.* Screenplay by Philip Dunne and Julien Josephson, from the novel by Louis Bromfield. Cast: Myrna Loy, Tyrone Power, George Brent, Brenda Joyce, Maria Ouspenskaya, Nigel Bruce, and Joseph Schildkraut. Fred Sersen and E. H. Hansen won an Academy Award for their special effects for this film: a spectacular earthquake and flood that destroy the Indian province of Ranchipur. The screenplay and acting are much less spectacular, concentrating principally on the clandestine (and unlikely) romance of a bored married Englishwoman (Loy) with a questionable past and an idealistic young Indian surgeon (Power). Much heavy-handed emoting, but the awesome climax is almost worth the wait.

The Real Glory. Goldwyn. *Henry Hathaway.* Screenplay by Jo Swerling and Robert R. Presnell, from the novel by Charles L. Clifford. Cast: Gary Cooper, David Niven, Andrea Leeds, Broderick Crawford, Kay Johnson, and Vladimir Sokoloff. Well-staged action scenes highlight this melodrama concerning a small contingent of American soldiers in the Philippines after the Spanish-American War, who are forced to repel an armed uprising by Moro tribesmen. Cooper plays a courageous doctor who saves the day for the troops in the climactic battle.

Son of Frankenstein. Universal. *Rowland V. Lee.* Screenplay by Willis Cooper, based on characters created by Mary Shelley. Cast: Basil Rathbone, Boris Karloff, Bela Lugosi, Lionel Atwill, Josephine Hutchinson, and Edgar Norton. The third entry in the "Frankenstein" series, this elaborately made thriller boasts stunning decor by Jack Otterson and a cast that knows its way around this sort of film. Rathbone plays the late Baron Frankenstein's son, whose efforts to restore his father's monster to full power wreak havoc on the community and nearly destroy his young son. Lugosi creates a memorable character with his grotesque, broken-necked Ygor.

The Story of Vernon and Irene Castle. RKO. *H. C. Potter.* Screenplay by Richard Sherman, Oscar Hammerstein II, and Dorothy Yost, from a book by Irene Castle. Cast: Ginger Rogers, Fred Astaire, Walter Brennan, Edna May Oliver, and Lew Fields. This nostalgic musical, the last of the Astaire–Rogers films for a decade, purports to tell the story of Vernon and Irene Castle, international dancing stars in the years before World War I. The film substitutes sentiment and decorous dances for the team's usual gaiety and wit, but some of the musical numbers are pleasing.

They Made Me a Criminal. Warner Bros. *Busby Berkeley.* Screenplay by Sig Herzig, from a story by Bertram Millhauser and Beulah Marie Dix. Cast: John Garfield, Ann Sheridan, Claude Rains, May Robson, Gloria Dickson, Billy Halop, Bobby Jordan, Leo Gorcey, and Gabriel Dell. Berkeley, usually associated with Warners' kaleidoscopic musicals, directed this gritty melodrama about a boxer (Garfield) who is falsely accused of murder and flees to a work farm for juvenile delinquents, where he finds romance and a new purpose in life. Garfield's forceful performance mixes well with the shenanigans of the "Dead End" Kids, the group of young actors who scored a triumph in the stage and movie productions of *Dead End.* Previously filmed by Warners in 1933 as *The Life of Jimmy Dolan.*

Tower of London. Universal. *Rowland V. Lee.* Screenplay by Robert N. Lee. Cast: Basil Rathbone, Boris Karloff, Vincent Price, Barbara O'Neil, Ian Hunter, Nan Grey, and John Sutton. A gory, efficiently made, and often effective historical thriller, with Rathbone as the evil Richard III, who tortures and murders his way to the throne in fifteenth-century England. Karloff plays his clubfooted executioner. The most startling death scene: Price (as the Duke of Clarence) is drowned in a vat of Malmsey wine.

You Can't Cheat an Honest Man. Universal. *George Marshall.* Screenplay by George Marion, Jr., Richard Mack, and Everett Freeman, from a story by Charles Bogle (W. C. Fields). Cast: W. C. Fields, Edgar Bergen, Charlie McCarthy, Mortimer Snerd, Constance Moore, Mary Forbes, Thurston Hall, and Eddie Anderson. The first of Fields's four comedies for Universal, this ramshackle but frequently hilarious farce places the inimitable comedian in a circus atmosphere, where he can cheat, swindle, and bamboozle to his heart's content. Ventriloquist Bergen and his wisecracking dummy are on hand, but the laughs belong to Fields as con man Larson E. Whipsnade. Highlight: Whipsnade creates an uproar at a high-society party. Also wait for Fields in disguise as "Buffalo Bella."

POSTSCRIPT

By 1940, the war in Europe no longer seemed quite so distant, and many Americans were beginning to wonder not if, but when, the country would be drawn into the conflict. The government's clear watchword was: Be prepared. In January, President Roosevelt asked $1.8 billion for defense, and by the end of the year, he had created the Office of Production Management to organize the U.S. defense industry. In September, the Selective Service Bill was signed into law, requiring all males ages twenty-one to thirty-five to register, and in the following month, the first numbers were drawn in America's peacetime military draft.

Inevitably, the war in Europe had a devastating impact on America's film industry. After the invasion of Poland, the entire market in Western Europe was lost to the studios. The home offices and bankers in New York began to insist on severe cutbacks in production and personnel. The government started to pressure the studios to produce films that would prepare the public, at least psychologically, for war.

Yet there were memorable films released in 1940. John Ford capped his triumphs of the previous year with his powerful adaptation of John Steinbeck's novel *The Grapes of Wrath*. Alfred Hitchcock created a tense, riveting melodrama out of Daphne du Maurier's novel *Rebecca*. George Cukor captured the wit and sparkle of Philip Barry's play *The Philadelphia Story*. And there was considerable merit in such polished productions as Robert Z. Leonard's *Pride and Prejudice*, Sam Wood's *Our Town*, and Frank Borzage's *The Mortal Storm*, one of the few films of that time to address the terror inside Nazi Germany.

With America's involvement in the war after December 1941, one era ended and another began. The threat to national survival from forces within the country suddenly became a greater threat from forces across two oceans. As Americans rallied to the battle, the film industry not only assumed its familiar role as a purveyor of cheerful entertainment in a grim time but also became a propaganda machine, exhorting citizens to victory over the Axis. The lighthearted fantasies persisted (America always needs its Shirley Temples and Betty Grables), but the social melodramas of the thirties gave way to the rousing, flag-waving films of the war years.

Between these two periods of the Depression and the Second World War, one year, 1939, witnessed a movie miracle: an unmatched succession of films that have never faded from memory.

Happily, a half-century later, we still celebrate their achievements.

FILM AWARDS: 1939

ACADEMY AWARDS

Best Picture: *Gone With the Wind*
    Also nominated: *Dark Victory; Goodbye, Mr. Chips; Love Affair; Mr. Smith Goes to Washington; Ninotchka; Of Mice and Men;* Stagecoach; The Wizard of Oz; Wuthering Heights*

Best Actor: Robert Donat in *Goodbye, Mr. Chips*
    Also nominated: Clark Gable in *Gone With the Wind;* Laurence Olivier in *Wuthering Heights;* Mickey Rooney in *Babes in Arms;* James Stewart in *Mr. Smith Goes to Washington*

Best Actress: Vivien Leigh in *Gone With the Wind*
    Also nominated: Bette Davis in *Dark Victory;* Irene Dunne in *Love Affair;* Greta Garbo in *Ninotchka;* Greer Garson in *Goodbye, Mr. Chips*

Best Supporting Actor: Thomas Mitchell in *Stagecoach*
    Also nominated: Brian Aherne in *Juarez;* Harry Carey in *Mr. Smith Goes to Washington;* Claude Rains in *Mr. Smith Goes to Washington;* Brian Donlevy in *Beau Geste.*

Best Supporting Actress: Hattie McDaniel in *Gone With the Wind*
    Also nominated: Olivia de Havilland in *Gone With the Wind;* Geraldine Fitzgerald in *Wuthering Heights;* Edna May Oliver in *Drums Along the Mohawk;* Maria Ouspenskaya in *Love Affair.*

---

*Although filmed in 1939, *Of Mice and Men* did not go into general release until February 1940.

Best Director: Victor Fleming for *Gone With the Wind*
 Also nominated: Frank Capra for *Mr. Smith Goes to Washington;* John Ford
 for *Stagecoach;* Sam Wood for *Goodbye, Mr. Chips;* William Wyler for
 Wuthering Heights

Best Art Direction: Lyle Wheeler for *Gone With the Wind*

Best Cinematography (color): Ernest Haller and Ray Rennahan for *Gone With the Wind*

Best Cinematography (black-and-white): Gregg Toland for *Wuthering Heights*

Best Film Editing: Hal C. Kern and James E. Newcom for *Gone With the Wind*

Best Score: Richard Hageman, Franke Harling, John Leipold, Louis
Gruenberg, and Leo Shuken for *Stagecoach*

Best Original Score: Herbert Stothart for *The Wizard of Oz*

Best Song: "Over the Rainbow," from *The Wizard of Oz*, music by Harold
Arlen, lyrics by E. Y. Harburg

Best Writing (Original Story): Lewis R. Foster for *Mr. Smith Goes to Washington*

Best Writing (Screenplay): Sidney Howard for *Gone With the Wind*

Best Special Effects: E. H. Hansen and Fred Sersen for *The Rains Came*

Irving G. Thalberg Memorial Award: David O. Selznick

THE NEW YORK FILM CRITICS AWARDS

Best Motion Picture: *Wuthering Heights*

Best Male Performance: James Stewart in *Mr. Smith Goes to Washington*

Best Female Performance: Vivien Leigh in *Gone With the Wind*

Best Direction: John Ford for *Stagecoach*

BIBLIOGRAPHY

Anderegg, Michael A. *William Wyler*. Boston: Twayne Publishers, 1979.

Anderson, Lindsay. *About John Ford*. New York: McGraw-Hill Book Company, 1981.

Astor, Mary. *A Life on Film*. New York: Delacorte Press, 1971.

Bainbridge, John. *Garbo*. New York: Holt, Rinehart & Winston, 1971.

Bayer, William. *The Great Movies*. New York: Grosset & Dunlap, 1973.

Behlmer, Rudy. *America's Favorite Movies: Behind the Scenes*. New York: Ungar Publishing Co., 1982.

——. *Inside Warner Bros.: 1935–1951*. New York: Viking Penguin Inc., 1985.

——, ed. *Memo from David O. Selznick*. New York: The Viking Press, 1972.

Capra, Frank. *The Name Above the Title*. New York: Macmillan, 1971.

Chierichetti, David. *Hollywood Director: The Career of Mitchell Leisen*. New York: Curtis Books, 1973.

Corliss, Richard. *Greta Garbo*. New York: Pyramid Publications, 1974.

Crowther, Bosley. *The Lion's Share*. New York: E.P. Dutton & Company, 1957.

Dooley, Roger. *From Scarface to Scarlett: American Films in the 1930s*. New York and London: Harcourt Brace Jovanovich, 1981.

Edwards, Anne. *Judy Garland: A Biography*. New York: Simon & Schuster, 1974.

Fairbanks, Jr., Douglas. *The Salad Days*. Garden City, New York: Doubleday and Company, Inc., 1988.

Fonda, Henry (as told to Howard Teichmann). *Fonda: My Life*. New York: New American Library, 1981.

Ford, Dan. *Pappy: The Life of John Ford*. Englewood Cliffs, New Jersey: Prentice-Hall, Inc., 1979.

Fordin, Hugh. *The World of Entertainment!: Hollywood's Greatest Musicals.* Garden City, New York: Doubleday and Company, Inc., 1975.

Gabler, Neal. *An Empire of Their Own: How the Jews Invented Hollywood.* New York: Crown Publishers, Inc., 1988.

Godfrey, Lionel. *Cary Grant: The Light Touch.* New York: St. Martin's Press, 1981.

Griffith, Richard. *Samuel Goldwyn: The Producer and His Films.* New York: Garland Publishing Inc., 1985.

Halliwell, Leslie. *Halliwell's Hundred.* New York: Charles Scribner's Sons, 1982.

Harmetz, Aljean. *The Making of The Wizard of Oz.* New York: Alfred A. Knopf, Inc., 1977 (Limelight Edition, 1984).

Haver, Ronald. *David O. Selznick's Hollywood.* New York: Bonanza Books, 1980.

Higham, Charles. *Bette: The Life of Bette Davis.* New York: Macmillan, 1981.

————. *Warner Brothers.* New York: Charles Scribner's Sons, 1975.

———— and Mosely, Roy. *Princess Merle: The Romantic Life of Merle Oberon.* New York: Coward, McCann, Inc., 1983.

Howard, Sidney. *GWTW: The Screenplay* (edited by Richard Harwell). New York: Collier Books, 1980.

Kerbel, Michael. *Henry Fonda.* New York: Pyramid Books, 1975.

Kobal, John. *Rita Hayworth: The Time, the Place, and the Woman.* London: W. H. Allen, 1977.

Lambert, Gavin. *GWTW: The Making of Gone With the Wind.* Boston: An Atlantic Monthly Press Book, Little, Brown and Company, 1973.

Lasky, Jesse, Jr., with Pat Silver. *Love Scene: The Story of Laurence Olivier and Vivien Leigh.* New York: Thomas Y. Crowell, Publishers, 1978.

Leyda, Jay, ed. *Voices of Film Experience.* New York: Macmillan, 1977.

McBride, Joseph. *Hawks on Hawks.* Berkeley: University of California Press, 1982.

McClelland, Doug. *Down the Yellow Brick Road: The Making of The Wizard of Oz.* New York: Pyramid Publications, 1976.

Madsen, Axel. *William Wyler: The Authorized Biography.* Thomas Y. Crowell, Publishers, 1973.

Marx, Arthur. *Goldwyn.* New York: W. W. Norton & Company, 1976.

Pasternak, Joe. *Easy the Hard Way.* New York: G. P. Putnam's Sons, 1956.

Phillips, Gene D. *George Cukor.* Boston: Twayne Publishers, 1982.

Pratt, William. *Scarlett Fever.* New York: Collier Books, 1977.

Quirk, Lawrence J. *Norma: The Story of Norma Shearer.* New York: St. Martin's Press, 1988.

Russell, Rosalind, and Chris Chase. *Life Is a Banquet.* New York: Random House, 1977.

Sennett, Ted. *Great Hollywood Movies.* New York: Harry N. Abrams, 1983.

————. *Great Movie Directors.* New York: Harry N. Abrams, 1986.

————. *Warner Brothers Presents*. New Rochelle, New York: Arlington House, 1971.

Sinclair, Andrew. *John Ford: A Biography*. New York: Lorrimer Publishing, Inc., 1984.

Swindell, Larry. *Charles Boyer*. Garden City, New York: Doubleday & Company, Inc., 1983.

Taylor, John Russell, ed. *Graham Greene on Film*. New York: Simon & Schuster, 1972.

Thomas, Bob. *Joan Crawford*. New York: Simon & Schuster, 1978.

Walker, Alexander. *Joan Crawford—The Ultimate Star*. London: Weidenfeld and Nicolson, 1983.

Wansell, Geoffrey. *Haunted Idol: The Story of the Real Cary Grant*. New York: William Morrow and Company, 1984.

Wolf, William, with Lillian Kramer Wolf. *Landmark Films*. New York and London: Paddington Press Ltd., 1979.

Wood, Tom. *The Bright Side of Billy Wilder, Primarily*. Garden City, New York: Doubleday & Company, Inc., 1970.

Zolotow, Maurice. *Billy Wilder in Hollywood*. New York: G. P. Putnam's Sons, 1977.

INDEX

Don Ameche • Jean Arthur • J

• Humphrey Bogart • Charles

Colbert • Joan Crawford • Geor

de Havilland • Marlene Dietrich

Douglas Fairbanks, Jr. • Geraldin

Fontaine • John Ford • Clark Gal

Greer Garson • Paulette Godda

• Rita Hayworth • Vivien Leigh

Merle Oberon • Laurence Olivie

• Mickey Rooney • Rodgers &

Shearer • James Stewart • John W